JOAN CHITTISTER

✠

MODERN SPIRITUAL MASTERS SERIES

JOAN CHITTISTER

✝

Essential Writings

Selected by
MARY LOU KOWNACKI
AND
MARY HEMBROW SNYDER

ORBIS BOOKS
Maryknoll, New York 10545

Third Printing, March 2015

ORBIS BOOKS
Maryknoll, New York 10545

Fathers and Brothers
MARYKNOLL

Founded in 1970, Orbis Books endeavors to publish works that enlighten the mind, nourish the spirit, and challenge the conscience. The publishing arm of the Maryknoll Fathers and Brothers, Orbis seeks to explore the global dimensions of the Christian faith and mission, to invite dialogue with diverse cultures and religious traditions, and to serve the cause of reconciliation and peace. The books published reflect the views of their authors and do not represent the official position of the Maryknoll Society. To learn more about Maryknoll and Orbis Books, please visit our website at www.maryknollsociety.org.

Library of Congress Cataloging-in-Publication Data
Essential writings / Joan Chittister ; selected by Mary Lou Kownacki and Mary Hembrow Snyder.
    pages cm. – (Modern spiritual masters series)
    Includes bibliographical references.
    ISBN 978-1-62698-091-4
    1. Christian life–Catholic authors. 2. Spiritual life–Catholic Church.
    I. Kownacki, Mary Lou, editor of compilation. II. Title.
    BX4705.C476A25   2014
    248.4'82–dc23   2014005449

Contents

Sources

Becoming Fully Human: The Greatest Glory of God. Lanham, MD: Sheed & Ward, Rowman & Littlefield, 2005.

The Breath of the Soul: Reflections on Prayer. Mystic, CT: Twenty-Third Publications, 2009.

Called to Question: A Spiritual Memoir. Lanham, MD: Sheed & Ward, Rowman & Littlefield, 2004.

The Cry of the Prophet: A Call to Fullness of Life. Erie, PA: Benetvision, 2009.

The Fire in These Ashes: A Spirituality of Contemporary Religious Life. Kansas City: Sheed & Ward, 1995.

Following the Path: The Search for a Life of Passion, Purpose, and Joy. New York: Random House, 2012.

For Everything a Season. Maryknoll, NY: Orbis Books, 2013; published as *There Is a Season,* with art by John August Swanson. Maryknoll, NY: Orbis Books, 1995.

The Gift of Years: Growing Older Gracefully. New York: BlueBridge, 2008.

God's Tender Mercy: Reflections on Forgiveness. Mystic, CT: Twenty-Third Publications, 2010.

Gospel Days: Reflections for Every Day of the Year. Maryknoll, NY: Orbis Books, 1999.

Happiness. Grand Rapids, MI: Wm. B. Eerdmans, 2011.

Heart of Flesh: Feminist Spirituality for Women and Men. Grand Rapids, MI: Wm. B. Eerdmans, 1998.

Illuminated Life: Monastic Wisdom for Seekers of Light. Maryknoll, NY: Orbis Books, 2000.

In Search of Belief. Revised. Liguori, MO: Liguori, 2006.

In the Heart of the Temple: My Spiritual Vision for Today's World. New York: BlueBridge, 2004.

The Liturgical Year: The Spiraling Adventure of the Spiritual Life. Nashville: Thomas Nelson, 2009.

The Monastery of the Heart: An Invitation to a Meaningful Life. New York: BlueBridge, 2011.

The Radical Christian Life: A Year with Saint Benedict. Collegeville, MN: Liturgical Press, 2011.

The Rule of Benedict: A Spirituality for the 21st Century. New York: Crossroad, 2010.

Scarred by Struggle, Transformed by Hope. Grand Rapids, MI: Wm. B. Eerdmans, 2003.

The Story of Ruth: Twelve Moments in Every Woman's Life. Grand Rapids, MI: Wm. B. Eerdmans, 2000.

The Ten Commandments: Laws of the Heart. Maryknoll, NY: Orbis Books, 2006.

Uncommon Gratitude. Collegeville, MN: Liturgical Press, 2010.

Welcome to the Wisdom of the World and Its Meaning for You: Universal Spiritual Insights Distilled from Five Religious Traditions. Grand Rapids, MI: Wm. B. Eerdmans, 2007.

Wisdom Distilled from the Daily: Living the Rule of St. Benedict Today. San Francisco: HarperCollins, 1990.

Other Sources Cited
Reprinted with Permission

Chittister, Joan D. "God Become Infinitely Larger." In *God at 2000,* ed. Marcus Borg and Ross Mackenzie. Harrisburg, PA: Morehouse Publishing, 2000.

Chittister, Joan. "God Our Father, God Our Mother: In Search of the Divine Feminine." In *Women, Spirituality and Transformative Leadership: Where Grace Meets Power,* ed. Kathe Schaaf, Kay Lindahl, Kathleen S. Hurty, and Guo Cheen, 60–70. Woodstock, VT: SkyLight Paths, 2012.

Chittister, Joan. Essay from *In a Dark Wood: Journeys of Faith and Doubt,* ed. Linda Jones and Sophie Stanes, 207–8. Minneapolis: Fortress Press, 2003.

Chittister, Joan. Essay from *What Does It Mean to Be Human?: Reverence for Life Reaffirmed by Responses from around the World*, gathered by Frederick Franck, Janis Roze, and Richard Connolly, 193–96. Nyack, NY: Circumstantial Productions, 1998.

Chittister, Joan. "The Power of Questions to Propel: A Retrospective." In *Spiritual Questions for the Twenty-First Century: Essays in Honor of Joan D. Chittister*, ed. Mary Hembrow Snyder. Maryknoll, NY: Orbis Books, 2001.

Reprinted with Grateful Acknowledgment

Chittister, Joan. "A Spirituality for the Long Haul." *Compass Magazine and New Designs: An Anthology of Spiritual Vision* (May–June 1992): 12–13.

Chittister, Joan, et al. "Dear Bishops: Open Letter on the Morality of Nuclear Deterrence Addressed to the U.S. Catholic Bishops," statement of Pax Christi USA, 1989.

Chittister, Joan. "The Bishop Who Said, 'Sorry.'" *The Tablet* (January 18, 1997).

Chittister, Joan. "Dangerous Disciple." *Sojourners* 3, no. 1 (January/February 2002).

Chittister, Joan. "Heart of Flesh: A Feminist Spirituality for Women and Men." *Call to Action Newsletter* (January 1998).

Chittister, Joan. "Three Choices at a Crossroads," Call to Action Conference: Prophets of a Future Not Our Own (Milwaukee, November 5–7, 2010).

National Catholic Reporter (NCR), established in 1964, began as a newspaper and is now a print and web news source for which Joan Chittister writes a regular online column, "From Where I Stand." www.ncronline.org.

The Monastic Way by Joan Chittister is a monthly print and online publication produced by Benetvision Publishing, an outreach of the Benedictine Sisters of Erie. Online at www.monasticway.org.

Acknowledgments

We are deeply grateful to all who supported us in myriad ways as we worked to complete this book for Joan. Most especially we thank Benedictine Sister Susan Doubet, who offered immeasurable help in providing access to Joan Chittister's archives; Sister Anne McCarthy for making the copyright process manageable, as well as proofreading the manuscript; Judy Allison for formatting and proofreading; Mercyhurst University's President Dr. Tom Gamble and Vice President for Academic Affairs Dr. Phil Belfiore for granting Mary Hembrow Snyder release time from teaching to complete this project; and Sisters Mary Ellen Plumb, Marlene Bertke, and Linda Romey for proofreading.

Grateful acknowledgment is made to the following publishers for permission to reprint from copyrighted material:

Augsburg Fortress Publishers for an essay by Joan Chittister from *In a Dark Wood: Journeys of Faith and Doubt* edited by Linda Jones and Sophie Stanes, copyright © 2003 by Linda Jones and Sophie Stanes.

BlueBridge, an imprint of United Tribes Media, Inc., for excerpts from *The Monastery of the Heart: An Invitation to a Meaningful Life*, copyright © 2011 by Joan Chittister; *In the Heart of the Temple: My Spiritual Vision for Today's World,* copyright © 2004 by Joan Chittister; and *The Gift of Years: Growing Older Gracefully,* copyright © 2008 by Joan Chittister.

Church Publishing for an essay "God Become Infinitely Larger," by Joan Chittister from *God at 2000* ed. by Marcus Borg and Ross Mackenzie, copyright © 2000 by Marcus Borg and Ross Mackenzie.

The Crossroad Publishing Company for an excerpt from *The Rule of St. Benedict: A Spirituality for the 21st Century* by Joan Chittister (New York: Crossroad, 1992).

HarperCollins Publishers for an excerpt from *Wisdom Distilled from the Daily: Living the Rule of St. Benedict Today* by Joan Chittister, copyright © 1990 by Joan Chittister.

Image Books, an imprint of the Crown Publishing Group, a division of Random House LLC, for an excerpt from *Following the Path: The Search for a Life of Passion, Purpose, and Joy* by Joan Chittister, copyright © 2012 by Joan Chittister.

Liguori Publications for excerpts from *In Search of Belief* by Joan Chittister, copyright © 1999 by Joan Chittister.

St. Martin's Press for an essay by Joan Chittister from *What Does It Mean to be Human?: Reverence for Life Reaffirmed by Responses from Around the World,* gathered by Frederick Franck, Janis Roze, and Richard Connolly, copyright © 1998 by Circumstantial Productions.

Sheed & Ward, an imprint of Rowman & Littlefield Publishers, Inc., for excerpts from *The Fire in These Ashes: A Spirituality of Contemporary Religious Life* by Joan Chittister, copyright © 1995 by Joan Chittister; *Called to Question: A Spiritual Memoir* by Joan Chittister, copyright © 2004 by Joan Chittister; and *Becoming Fully Human: The Greatest Glory of God* by Joan Chittister, copyright © 2005 by Joan Chittister.

SkyLight Paths Publishing for an excerpt by Sr. Joan Chittister from *Women, Spirituality and Transformative Leadership: Where Grace Meets Power* © 2012, ed. Kathe Schaaf, Kay Lindahl, Kathleen S. Hurty, and Guo Cheen. (Woodstock, VT: SkyLight Paths Publishing).

Thomas Nelson, Inc., for excerpts from *The Liturgical Year* by Joan Chittister, copyright © 2009 by Joan Chittister.

Twenty-Third Publications, a division of Bayard, for excerpts from *The Breath of the Soul: Reflections on Prayer,* copyright © 2009 by Joan Chittister and *God's Tender Mercy: Reflections on Forgiveness,* copyright © 2010 by Joan Chittister.

Wm. B. Eerdmans Publishing Company for excerpts from *Heart of Flesh: Feminist Spirituality for Women and Men* by Joan Chittister, copyright © 1998 by Wm. B. Eerdmans; *Happiness* by Joan Chittister, copyright © 2011 by Joan Chittister; *Scarred by Struggle: Transformed by Hope* by Joan Chittister, copyright © 2003 by Wm. B. Eerdmans; *The Story of Ruth: Twelve Moments in Every Woman's Life* by Joan Chittister, copyright © 2000 by Wm. B. Eerdmans;

Introduction

BY MARY LOU KOWNACKI, OSB

She absolutely electrified that audience and brought them all to their feet. I still remember what I felt at that moment. Afterward I went to Joan, gave her a big hug, and said, "You are a revival preacher, Joan Chittister. Want to go on the road together?"

—Jim Wallis, *Sojourners*

The theme of this book is passion. To anyone who has met, read, or heard Joan Chittister that choice is obvious.

Spend a short amount of time with Joan and you will feel the intensity of Jeremiah's cry, "God's word was imprisoned in my body like a fire blazing in my heart" (Jer. 20:9).

For over forty years she has tirelessly crisscrossed the country and the globe driven by God's fiery word. The reason for such steadfastness might best be explained in the novel *My Name Is Asher Lev* by Chaim Potok. In that book, Asher says, "My father's great grandfather in his middle years began to travel. Why did he travel so much I began to ask. To do good deeds and bring the Master of the Universe into the world, my father would respond. To find people in need and to comfort and help them, my mother would say." To bring God into godless places, to do righteous deeds, to comfort and help the poor and powerless of the earth are what impel Joan, too.

In the final years of the Cold War, she was part of two groundbreaking peace delegations to the Soviet Union. She visited Haiti as part of a Pax Christi peace delegation in 1989, meeting secretly with leaders of the peasant movement and other leaders seeking to oust the then-illegal military junta. She has stood in Hiroshima with survivors of the nuclear bombings and prayed for peace; she did the same on the border of North Korea and South Korea.

1

Joan has sat with the peasant revolutionaries in Chiapas and listened to their tragic stories of torture and oppression. She has visited the apartheid settlements of South Africa and joined Egyptians in Cairo's Tahrir Square as they demonstrated for freedom.

"I have walked with Sister Joan through the checkpoints of Israel and Palestine," writes Dena Merriam, convener and co-chair of the Global Peace Initiative for Women, of which Joan is also a co-chair. "I have sat by her side as she mediated the emotional tirades of Israeli and Palestinian women. I have walked with her through the streets of Damascus when we went as envoys of peace from the American people. I have seen her compassion and tears as she held Iraqi refugees in Syria. Her heart has taken them all in. They won't forget her and she won't forget them."

And Joan doesn't forget them. It is their tragic stories that she carries to places of power, becoming their voice, their stead. It is their message she takes into churches and temples and mosques; into banquets, public lectures, and forums; into books, articles, and interviews.

People who have heard her speak use words like "electrifying," "soul-stirring," "afire." Here's how one interviewer tried to capture her passionate presence: "The sheer authority of her voice and the force of her indictment made me feel as if I were being pressed back against my plush, red-cushioned seat, as when a plane takes off." The same holds true when you read her voluminous writings.

Her passions are weighty: justice for the disenfranchised, especially women; an end to militarism and war; and a call to discipleship that costs. She writes, "We talk religion in a world that worships the bread but does not distribute it, that practices ritual rather than righteousness, that confesses but does not repent." And, yet, Joan is not a doomsday prophet who leaves audiences and readers depressed and impotent. The words that burn also ignite the listener's soul and melt away layers of fear, apathy, and helplessness. And she's funny, too. It's a matter of course to attend a Chittister lecture on the most serious of topics and find the audience laughing uproariously at stories and one-liners.

Not only do her words radiate energy and hope, but, like sparks against a black sky, they poke holes in the darkness, enabling others to mark their way. An outstanding leader of great vision, she has served as president of the Leadership Conference of Women Religious, president of the Conference of American Benedictine Prioresses, and prioress of the Benedictine Sisters of Erie.

She is the recipient of dozens of honors and awards from universities, press associations, and organizations devoted to a more just church and world. For over thirty years, she has been a columnist for the *National Catholic Reporter* and covered the U.N. Fourth World Conference on Women in Beijing, the funeral of Pope John Paul II, and the election and inauguration of Pope Benedict XVI.

Impressive as Joan's vita is, perhaps her greatest passion is reserved for people and for life itself. She plays as intensely as she preaches and can always be counted on to party. The bulk of her writing is devoted to helping ordinary people develop into their best selves. She sets a standard for a mature spirituality, and the power and passion of her vision compel people to reach beyond the possible.

"I turn to Sister Joan because she lives between water and fire—between the tenderness of love and the fierceness of conviction," wrote Elizabeth Lesser, co-founder of the Omega Institute.

It is this life of passion lived with abundant love and unwavering conviction that we attempted to capture in this collection of Joan Chittister's essential writings.

EARLY INFLUENCES

Joan's is a prophet's voice telling us that when love breaks through in even one person, the effect for the world is immense. —Paula D'Arcy, author

When she received the 2007 Leadership Conference of Women Religious Leadership Award, the video presentation of her life described Joan's childhood as "grim and demanding."

Joan Chittister was born in DuBois, a small town in western Pennsylvania, to Dan and Loretta Dougherty. Three years after her birth her father died. Family members told her that she never smiled for a photograph for years after that loss. Her twenty-one-year-old mother was left, in the midst of the Depression, with a small child and no skills or means of support. Within a year and a half her mother remarried and moved with her new husband, Dutch Chittister, to the Pittsburgh area. Joan's new father formally adopted her and always treated her as his own. Joan writes and speaks of genuine fondness for her stepfather, who, when not drinking, was a decent man. He was, however, an alcoholic and often became violent toward her mother.

Indeed, one could agree that "grim and demanding" was an apt description for Joan's early years. But there were saving graces as well.

The extraordinary bond between Joan and her mother is without question the major influence in Joan's life. Joan speaks of her as lovingly tactile, a woman with whom she shared every discovery, every book, every question; a mother who adored her daughter, yet pushed her to personal independence. Joan writes that her mother was "brilliant . . . there was great intelligence, but she was totally uneducated."

Through her mother's plight, Joan lived the reality of what happens to a woman trapped in economic dependency. When she asked her mother why she had married her stepfather or why they didn't leave him it was always the same answer: "There was nothing else a woman could do. There was no money, no financial security, no home for us."

Joan writes, "The answer seared then and only burned more deeply over the years: there was nothing else a woman could do. I have never been able to get that answer out of my mind." Years later, when Joan met the idea of feminism, she simply said, "Yes," and jumped off the high diving board. Concern for women's roles and welfare were her bone and marrow.

Loretta did, however, recognize her daughter's unusual intellectual gifts and relentlessly insisted that she read, study, and work hard so that "you can take care of yourself." One has to greatly admire this mother, who, when Joan decided to enter the convent at sixteen, convinced the reluctant prioress of the Benedictine Sisters of Erie to accept her daughter.

Joan writes, "That was 1952, and after I had plagued the prioress, Mother Sylvester, for two years to take me. She hesitated because I was an only child, and said my mother would need me. So I took my mother to meet her and my mother supported me, telling Mother Sylvester that if I had made up my mind, that was what I was going to do."

Certainly Joan's determination cannot be dismissed, but if Loretta's driving force was to make certain that her daughter got a different chance at life, this was a rare instance of unconditional love. Up till then it had been Joan and her mother—together—facing the "grim and demanding." Now they were separated.

Joan's mother lived to see her act of "letting go" rewarded: clipped every news story about Joan, organized one Joan scrapbook after another, basked in Joan's awards and recognition.

Joan writes poignantly of losing her mother to Alzheimer's in *Welcome to the Wisdom of the World* and her regret at not recognizing the disease that so drastically changed her mother's personality. The actual death of her mother, however, was perfect closure to a most unusual relationship. In her final years, Joan's mother moved into the monastery. Joan, who was traveling 300 of the 365 days of the year, had attended a community meeting and was preparing to leave for a trip abroad. She was at the monastery door when she was paged. Her mother had taken a turn for the worse. Joan crawled into bed with her and sang the songs her mother sang to her as child. Her mother died wrapped in her arms.

After her mother, women religious were the next strongest influence in Joan's formative years. When living outside of Pittsburgh, she attended Saint Veronica's Elementary School and was taught by the Sisters of Saint Joseph of Baden. The sisters took special care of their precocious student. They challenged her intellectually, of course, providing advanced reading materials, including the novels of Charles Dickens. But more importantly they showered her with special kindness and care. Saint Veronica's became a home away from home, a safe place for Joan to learn and develop. "I was crazy about the Baden Josephs," Joan says, "I can't imagine what my childhood would have been without them."

Joan was in fourth grade when the family moved to Erie, Pennsylvania, and she chose Saint Benedict Academy as her high school. There she met the Benedictine Sisters of Erie and in her sophomore year applied for entrance.

What D'Arcy wrote: "When love breaks through in even one person, the effect for the world is immense," held true in Joan's life. The remarkable love of her mother and love of sisters who taught her had an immense effect on Joan and, consequently, on the world.

PERSONAL SPIRITUALITY

Joan is a passionate contemplative who lives and exudes a mystical life. The fruits of such mysticism are boundless energy, great enthusiasm, and a hope-filled spirit of presence to the now which is both embracing and contagious. —Theresa Kane, RSM

To be called a "passionate contemplative" is no small praise. And if it's true, how did Joan Chittister become that fire of God? What kindled the passion? What formed the contemplative?

Joan Chittister does not disclose much about her personal spirituality. A reading of her sizeable library of interviews, articles, speeches, and books gives only glimpses into her personal relationship with God.

Joan had a direct experience of God at a very early age but only revealed it some fifty years later during a public lecture. In that speech, she recounted praying one night as a teenager in the dark Erie cathedral with only the sanctuary lamp for light. Suddenly she had an experience of intense light. She joked that it might have been a janitor working late or a bad light switch, but for her it became an insight into God that remained—"I knew then that the light was God and that God was light."

A second incident that affected her spirituality occurred in her early twenties, when, as a young Benedictine sister, she was given the book *Abandonment to Divine Providence* by Jean-Pierre de Caussade. What Joan discovered in de Caussade was the concept of the sacrament of the present moment. The awakening for her was God's abiding presence in every moment of life. For her, then, the spiritually developed person—the contemplative—is one who grew in God consciousness. Everything else—all the prayer rituals, the retreats, the readings, the spiritual practices—were only means to finding God in the here and now.

And the third major influence in her spiritual development was the monastic life itself. From the age of sixteen, she immersed herself in the Benedictine way of life: she recited the Psalms and listened to the scriptures in choral prayer three to five times a day; she spent daily personal time reading and reflecting on sacred literature; and she went to do good work every day, with a community of women committed to making the reign of God on earth as it is in heaven.

She writes of this experience: "I wasn't long in the monastic life when I realized, like a teabag, I was being steeped in an environment that spoke to me of another layer and level of life."

And that layer of life was the sacrament of the ordinary—a gradual understanding that the acceptance of every single moment of life and whatever came to her was of God. Washing dishes, intoning an antiphon, speaking to 2,000 people, playing the accordion, mediating conversation between Palestinian and Israeli women, being elected prioress, casting a fishing line into Lake Erie—all were of God.

The daily rhythm of the monastic life reinforced her initial attraction to the sacrament of the present moment. The daily listening to the Psalms and the rest of scripture called her to see the world through the eyes of God and then respond as God would. She writes, "The scriptures become the heartbeat of your life. It is the application of scripture that drives every day of your life,

it is your mission, it is your ministry, it's the ground on which
you stand."

What turned Joan into a passionate contemplative? A life-
changing book. A commitment to an ordinary life of prayer and
work with a community of seekers. A listening heart that grappled daily with the scriptures until it stretched wide enough to
embrace a suffering world. And a memory of intense light that
became "a God without a face of any color or gender, a God
who came in light and fire, God with us—Emmanuel. That God,
I knew, lived in the light. And the light, I could feel, was inside
of me."

THE WRITER

*Joan Chittister has left her mark upon America's book
reading public in ways that few writers could ever hope
to do and most can only envy. Not just in sales—though
her books are bestsellers—but in effective impact. She
enjoys that rare, rare ability of thinking deeply, clearly,
imaginatively, and devoutly at one and the same time and
then, afterward, of conveying her thoughts accessibly
and unpretentiously. Because of that, she has tended to
thousands of mindful souls in this country and abroad.
And in doing so, Sister Joan Chittister has enriched the
Christian life of our times, even as she simultaneously
added grace and a beautiful compassion to our ways of
being in this world.*

—Phyllis Tickle, author and founding editor
of the Religion Department of *Publishers Weekly*

Joan's primary image of herself is as a writer. From the age of
seven she was writing plays for the neighborhood children and
stories about imaginary brothers. But it wasn't until she was in
ninth grade at Saint Benedict Academy in Erie that her call was
recognized, nurtured, and confirmed. As Joan explains it, she
was summoned out of an algebra class by her English teacher to
explain an essay assignment. Did Joan copy this essay? Did one
of her parents write it? Who suggested the topic for the essay?

When Joan assured her that it was an original paper, she was told to report to the journalism room immediately.

From that moment on, according to Joan, "I lived to write. I wrote all the time. I wrote in small notebooks and tiny date books and on sheets of blank white typing paper." She wrote for every section of the newspaper and she wrote short stories in secret. "Writing was all I wanted to do in life."

And then, in her sophomore year of high school, she entered the monastery.

> Saint Benedict did not devote a chapter of his Rule to "Artists of the Monastery" because he was running out of material. My experience in monastic life leads me to believe that even in the sixth century artists of any kind must have been a problem in community. It's true that Saint Benedict wanted to guard the unusually gifted from pride, but I also think he desired to legitimize the role of artists and to deflect, as much as possible, the jealousy and fear and judgment against those who had a talent beyond the ordinary—the painters, potters, photographers, composers, musicians and, yes, the writers.

Two events in Joan's life bear out this mistrust of the community's gifted that usually masks as a need to teach them "humility."

Joan tried to carry her writing practice into the monastery in the form of a spiritual journal. She remembers, "I recorded every thought I had about the spiritual life, every reaction I had to the newness of monastic life, every response I had to the structures of formation and the nature of community life. I worked on the journal every night in the novitiate just before lights out and then tucked it into the corner of my tiny desk, only to begin again on every day that followed. I knew, somehow, that someday I would look back on this work as a treasure house of idea development, a map of my own spiritual coming of age."

Imagine, then, going to her desk one morning and finding the journal missing. Imagine being summoned by your former novice director, five years later—on the eve of your final profession—to the incinerator in the basement and told, "Open it." Imagine seeing your private journal brought out from under her apron. Imagine being asked to throw your journal into the flaming furnace because, "You don't want to do this kind of thing anymore."

In retrospect the destroyed journal was an immeasurable loss. What biographer wouldn't desire to trace Joan's spiritual development from the earliest possible source?

Though the journal went up in flames, her passion for writing persisted, smoldering in the ashes. So imagine her deep joy, when as a young English teacher, she was told by the prioress to apply to the prestigious University of Iowa for the summer writing program. And then the euphoria when she was accepted. Next imagine receiving a phone call from the prioress forbidding her to attend because the prioress woke up that morning and decided Joan needed a lesson in humility. Instead of writing, Joan would serve as an assistant cook at the community's children's camp that summer.

Joan painfully describes this life-changing event and its ensuing consequences in *Scarred by Struggle, Transformed by Hope*. These two events happened prior to Vatican Council II, when religious life was punitive and controlled by the whim of a superior. But they happened. She ends that book by recording her moment of enlightenment, when she recognized that writing was still her path but, "I began to understand that I wasn't called to write fiction; I was called to speak the pain of reality. I began to write about the conflict between theology and the Gospel." And write she did.

As this text goes to press, Joan Chittister has authored more than fifty books, most of them bestsellers, thirteen of which received Catholic Press Association Awards. She has written over seven hundred articles and columns for journals, magazines, and newspapers around the world. She is a regular columnist for the

National Catholic Reporter and writes a blog for the *Huffington Post*. She has written chapters in a hundred other books, thousands of letters to her readers, and, yes, she has kept journals through most of her adult life.

Joan's writing sustains so many because, as Sister Helen Prejean notes, "She writes in a way that ordinary people can understand. She makes Jesus come alive in the twenty-first century." Her readers do not meet a "cheap" Jesus. Her Jesus is both unlimited compassion and unreasonable challenge. Her Jesus desires human wholeness and sees no face as enemy. Her Jesus embraces human weakness and unleashes anger at injustice. Her Jesus stands with the most vulnerable and unmasks the mighty. Her Jesus both comforts and discomforts. Joan met this Jesus through writing.

Joan prays best with a pen or computer keyboard. When she was prioress of the Benedictine Sisters of Erie for twelve years, she sat in her choir stall jotting notes during the daily morning and evening recitation of the Liturgy of the Hours. For some people this was a bit of a scandal—why is she writing during prayer? At the end of prayer, when it was time for her to bless the community, she used her notes to give a three-minute meditation on one of the Psalms prayed. I always marveled at the depth and insight of the message given—off-the-cuff, with no time for preparation and editing—and was equally taken by its realistic application. "Here, Sisters, is how you might live the Psalm today"—nothing pious or sanguine or dogmatic or unreachable, just solid Christian living, with a new twist. This daily exercise not only provided excellent teaching but modeled how to pray, really pray, the Psalms.

"I'm not sure I could contemplate at all if it weren't for the fact that I have spent most of my life surrendering to the experience of going down into the dark of the writing process," Joan said in an interview. "Contemplation is more than 'prayer without words.' It is coming to see the world as God sees the world, or learning to put on the mind of Christ. That takes a stripping away of the old thoughts, the old assumptions, the old world-view. For me, writing is a necessary part of that exchange."

Joan was once asked in an interview, "What do you want to be remembered for?" to which she answered, "For writing at least one sentence that changed a person's life."

If Phyllis Tickle of *Publisher's Weekly* is anywhere near the target, it is certain that Joan will be remembered for far more than one sentence. Tickle said that Joan "has left her mark upon the reading public in ways that few writers could ever hope to do and most can only envy. . . . She has tended to thousands of mindful souls in this country and abroad . . . has enriched the Christian life of our times, even as she has simultaneously added grace and beautiful compassion to our ways of being in this world." Not a shabby accomplishment for someone who once watched her journal go up in flames and was told that becoming a religious meant letting go of writing.

PASSION FOR JUSTICE

Joan, you have a talent for seeing what you're looking at, and saying what you saw. Don't let anyone ever destroy that in you.
> —Carroll Arnold, Joan's doctoral advisor
> at Penn State University

Joan is both revered and reviled for her courage with pen, pulpit, and podium. But one thing cannot be denied—Joan never let anyone destroy her talent "for seeing what she was looking at, and saying what she saw." Though, by her own admission, she came to the issues of the times late, once there Joan proved relentless in the pursuit of justice, becoming one of the most articulate and outspoken critics of church and society. What she saw, she named.

When the Vatican acted punitively to punish those who asked controversial questions or acted out of conscience—Sister Agnes Mary Mansour, Bishop Thomas Gumbleton, Roy Bourgeois—Joan ascended the public pulpit and raised a voice of dissent.

In forums around the globe she calls the church to task for its exclusion of women in liturgical language and from decision-making positions, and its refusal to address the ordination of women. She asks searing questions about whether the church is really pro-life or pro-birth, since it raises nowhere near the political clout to fight poverty, war, and women's health issues as it does to advocate against abortion. She names the church's sins publicly: its pomp and hypocrisy, its secrecy and politicking, its misuse of obedience and authority.

She questions the state with the same urgency as she does the church—challenging any policy that contradicts the gospel message. Like the prophets of old, she charges full force into any system of power that tramples the lowly and powerless, be they victims of war, militarism, sexism, economic exploitation, racism, abuse, or the prison systems. "Don't be afraid to speak," she has written. "Be afraid of what will happen to the whole truth if you don't."

Her dogged insistence that her bit of truth matters has earned her legions of ardent admirers and scores of zealous detractors, many who accuse her of overstepping the line between politics and religion.

When asked in an interview to explain how a religious person could be involved in political affairs, Joan answered, "I am not a politician. Nor was Jesus. But he kept pointing out how the system failed the people it purported to serve. If you have a religious heart, how can you not be there with the poorest of the poor, who are bearing the brunt of the sins of this system. This, for me, is a religious and spiritual obligation—nothing more and nothing less."

Hers is a fierce voice for gospel justice, a compelling one, a voice that comforts the weary and confronts the comfortable. But it is an authentic one? I think an authentic voice for justice can be measured by three criteria: Is it fearless? Is it self-critical? Is it humble?

To be fearless, a voice for justice must speak its truth to benefactors at cocktail parties and family members at holiday meals with the same zeal as it does to popes and presidents in public forums. Here are three instances where Joan's authentic voice can be judged.

Writing an opinion piece on the fortieth anniversary of the *National Catholic Reporter*, Joan recalls her first act of protest. She writes of being appalled when, as a young sister, she heard that a renewal-minded young prioress of a Benedictine monastery was removed from office. What appalled Joan, besides the fact that Rome listed as a reason for removal "too much of her hair showed under the headband," was that the sister-president of the Benedictine Federation had issued the decree at the bidding of the Vatican. She immediately sat down and wrote the Federation president a letter. Joan writes, "She had, I told her from my young perch, allowed herself to be used as an instrument of oppression in the name of faith, which I felt convinced was bigger than authoritarianism, bigger than obedience to a system." This simple act of courage coming from "a little nobody from nowhere," as Joan describes herself in the written account, is in retrospect alarmingly brave. Given the nature of religious life at the time, it was unheard of not only to question but to chastise the leader of her Benedictine family.

In the 1980s, Joan was in Texas to give a lecture. Prior to the event there was a hospitality party, and Ronald Reagan suddenly appeared on a large-screen television in the room to announce that he had just signed a piece of legislation instructing U.S. border guards to shoot anyone coming over the Rio Grande. Joan writes, "I heard people around me making comments like, 'Well I hate to have something like this happen, but what else can Reagan do for Pete's sake; after all, you gotta get tough with these people.' And at that point I said aloud, out of quiet desperation, 'Well, we could give Texas back.' And the room went perfectly still, like one of the E. F. Hutton ads."

Admittedly, outrageous. These two lasers of uncensored truth, delivered with fearless abandon, make an audience gasp audibly and then respond in thundering applause. Here's a third instance, this one directed at church authority. When *Newsday* asked her

what she would say to Pope John Paul II if she had three minutes with him, part of Joan's response was "I am grateful for the
pope's recent letter in support of equality for women and his
apology for the church's role in denying full equality. But when
I was in the second grade, Sister told me that confession of guilt
was not enough, that you had to have a firm purpose of amendment. It's the firm purpose of amendment I'm looking for."

The second measure of an authentic voice for justice is the
ability to be self-critical. I have always admired Joan for putting in print a time when she let herself down, when she failed
to match her own standards of justice. It happened in 1976,
when Joan was president of the Leadership Conference of
Women Religious, and the Vatican issued its first explanation
for the nonordination of women. Instead of confronting the
theological shortcomings of the Vatican statement and challenging it on behalf of women everywhere, Joan writes, "My
official response was short and bland; oh, very true, yes, but
very, very political. The statement I put out said, 'Now that we
understand what the issue is, we can study it.' It was the perfect answer of the perfect victim in the face of perfect power.
It was 'nice.' It wasn't 'aggressive.' And it did nothing at all to
advance the question of the role of women in the church or
to invite dialogue. I had opted to save the organization rather
than to 'speak truth to power.' And in that act, truth, as I knew
it in the depths of me, wasted away." And then comes her firm
purpose of amendment: "I knew then and there that I would
never do that again. I would never again squander the tiny
space a woman has to say anything of value."

And finally, is the voice for justice humble? It might surprise
the large audiences that Joan addresses to know that when she
confidently strides across the stage to the microphone, usually to
a standing ovation, Joan is silently reciting a prayer. It is a Prayer
for a Happy Death that she found in the back of a missal in
her early twenties and memorized, not to prepare for death, but
to prepare for acceptance of the present moment. She changed
"death" to "deaths," and prior to a speech, opens herself to

accepting whatever God has in store for the sake of her spiritual development. As she grabs the podium and begins to tear down the mighty from their thrones of power, she prays, "Lord Jesus, at this moment, I do accept from Thy hands with a quiet and trusting heart, whatsoever deaths Thou shalt choose to send me, with all their pain and grief."

It is a tradition of the Benedictine Sisters of Erie to give a "title" to each sister on the day of her final profession. For example, one sister might be given "The Compassion of God," another, "The Immaculate Heart of Mary," a third, "The Peace of Jesus," and so on. Joan was given the title "The Justice of Benedict." When she received it at the age of twenty-one, she was both disappointed and clueless as to its meaning. Call it providential or mystical, even, but it was a title that eventually tapped her deepest passion and defines her life.

PASSION FOR RELIGIOUS LIFE

The leadership team of my congregation, the Sisters of St. Agnes, sent each of us a copy of your book The Fire in These Ashes. *I could not put it down. It is the best treatment of aspects of religious life that I have read in years. You very honestly address pressing and even painful issues, but you do it in such a hopeful manner. I am most grateful to you for this work.*

—Dianne Bergant, CSA, the Carroll Stuhlmueller, C.P.,
Distinguished Professor of Old Testament Studies
at Catholic Theological Union, Chicago

Joan claims she decided to become a sister at the age of three, when her father died and her mother took her to the funeral parlor. She remembers seeing "the strangest looking people" sitting at the end of the casket, "all wrapped in black."

"What are those?" she asked her mother. "Joan, those are very special friends of God," her mother answered, "and they're very special friends of your Daddy's. They give little girls' daddies to God. So they'll stay here. When the angels come tonight, they'll say, 'This is Joan's daddy. He was a very good man. You take him

straight to God so that he doesn't have to wait anyplace else.'"
According to Joan, this was such an exalted work that she resolved
right there to become a nun and never wavered in that decision.

But it was a decision that was tested. The first test came with
shocking immediacy—five weeks after her entrance when she
was stricken with polio. She was hospitalized, placed in an iron
lung, and then confined to a wheelchair. Joan credits her eventual recovery, in large part, to Sister Theophane Siegel, a nurse
who was subprioress at the time and worked with Joan through
four years of daily therapy. Sister Theophane was also a visionary and brilliant woman. She recognized the rarity of Joan's gifts
and mentored her, smuggling her formative reading material
that was not permitted in the novitiate library, but provided a
solid base in Joan's spiritual development.

The polio incident also meant years of turbulence for the
Erie Benedictines who were divided about whether or not
to send Joan home. What was the fair thing to do for both
Joan and the community? Joan was adamant about staying
and did the impossible to keep a normal schedule, dragging
her heavy leg brace down long halls and high stairwells, to
attend hours of daily prayer, and meals in the refectory, and
to keep up with study and chores. In the end, her desire for
religious life, her unyielding resolve and stern courage, convinced the community that they were dealing with a unique
vocation, and it might be best not to intervene.

A second major test came during Vatican Council II and the
turmoil that ensued as religious orders were mandated to renew
their lives by "returning to the scriptures and the charism of
the founder." In the Erie Benedictine community, Joan was not
an early proponent of renewal. She cared deeply about the tradition, was not satisfied with the reasons given for such drastic
change, and so questioned every tenet behind the rationale. To
those seeking change, she was a scorned though formidable
opponent. When it became apparent that change was inevi-
table, but the reasons were still not satisfactory to her, Joan
considered leaving and even went to inform her parents. They

cautioned her to examine her motives carefully—why had she entered religious life, really?

She described that period for herself—and for most religious—as akin to "walking through the outskirts of hell." Communities were frightened, confused, and polarized. Everything was up for grabs—schedules, clothing, ministry, living situations, the nature of the vows and of religious life itself. Since one of her main concerns was the wearing of the habit, she remembers clearly asking herself, with typical Chittister humor, "Joan, it comes down to this. Are you or are you not a Benedictine in the bathtub?"

She emerged from the agonized soul searching with what she calls her greatest life lesson—the ability to make the transition from the nonessential to the heart of the matter. "I had to get to the point where I asked myself, 'What really matters?' The only answer that I could come up with was that Christ mattered, the gospel mattered, the people mattered. That was it."

Within those pivotal renewal years, Joan began her doctorate at Penn State University in communications theory, with an emphasis on organizational and social psychology. What she was unable to hear in her own community about organizational decline, renewal, and revitalization, she was "now being taught, three credits at a time."

Having gained both interior freedom and certitude about the future direction of religious life, equipped with a background in organizational theory and a gift for making academic theory both understandable and doable, Joan was positioned to make an impact. Though Joan's prodigious abilities were always evident, a series of elections to major religious positions, beginning while she was in her thirties provided opportunity for her charismatic leadership to thrive in a national arena: president of the Federation of Saint Scholastica, president of the Conference of Benedictine Prioresses, president of the Leadership Conference of Religious Women and prioress of the Benedictine Sisters, and the U.S. delegate to the International Union of Superiors General (UISG) for four years.

In this new venue, Joan became one of the most articulate analysts and advocates for religious life. Not only was she able to champion the new face of religious life to the media, the person in the pew, and the hierarchy, but she was able to express clearly the reasons behind the changes and, more particularly, reexamine the role of religious in the church.

The group that received her concentrated attention, however, were the sisters themselves. Joan made it her mission to complete the renewal process: "The early years of renewal enabled us all to grow up," she would tell audiences of sisters. "Now it's time to ask ourselves what did we grew up for." With burning zeal she pursued that question in religious communities across the United States and the world.

The synthesis of Joan's thinking, based on over thirty years of experience, became the book *The Fire in These Ashes: A Spirituality of Contemporary Religious Life* (Sheed & Ward, 1995). She writes in the preface:

> I have watched religious life both from an intensely personal position and from an internationally public perspective, both from the bottom of the institutional ladder and, like Simon Stylites, from the top of it, as a young nun before Vatican II and as a national administrator in the decades following it. I have watched it close-up in convents from Washington to Rome, from coast to coast, from Erie, Pennsylvania, to Australia and back. I have chaired and presided and interviewed and organized and researched religious life through phase after phase of the renewal project. As a communication theorist and social scientist, I looked always for signs of life and signs of holiness, asked myself what, if anything, was bringing life to religious communities, despite the struggles of change, and what was not.

In the book, Joan directly addresses the questions still facing religious today: What is religious life for? Is it still viable? Are those who stay wasting their time? Should we encourage others to enter? Is religious life dead? And her answer strikes at the heart of the call: The only purpose of religious life is the single-minded search for God. Religious must own this call, proclaim it, and be so afire with God that they cannot rest until the world is ablaze with love. The human quest for God is made visible in "professional" seekers of every religious tradition, and it is this desire for God that is their reason to be. "It is the function of religious life," Joan wrote, "to concentrate on fanning to flame the spiritual lights within them that enable a people to go on treading the path to wholeness."

Though some in the church blame renewal efforts and leaders like Joan Chittister for the decline in the number of women entering religious life, Joan maintains that religious life is more authentic now, and numbers do not measure viability. She is less concerned with survival than with staying the path to holiness. "The fact is that religious life was never meant simply to be a labor force in the church," Joan wrote. "It was meant to be a searing presence, a paradigm of search, a mark of human soul, and a catalyst to conscience in the society in which it emerged." Religious, she believed, simply find what is not being done and do it so that others will see the need to do it, too. At one time that meant starting schools and opening hospitals for the poor and uneducated Catholic immigrants who could not afford education or health care. Now it means identifying the new poor and responding to the burning issues of the day.

The community of sisters worldwide recognized in Joan a woman they could trust. She never shied from asking the difficult questions or posing the challenges to be surmounted or weakened the personal transformation needed for religious life to embrace gospel authenticity. Not everyone agreed with her vision, but few could question that it emanated from a woman deeply passionate about religious life, for the treasure it held "to transform the world, to bring the foolish standards of the gospel to the issues of the age."

It is no exaggeration to write that at the age of three Joan began a love affair with religious life. It continues to this day.

A WOMAN OF THE CHURCH

Already one of the true voices of the post–Vatican II
age, she speaks to us as a woman, as church, as spiritual
guide, but most of all, as following the mystical poet
Blake in a voice that cleanses the doors of perception
so that we may see the universe as it is—infinite. Joan
understands that religion is not the work of the will but
of the imagination and that the church is the sacrament
of the world, just as it is.

—Eugene Kennedy, professor emeritus
of psychology at Loyola University

Joan Chittister traces her questioning attitude toward the Roman
Catholic Church to second grade when the sister who was teaching religion told the class that only Catholics went to heaven. Joan
remembers racing home after school and telling her mother who
asked, "And what do you think about that, Joan?" Joan replied
that she thought the sister was wrong because "Sister doesn't know
Daddy." Joan knew her Protestant father and his family to read
the Bible, to attend Sunday school, to sing hymns and to pray. Sister, she concluded, had not seen what God saw. Her mother held
her closely and said, "That's right darling. That's right." Affirmed
by a mother whom she worshiped, and trusting her own experience, Joan eventually concluded, "That day I learned that keeping
the faith requires more than keeping the rules."

If the seven-year-old could not publicly question the church
doctrine being taught by a grade school nun, the adult Chittister
made it her mission to question controversial church teachings
that were locked to discussion. If the church could be in error
about this particular official teaching, might there be others and,
if so, wasn't there a burning responsibility to differentiate institutional obedience from gospel obedience?

Though she has challenged the church for its tepidity and
inconsistency on the immorality of modern warfare, for devot-
ing its resources to anti-abortion efforts rather than to a full pro-
life spectrum, for being punitive toward theologians and activists

who speak out for inclusivity in the church, Joan has reserved most of her searing critique for the church's treatment of women.

When asked in a book interview what she would do if she were "Pope for a Year," Joan replied, "The first thing I would do is to bring women into all arenas of the church . . . and I would do it overnight. Why? Because that's the only way you're going to hear and develop a full theology of church. Don't talk to me about social justice and do nothing about the case of women. Don't talk to me about the sanctity of marriage and do nothing about the training of men and male attitudes toward the way the family goes together. Don't talk to me about justice and assume that half of the human race can simply carry the injustice of the other half and 'offer it up.' I won't go there."

Joan's outspoken challenges to the institution have made her a target of those in the church with differing views who brand her as "insubordinate," "arrogant," "scandalous," "disobedient," "defiant," and "dangerous." She is banned from speaking in many dioceses in the United States. When she was to give the 2001 keynote address at the National Catholic Education Association's annual convention in Milwaukee, the bishops of Pittsburgh and Peoria asked their teachers not to attend and refused to permit diocesan funds to those who went anyway. (A side note: The Institute Leadership Conference of the Sisters of Mercy was meeting when this ban was reported and quickly and publicly announced a pledge to "offer economic assistance to teachers of both dioceses who wish to attend.") In 2007, Bishop Barry Jones refused to let Joan speak in New Zealand. When the Benedictine Abbey of Schuyler in Omaha, Nebraska, refused a request by neighboring Bishop Fabian Bruskewitz in Lincoln, Nebraska, to cancel Joan's speaking engagement at their monastery, the diocese refused to advertise any of the abbey's retreats or vocation material in its publications.

Her greatest crisis with church authorities occurred in 2001, when Joan was scheduled to address the First Annual Conference on Women's Ordination Worldwide in Dublin, Ireland. Because the Holy See had decreed that the topic of women's ordination could not be discussed in a church, Sister Christine Vladimiroff, the then prioress of the Benedictine Sisters of Erie, was sent a letter by the Congregation for the Institutes of Consecrated Life and Societies of Apostolic Life—that soon became public—instructing her to forbid Joan to attend the conference, under obedience, on pain of unspecified "just penalties."

Sister Christine declined to administer the decree and issued a press release. She explained: "There is a fundamental difference in the understanding of obedience in the monastic tradition and that which is being used by the Vatican. . . . Benedictine authority and obedience are achieved through dialogue between a member and her prioress in a spirit of co-responsibility. . . . Sister Joan Chittister, who has lived the monastic life with faith and fidelity for fifty years, must make her own decision." The Benedictine community voted 127 to 1 in support of Sister Christine's decision. Joan attended the conference and spoke on discipleship and the ordination of deaconesses, but reading the speech, included in this book, makes her stance on women's ordination clear.

The "just penalties" for disobeying were reserved for Sister Christine and the Erie Benedictines who were subject to an extraordinary Apostolic Visitation by the Holy See. The entire episode brought enormous tension and conflict to the Erie community—some wanted to make the entire process public and others preferred a private handling. In the end, the negotiations and sanctions were handled behind closed doors. Sister Joan, herself, received no official reprimand, nor was she silenced. Nevertheless, the Vatican adroitly tightened the vise around Joan's heart, making it clear that deciding to follow her conscience in the future meant pain and suffering for the community she loved.

The irony is that though differing voices in the church believe Joan is "leading the faithful astray," a large number of Catholics return or stay in the church because of her words and witness. For instance, in January 2008, readers of *U.S. Catholic* magazine voted Joan Chittister "by far the most inspirational woman currently alive." The reason given by one reader was echoed by most: "She works for change from within the community she calls her home. She is an example of what it means to be on fire with the Spirit, loving her church so much that she cannot sit quietly in the face of injustice."

Her archives contain letter upon letter with sentiments similar to this one from a woman in Richmond, Virgina, following Joan's appearance on *NOW with Bill Moyers*: "I have been struggling with my Catholic identity. . . . I was starting to think that maybe I didn't have a real understanding of the Catholic church . . . that maybe social justice wasn't as important to the church as I thought it was. . . . I even stopped going to Mass. Sister Joan gave me some hope. She has inspired me to seek a less conservative, more social justice-oriented Catholic church in my new hometown. Thanks for the hope and inspiration."

It is no small matter to remember that Joan does not challenge church decrees and behaviors only on the basis of outside observer. For many years, she attended meetings in Rome for the worldwide network of Benedictine women, as a representative of the Leadership Conference of Women Religious (LCWR) and as the U.S. representative to the International Union of Superiors General (UISG), which met in Rome annually. The UISG brought together women religious superiors from around the world "to foster religious life through research, reflection, and collaboration." Joan's personal journal from the 1983 meeting, for example, gives an inside view of how leaders of women's communities were treated by the Vatican. Joan writes how the women themselves, all at varying degrees of renewal and coming from diverse cultures, are awakening to the women's issues and desiring more collaboration. But the LCWR officers, who met with the Institute of the Sacred Congregation of Religious, reported that they "spent three terrible hours with the head of SCRIS, Augustine Mayer, who says our constitutions will not be approved unless we require and describe a habit, that if not we 'can be Secular Institutes.'" Joan continues, "The frustration and anger and alienation is high. Harassment and control is the order of the day. . . . [One superior] has heard from Washington that Rome is beginning an 'observation' of all American religious communities." This is 1983, remember, twenty-five years prior to when the official Vatican observation—visitation—takes place in the United States. And during all those years, outstanding women leaders, Joan included, traveled faithfully to Rome in hope of honest dialogue and were treated instead with suspicion and disdain.

It takes no stretch of the imagination, then, to understand that the question Joan gets asked most frequently is: Why do you stay in the church?

An essay included in this book, "Why I Stay," gives an eloquent answer. And in a magazine interview, Joan explained that for her the church was "The keeper of the history of our journey together . . . A sacramental system that renders all life holy . . . A pillar of light." She noted that even if a family is dysfunctional, you still have love for it and hope for it. "For me," she said, "it isn't a matter of being upset with the church. It is a matter of wanting a better world and more light, even for the church."

In the final analysis, Joan believes that pursuing the questions honestly while remaining faithful is evidence that she cares deeply about the church. Furthermore, she wants to be true to her calling. "If all those years of prayer and service and immersion in the scriptures are to mean anything, then the Jesus who raised questions to the Pharisees must not die in religious life. . . . If the unacceptable question is to come from anywhere, it should come from the religious community. It is a question of naming the questions. That is the function of religious life."

JOAN THE PERSON

I'll get straight to the point: the laugh. Not a timid one, not a polite let's-be-civil one, certainly not one that suggests timidity or nervousness. No, hers is a laugh, genuine, from the belly, a laugh that embraces where her arms can't reach. It is a laugh that removes from us the weight of pieties and strained holiness; it is a laugh as loud and raucous and warm and indiscriminate as the love of God for the real world. —Tom Roberts, journalist

"Nothing great in the world has been accomplished without passion," wrote the German philosopher Hegel.

Joan's passion for the spiritual, for justice, for ideas, for writing, have accomplished much, but must be measured by the fire that fuels them—her passion for life and for people.

Joan loves people, and they respond in kind. Take this account from a 1987 story in *National Catholic Reporter,* when she was part of a peace delegation to the Soviet Union. Asked by the Soviet Peace Committee of Baku to address a packed congregation at the local Russian Orthodox Church of Mary, Joan nervously stepped forward. We were still mired in the Cold War, and the Russian people in the church were serious, grim even, with no smiles of welcome or trust. What's more, they were confronted with a woman, head uncovered, speaking in an Orthodox house of worship.

Joan began to speak, slowly and simply. She told them that this moment was the highlight of her trip because she was able to look Russian people in the eye and tell them that the U.S. delegation cared for them and did not want war. *The people looked up.*

She assured them that this delegation was only a hint of the church people all over the United States who held in their hands olive branches of peace. *People standing outside the church moved in through the doors to listen.*

She told them that this group and others in the United States protested the arms race and the arming of the heavens (Star Wars). *The people blessed themselves.*

Then she told them that the delegation pledged, on behalf of the Russian people, to double their peacemaking efforts when they returned to the States. *The congregation nodded vigorously and many began to cry.*

She ended by telling them this story:

> An old rabbi once asked his pupils how they could tell when the night had ended and the day had begun.

"Could it be," asked one of the students, "when you can see an animal in the distance and tell whether it's a sheep or a dog?"

"No," answered the rabbi.

Another asked, "Is it when you can look at tree in the distance and tell whether it's a fig tree or a peach tree?"

"No," answered the rabbi.

"Then when is it?" the pupils demanded.

"It is when you can look on the face of any man or woman and see that it is your sister or brother. Because if you cannot see this, it is still night."

—*Tales of the Hasidim*

Then she prayed, "Mary, the Mother of God, lead us to the morning when all people, for the sake of the whole human race, are 'able to see in every human face, the face of a brother or sister.'" *Now the whole congregation began to talk aloud and smile and bow. They moved toward the delegation with handshakes and hugs.*

As Joan started off the platform she was grabbed by the crowd and kissed and blessed and passed from one set of arms to another. *"They cried," she said, "and so did I."*

This passionate response to Joan in this incident, dramatic for its context, is repeated almost every time she enters a room or addresses an audience. She exudes an energy that propels people into its sphere of acceptance and hope. She has the ability of concentrating her entire attention on you, even in the midst of a crowd, and assuring you that she sees you at your best, no matter the circumstances.

Not only is there a constant stream of people coming to Joan for direction but there are file cases filled with correspondence from strangers pouring out their hearts on such weighty matters as depression, divorce, sexual identity, and alienation from the church. Joan personally answers every letter received and in many instances writes to the person for months until the writer finds some peace.

Here's a letter from a mother whose son's promising football career was cut short in his last high school game by a head-to-head collision that put him into a three-month coma from which he emerged barely functional. "I thought I was going to have a complete breakdown, but I had to hold it together for my son. No one was of any help to me. Then someone recommended your book, *Scarred by Struggle*. That book saved my life. Finally, finally someone understood what I was going through. I thought to myself, 'She wrote this book for me.' I was undergoing every stage of suffering that you described and, most importantly, you held out to me an eventual healing point."

Another woman who was on the verge of breakdown because of an unresolved childhood trauma told me, "I remember Joan saying over and over again, 'We are going to walk into that dark cave together and find only a toothless dragon.' Like all abuse victims, I blamed my six-year-old self for what had happened to me. But she freed me from a shame and burden that I had put on myself and eventually I was able to laugh at the toothless dragon. It was in my thirties and it was the first time that I told my entire abuse story to anyone. I could only do it because she made me feel so safe and so loved. She saved my life."

When you consider the number of people who attest that their lives were changed by Joan's writings, speeches, and personal interactions, it is difficult not to conclude that she is at her core an enormously gifted pastor and spiritual healer. Her twelve years as prioress of the Benedictine Sisters of Erie were further proof of this when, under Joan's leadership, the monastery was transformed into a hearth of hospitality, where the poor, the rich, refugees, peace activists, families, gays, women, and travelers from around the world found a home. Community numbers also grew significantly during these years with new vocations and many sisters who transferred from other communities to Erie.

Joan is also a good time, a lover of life who enters every situation with gas pedal floored. She mixes easily with both the wealthy and the destitute. Maria Shriver starts her day by reading a daily inspiration from Joan's newsletter, *The Monastic Way,* and writes Joan: "I am in awe of your passion to serve and make a difference. . . . Your writing has guided and inspired me." Norma, a prisoner in California, receives a pamphlet free from the Joan Chittister Fund for Prisoners, and also reads it faithfully each day. She writes: "It is a blessing to have found your beautiful and inspiring pamphlet *The Monastic Way.* Your publication is a light in a dark place."

Following her term as prioress, Joan moved to a small priory in inner-city Erie where she's lived for twenty-five years. "You listen with the ear of your heart in a different way here," she explains. "Angry voices awaken you in the middle of the night; your doorbell rings and there's someone asking for food; a neighborhood child we befriended comes in for homework help. I read the scriptures a bit differently now." Despite international and national demands that consume her schedule, she takes time for the poor in her hometown. Joan was instrumental in starting a Benedictine Sisters Inner City Neighborhood Art House in Erie that provides free instruction in the visual, performing, and literary arts to at-risk children, and she serves on the board of the community's soup kitchen.

Joan collects jokes and opens most lectures with one from her collection—"They help me see the silly irony of the human condition," she says. Joan is crazy about animals. So far she has owned two large dogs—a golden retriever and Irish setter—and two birds, the present one named "Lady" after Hildegard of Bingen. She dotes on Lady and thinks she'd be content living in one room with her computer and pet bird. That would hold true for about two days, and then a neighbor would knock and then another. She loves music and led many community parties playing a mean accordion until a bad back switched her to a keyboard that she plays for relaxation.

There isn't a technological gadget that Joan doesn't lust after. However, she must hold the Guinness world record for computer glitches, breakdowns, and hours spent on the phone getting help from computer geeks, who all know her personally and probably are invited for Christmas. She once raced a small motorboat, the *Abbey*, across Lake Erie to get away from the barrage of personal demands. (Phone rings: "Is Sister Joan in?" "No, I'm sorry. She's at the *Abbey*.") On the *Abbey*, she spent long, lazy summer afternoons fishing. On the *Abbey*, she also was cited twice within the same hour for speeding by the Coast Guard, despite the fact she had a bishop on board. She loves to cook but don't expect meatloaf—it will be something exotic that takes twenty-four hours to prepare and an army of volunteers to gather ingredients and clean up afterward.

Joan does not "suffer fools gladly," so be prepared to have your talking points in place if you decide to debate with her. Though she is available to all and can count legions of acquaintances, she has a handful of strong and intimate friendships that have endured for decades. She can start a party by walking in a room, and no one enjoys a good time more. "She has a razor wit and a full-throttle laugh. She tells a good joke. After a working session she relaxes with you, delights in good wine, belts out a solo of 'I Am Woman, Hear Me Roar,' in a karaoke bar," wrote Helen Prejean, author of *Dead Man Walking* and a leading advocate for abolishing the death penalty, who has shared a few conferences and happy hours with Joan.

Prior to the election of Pope Francis, theologian Matthew Fox wrote a column listing his two nominees for the papacy. The first was the Dalai Lama and the second was Joan Chittister. And in a column dealing with the naming of Benedictine Abbess Hildegard of Bingen as Doctor of the Church, Robert McClory wrote, "In a sense, St. Hildegard of Bingen could be considered a twelfth-century combination of Joan Chittister, Hilary Clinton, and Joan Baez." Fox and McClory both recognized in Joan a woman of largesse, outrageous and extravagant in vision and heart, a woman who took Jesus at his word when he proclaimed, "I have come that they may have life, and have it more abundantly." Both of them saw her as a woman who has loved the church enough to challenge its unjust structures and has loved people enough to beckon them to beatitude living, because she loves God enough to bring a brilliant new spiritual vision to the times.

Mary Lou Kownacki is a Benedictine Sister of Erie and has been a friend and co-worker of Joan Chittister for forty-five years.

1

PASSION FOR GOD

God is not now who God was for me in 1950.

—Joan Chittister

Sister Joan Chittister's desire for union with God is the defining characteristic of her life. Her spiritual and intellectual depth and insight are the fruit of decades of disciplined commitment to personal growth in self-knowledge, in contemplative prayer, in community life, and in an ever-emerging consciousness of the plight of the crucified people of this age.

If the reader is also a seeker, she will discover that Joan's passion for God is a graced invitation to join her on a journey to spiritual adulthood. It will be a "long haul," populated with demanding challenges, surprising adventures, unanticipated detours, painful obstacles, and gratuitous blessings. Companions on this journey with Joan are asked only the following:

- ◆ *To honor their questions;*

- ◆ *To "listen with the ear of their heart";*

- ◆ *To be open to conversion;*

- ◆ *To pray deeply;*

- ◆ *To confront injustice; and*

- ◆ *To embrace the journey with joy, gratitude, and uncommon hope.*

A SEEKER'S PATH
Seeking God

The search for God
is a very intimate enterprise.
It is at the core
of every longing in the human heart.
It is the search for ultimate love,
for total belonging,
for the meaningful life.

It is our attempt
to live life and find it worthwhile,
to come to see the presence of God
under all the phantoms and shadows—
beyond all the illusions of life—
and find it enough.

But the search depends,
at least in part,
on the complex of energies within us
that we bring to the challenges
of this seeking.

We do not all hear the same tones
at the same volume,
or see the same visions
in the same colors,
or seek the same goods of life
in the same way.

The search for God depends, then,
on choosing the spiritual path
most suited to our own
spiritual temper and character.

For some seekers,
it is in withdrawal from society

or by immersion in nature
that God is most present.

For others, the face of God
shows most clearly
in the face of the poor,
or is felt most keenly
through the support of those
with whom they share
a common spiritual regimen.

For many, it is a bit of both,
a balance of community,
contemplation,
and commitment
to the people of God.
It is the search to belong
to a group of fellow travelers
who will hold us up
when we fall,
and urge us on to greater heights
when we are afraid to strain for more.

These are the seekers who are looking for others
who seek what they seek,
who care about what they care about,
and who set out with them
to make life richer
and the world better
than they know they could ever do alone.

But whatever the nature
of a seeker's lifestyle,
the search for God
depends, as well,
on the spiritual maturity it takes
to move from one level
of spiritual insight to another—

rather than cling to the spiritual satisfaction
that comes with earlier,
less demanding, practices.
The search for God depends on the desire
to grow to full stature as a spiritual adult,
to come to know the God
who is as present in darkness
as in light.

It depends on the willingness
to let God lead us
through the deserts of a lifetime,
along routes we would not go,
into the Promised Land of our own lives.

Most of all, the search for God
depends on fidelity
to the demands of the search itself.
It is the constancy of commitment
which we bring to the spiritual path
that prepares us
to recognize and receive
the fullness of it.

There is, as a result,
more than one way
to go about the journey
to God.   —*The Monastery of the Heart*

God Become Infinitely Larger

Joan has spoken for many ecumenical and interfaith gatherings around the globe. This invitation was sponsored by the Hundere Endowment for Religion and Culture at Oregon State; the Chautauqua Institution of Chautauqua, New York; and the Trinity Institute of Trinity Parish, New York City. It was held in Portland, Oregon, and hosted by biblical and Jesus scholar, Marcus Borg. The topic was "God at 2000." This opportunity gave Sister Joan a chance to speak about who God had become for her at that point in her life. Her unfolding understanding of the Divine remains an integral aspect of her writing and speaking engagements. Sister Joan is convinced there is a deep correlation between a person's image of God and one's spiritual maturity.

Two seekers inspire a sense of the possibility and potential of this topic, and shape these reflections of mine on "God at 2000."

The first is an old Sufi who was found scratching through the sand in the middle of the road. "What are you doing, Sufi?" pilgrims asked as they passed him, digging and scratching, on their way to the temple.

"I am looking for the treasure I have lost," the old man said. So the pilgrims, good people all, dropped to their knees to help—sifting sand, digging under stones, and sweating under the waxing midday sun. Finally, hungry, soaking wet, and exhausted, one of the travelers said to him at last, "Sufi, are you sure you lost your treasure here?"

The old man said, "Oh my! No. I did not lose my treasure here. I lost it over there on the other side of those mountains."

"Well, if you lost it on the other side of the mountains," the people shouted at him, "why, in the name of Allah, are you looking for it here?"

And the old man said, "I am looking for it here because there is more light here."

My second guide through the complexities of this question is the seeker who asked the holy one: "How are we to seek union with God?"

And the holy one said, "The harder you seek, the more distance you create between God and you."

"Then what does one do about the distance?" the disciple persisted.

And the holy one said, "Understand that it isn't there."

"But does that mean that God and I are one?" the seeker asked.

And the holy one said: "Not one. Not two."

"But how is that possible?" the seeker said. And the holy one said: "The sun and its light, the ocean and the wave, the singer and his song: Not one. Not two."

Ideas about God

What I have learned about God after a lifetime of seeking is that, first, God must be sought in the light, and that, second, God does not have to be found.

If there is anything in the world, however, that may deserve our pity, it may well be the very idea of "God." What else in the history of humankind has been more reviled as fraud, more ridiculed as unprovable or, on the other hand, more glorified out of existence—more condemned to unattainable remoteness—than the notion of God?

A wag wrote once: "First God created us, and then we created God." The insight may be far too true to ignore, and the consequences of it far too distancing to celebrate.

The marketplace is, in fact, full of ideas about God—religious tradition itself not the least of the purveyors of them. Some of these ideas have been helpful to the development of a God-life within me, some of them not.

Whatever the images of God we offer, whatever the effects of them spiritually and socially, I have come to the conclusion over the years that it is precisely our idea of God that is the measure of our spiritual maturity. What we believe about God colors everything we do in the name of God, everything we think about other people, everything we determine about life itself.

It is the kind of God in which we choose to believe that in the end makes all the difference. And each of us fashions a private God the face of whom shapes our own.

Some believe, for instance, in a God of wrath and so themselves become wrathful with others as a result. Some believe in a God who is indifferent to the world and, when they find themselves alone—as all of us do at some time or another—they shrivel up and die inside from the indifference they feel in the world around them.

Some believe in a God who makes traffic lights turn green and so become the children of magical coincidence in a world crying out for clear-eyed, hard-headed, responsible shapers of this clay called life.

Some believe in a God of laws, and crumble in spirit and psyche when they themselves break those laws or else become even more stern in demanding from others standards they themselves cannot keep. They conceive of God as the manipulator of the universe rather than its ground. God, they hold, is the part of the scene that lies behind the objects in the forefront. They project onto God humanity's own small desires and indignities and needs.

I have known all of those Gods in my own life, and they have all failed me.

I have learned that law-keeping did not satisfy my need for meaning. I learned that, to be properly wicked, it was not necessary to break the law—just to keep it to the letter! I have learned that the fear of wrath did not seduce me to love. I have learned that God, the distant doer of unpredictable and arbitrary magic, failed to engage or enliven my soul. I have learned that life was surely about far more important things than that. If the question, then, is "Who is God for me in the year 2000?" my answer has to be: "God is not the God I thought I knew in 1950."

One of the best things I was ever taught about God was by a philosophy professor who told us that we could not "think" God. And he was obviously right, though clearly, think God we did— and aplenty. In my own case, God has been a changing, moving, inviting, disturbing, and totally engrossing mystery, and the more I thought about God, it seemed, the less I knew God at all.

I have feared the God of judgment and been judgmental of others. I have used God to get me through life. I have called the intolerable "God's will" and called our failure to stop evil God's failure to stop evil. I have expected God to be the crutch that would make the unbearable bearable. As a result, I often failed to take steps to change life either for myself or others when injustice masked itself as God's will and oppression as God's judgment.

I thought about God "out there" and became blind to God within me. And so, thinking of God as far away, I failed to make God present to others who were in my presence.

I have, in other words, allowed God to be mediated to me through images of God foreign to the very idea of God:

God the puppeteer, who created free will but takes it back when it gets inconvenient;

God the potentate, whose interest is self-love;

God the persecutor who created life to trap it in its own ignorance;

God the mighty male to whom obedience, subservience, and deference were the only proper response, and in whose being women were apparent only by their absence.

I have come to the conclusion, after a lifetime of looking for God, that a divinity such as these is simply a graven image of ourselves, not a God big enough to believe in.

The God in whom we choose to believe determines the rest of life for us. In our conception of the nature of God lies the kernel of the spiritual life. Made in the image of God, we grow in the image of the God we make for ourselves.

Knowing God

I learned as life went by that the God I make will be the God I seek, the spiritual life I live, and the quality of my own heart. Until I discover the God in whom I myself believe, then, until I unmask the God who lives in my own heart, regardless of the panoply of other God-images around me, I will never understand another thing about my own life.

I learned as life went on that clearly the professor was correct: I could not think God. But, I have now learned, the professor was also incorrect at the same time. Not to be able to think about God is only to make God unthinkable; it is not to make God unreal. The great spiritual truth, I learned over the years, is that, indeed, we cannot think God. We can only know God. And when we do think God into some single separate stultifying shape, it is only a sign that we now run the risk of knowing God less and less.

Each of these separate dimensions of God—justice and law and reason and omnipotence and a kind of "tsk-tsking" love at a distance—marks a stage of my own life. Each of them has been a highway marker through a complex of religious practices. Each of them has been good for the sake of the focus they gave me but false when they became an end in themselves and dimmed the sacramental nature—the divine depths—of the rest of life.

I became more and more convinced that God was to be found in other places and that only the search itself could possibly save me from the worst consequences of each.

I have seen God grow. Or maybe I have seen me grow and couldn't tell the difference.

I have become sure that if all I know about God is that my God is the fullness of life and the consummation of hope, the light on the way and the light at the end, then I will live my life in the consciousness of God and goodness everywhere, obscure at times, perhaps, but never wholly lacking.

So now God, that old rascal, is doing it again. I am moving in my heart from God as a trophy to be won, or a master, however benign, to be pacified, to God as cosmic unity and everlasting light.

The change has been gradual but very, very clear. It has come at the juncture of five divides, all seemingly separate, but all of a piece: spiritual tradition, personal experience, science, globalism, and feminism. These have all come together in my life to show me a God whom I cannot think but do deeply know to be true. I have learned from them all to know a greater God than I had been given. Let me explain.

The spiritual tradition that guides me is an ancient one: The *Rule of Benedict* of Nursia (a Catholic document written in the sixth century and still the way of life for thousands of monastics today). Chapter Seven—"On Humility"—sums up Benedict's spiritual theology. In light of the spirituality of the last several hundred years, what he says is at least startling if not unsettling.

The first degree of humility, the first step on the way to God, is to have always before our eyes what the ancients call the fear of God—what we know as the sense of God, the awe of God, the awareness of God, the presence of God.

The religious culture of Benedict's time was immersed in merit theology, a theology that sought deliverance from damnation by earning God. So many Masses equal so much union with God, so many rosaries equal so many units of God, so many penances and sacrifices and formulas of the faith equal so much fullness of God. Into this religious culture came an astounding revelation. The first step to union with God is knowing that you already have God, you already enjoy God, and you already contain within yourself the life that is God.

Both the Jewish mystic Isaac Luria (1534–1572) and the Catholic theologian Pierre Teilhard de Chardin (1881–1955) speak of the sparks of God—the residue of the creator in all of us—as common to the entire human race. The idea goes back to Moses at a flaming bush; to Jesus aglow on a mountaintop; to Benedict's first degree of humility that teaches us the grandeur of us all; to the mystic Julian of Norwich, who saw God as nurturing mother and "all that is" in a hazelnut. It links us in turn to the here and now, to a kind of spirituality that breaks down barriers and jumps boundaries. This is a spirituality in which I know that wherever I am, whatever my state of mind, God is the spirit with me and the life in me. God is there for the taking. God is the air I breathe, and God is the path I take. God is the womb in which I live. As the Zen proverb reads: "If enlightenment is not where you are standing, where will you look?" This was the Benedictine spirituality, steeped in the Jewish and Christian scriptures, that changed my awareness of the living God as alive around me, existing beyond me, and breathing within me.

An Experience of Intense Life

My ideas about God shook themselves free of legal lists and the golden calves of denominationalism, maleness, and race. It took another half a lifetime to come to trust them. As a young teenager, kneeling in a dark cathedral one night, with no illumination in the church but the sanctuary lamp, I had an experience of intense light. I was thirteen years old and totally convinced that, whatever it was and wherever it came from, the light was God. Perhaps it was a good janitor working late, or a bad switch that did not work at all, or a startling insight given, given to a young woman, given gratuitously. I did not know then and I do not know now. But I did know that the light was God and that God was light.

After that experience, whenever God was shrunk to meet someone's then-current need to control or frighten or cajole me, whenever God the vending machine or God the theological Santa Claus did not give me what I wanted, or whenever God the judge let evil go by unchallenged, I knew now that God was bigger than these gods, because I was never able to stop feeling the unshaped, uncontrolled, undiminished light.

For me as an adult, two different texts confirmed the image of God that I learned that night in the cathedral and lived for years in the presence of God in a Benedictine community. The first text that called me to images beyond images was the Hebrew-Christian scriptures, an ancient commentary and testimony on God's ways in the world. The scriptures showed me the God whose own identity was revealed to Moses simply, profoundly, as "I Am Who I Am," "I Will Be What I Will Be," and to Jonah as "mercy upon mercy upon mercy," and in the Jesus of the Mount of Transfiguration bathed in light. This was a God without a face of any color or gender, a God who came in fire and light, God with us—Emmanuel—but unseen, God with me, but hidden in the obvious. That God, I knew, lived in the light. And the light, I knew, was inside of me.

The second text was a tiny book by Jean Pierre de Caussade called *Abandonment to Divine Providence*. It brought me beyond the God of the distant and the partial, the punitive and the parental. It kept an ancient stream of thought alive under the avalanche of legalism, denominationalism, and doctrinal rules. The title of the book sounds like some kind of professional quietism or per-sonal masochism but it brought the distant God as close to me as the minute I am in. Then all the thinking stopped and the know-ing began, and the light burned the images away.

After that growing awareness of the immersing presence of God, I became conscious of three other present and obvious, but long-standing threats to traditional religious belief. Each became a spiritual revelation to me that was both logical and undeniable.

The first burst of insight was science, once the champion of the "material" and the skeptic of the spiritual. Science had made the split between the two seem irreconcilable. But then scientists unexpectedly discovered that the only difference between solids and space was the degree to which the same atoms that composed both were packed more or less closely together. The old line—the heretofore uncompromising dividing line between matter and spirit—had suddenly blurred. How could we really separate the two? So why not the material in the spiritual and the spiritual in the material? I learned, too, that the God who could not be verified was no greater an assumption than the scientific "facts" of modern physics, astronomy, or cosmology. These could not be verified experientially either, unless you know someone who has walked to Mars with a pedometer in her hand.

The mathematical findings of quantum physics, chaos the-ory, and the Big Bang forced classic scientific theory to turn in a different direction. The limits of knowledge ran out. Knowl-edge of the unlimited consumed us, and broke open our spirits to spiritual things greater than ourselves. A universe which, in 1900, we had taught with confidence had one galaxy, the Milky Way, now revealed to the telescope's eye in the year 2000 that there were at least forty billion galaxies out there. In such a world newly revealed as this, even the agnostic physi-cist Stephen Hawking asked in wonder who or what it was that "breathes fire into the equations?" Who or what is the beginning behind the universe? Suddenly science was a great spiritual teacher for me. Science became the guide to a God far greater than the God of petty sins and trivial traps and privatized religion. God was the God of the universe whose creating life lives in us, in me and in others, and in the stars, and whose light is bringing us home.

A New Kind of Dissonance

The second burst of insight across the sensors of my soul that changed the image of God for me was far less ethereal than science and cosmology. The melting of national boundaries and the free flow of peoples and ideas across the globe introduced for me a new kind of cognitive dissonance. The white, male, Catholic, American God was suddenly suspect. Were all these others—over four-fifths of the world—really "godless," without revelation, without any or all truth? Globalism, I came to realize, was a less startling, less dramatic revelation of the presence of God. Perhaps in the end it was, at least for me, an even more revealing one than scientific equations could ever be.

Sprung from the Catholic ghetto, however good that may have been in my spiritual formation, I found God at work everywhere, revealed everywhere, known everywhere. Jesus' insight that in the house of God there were many dwelling places (John 14:2) took on new meaning. So did Benedict's vision of having seen "the whole world in a single ray of light," and the injunction of Vatican Council II to "accept whatever was true in other religions." Clearly, then, something was happening to me. I had learned the greatest truth of all. God was bigger than parochialism. God had many faces. God had many names. God was a magnet in many hearts, all of which, according to the Parliament of the World's Religions meeting in Cape Town in December 1999, embraced a common global ethic: not to lie, not to steal, not to kill, and not to exploit others sexually. Or to put it in more religious terms: to hold all life sacred, to honor every truth, to deal with all people justly, and to love all life rightly. Clearly, the God of differences spoke in one voice, under whatever form that God might be enshrined, anywhere, everywhere.

So, as my world became smaller, God became infinitely larger. God became present for me not just everywhere, but in everyone, in many ways. God became a cataract of otherness, the likes of which I had never dreamed. God, as Anselm said in the eleventh century, had become for me "that than which nothing greater can be thought."

The third burst of insight was ecofeminism, the growing awareness that both an androcentric (male-centered) and an anthropocentric (human-centered) world are insufficient, even warped, explanations of life if God is really the fullness of being and no single being is the fullness of God.

When the question is "Are women fully human?" and the scientific answer is a resounding yes; when the scriptural explanation of creation is Adam's declaration that Eve is "bone of my bone, flesh of my flesh," someone just like me; when nothing on earth is dependent on human life for its existence and humans are dependent for theirs on everything else on the planet; and if God, to be God, must be pure spirit, then Augustine's hierarchy of being—maleness and a God made in a male image—has got to be at best suspect, at least incomplete, and in the end bogus.

This male construct of a male God in a male-centered world is no picture of God at all. God is not maleness magnified. God is life without end: all life, in everything, in everyone, in men and women. The light of the divine shines everywhere and has no gender, no single pronoun, no one image.

Life for me has been one long struggle between those limited and myopic images of God and the lifelong prevailing sense of a far greater experience, a more encompassing presence, called God.

If the question is: "Who is God for you in the year 2000?" then for me at least—in the face of new glimpses into the universe, the findings of science, the continuing insights of an ancient tradition, the piercing experience of light, the many faces of God around the globe and the revelations of ecofeminism— the answer is certainly "God is not now who God was for me in 1950." The God at the other swing of my trapeze is fierce but formless presence, undying light in darkness, eternal limit-lessness, common consciousness in all creation, an inclusiveness greater than doctrines or denominations, who calls me beyond and out of my limits.

I have learned clearly that in this new world I must allow no one to draw too small a God for me.

We must know that we have already found what we seek. "Not one. Not two."

And we must realize that, for the sake of the people, for the sake of the planet, for the sake of the empowering presence of God in an increasingly godless world, we must search for God with all the new lights we have.

As Augustine concluded at the end of his own struggle between the intellectual and the religious images of God, "It is better to find you, God, and leave the questions unanswered, than to find answers without finding you."   —*God at 2000*

In Search of the Divine Feminine

Why is the concept of the Divine Feminine important? The implications of this question shake the spiritual ground under our feet. In the attempt to lay out the dimensions of the subject, however, I found myself haunted by a story—at first seemingly irrelevant to this topic—but, at the same time, down deep, revelatory of the impact and import of this issue, not only to our spiritual life but to our daily life, as well.

In the story a tribal elder is explaining to a child the nature of life: "Remember, child," the elder teaches, "there are two wolves fighting for dominance within each of us. One wolf is good and the other wolf is evil." "But, Elder," the youngster asks, "which wolf will win?" The elder answers, "It depends, dear child, on which wolf you feed." The story is clear: Who we become as persons depends on what we decide to develop in ourselves, in us, and around us. Neurologists tell us now that it is experience that forges our brain patterns. What we think depends on what happens to us. We are not born as we are, we become it. What we believe derives from what we experience. The relationship of this story to the importance of the Divine Feminine in our own lives is obvious. First, if we fail to nourish the fullness of life in us, male and female, as the tribal elder implies—both the feminine and the masculine side—in both women and men, the lack of that inclusiveness will warp our personalities and stunt the growth of our souls. Second, it is useless to say that we truly embrace the feminine dimension of life but refuse to be part of the public process that makes respect for the feminine an equally important part of the social fabric.

Newspapers ask, Can a woman really be president? Magazine articles ask, What makes a real man? Researchers ask, Are women and men different or the same? Theologians ask, Can a woman really image God? We ask, How does God really deal with women? Face-to-face or only through male or clerical intermediaries? For example, take our public language. Eskimos have forty words for snow. They see forty different kinds of snow. It's important to them, to make the distinctions between them because snow is the very context of their lives. We have the same snow, yet we see only one kind, name one kind, because it's not as important to us. However, we have forty words for dog—we call them shepherds, poodles, chihuahuas. We have forty words for car—Kia, hatchback, SUV, limousine, convertible. But we have only two words for the human race—one of which we collapse into the other.

We are still teaching our children that when the gender of a group is clear, we may use the appropriate male or female pronoun. "Everyone attending the Women's Athletic Club presented her card," for instance. But when the gender of the group in question is unclear or mixed it must be male, "Anyone may have his money back" or "Someone left his pen here." In this linguistic system, women become invisible. Clearly, language shapes the mind: if it's not in the language, it's not in the mind. What that says about the importance of women to society, however, is clear: they are simply not seen. What we see creates perception, signals the very importance of a thing.

Ancient Roots

The book of Genesis reads, as does every scripture of every religion on earth, about male/female dual creation out of the same substance: "Let us make humans in our own image, in our own image let us make them; male and female let us make them" (Gen. 1:26–27)—that is, God is male and female, not male. The scriptures reflect the reality of it, and the meaning is clear: the way we see God determines the way we see ourselves. The language we use shapes public perceptions about God. If we see God only as maleness, maleness becomes more Godlike than femaleness. Maleness becomes the nature of God and the norm of humankind, rather than simply one of its manifestations. If we limit ourselves to the Divine Masculine, we will never see the Divine Feminine.

The great figures of early Christianity centuries ago—Origen, Irenaeus, Anselm, Bernard of Clairveaux, and Aelred—believed that the womb of God is the Divine Feminine, and that without that awareness of the motherhood of God, as well as the fatherhood of creation, we will never know the fullness of God in our own lives. None of us, neither women nor men. In the end, the real depth of the spiritual life, the real development of the psychological, emotional life, depends on whether or not we each nourish the feminine image of God in us and around us as fully as we do the image of the fatherhood of God. When churches refuse the language of the feminine dimension of God, when they delete female pronouns and so collapse the male and the female into "all men" and "dear brothers," and "God, our mother," into "God, the father" they deprive us of the whole spirit of God.

However much we mock the idea, the truth is ironically that every major spiritual tradition on earth carries within it, at its very center, in its ancient core, an awareness of the Divine Feminine. In Hinduism, Shakti—the great mother, the feminine principle—is seen as the sum total of all the life-giving energy of the universe. She is the source of all. In Buddhism, Tara is seen as the

perfection of wisdom, and, in Buddhism, wisdom is life's highest metaphysical principle! Tara is considered the light and the
prime source of Buddhahood and so of all Buddhas to follow.

In the Hebrew scriptures—the ground of the entire Abraha-
mic family (Jewish, Christian, and Muslim) the God to whom
Moses says, "Who shall I say sent me?" answers not, "I am he
who am"; not "I am she who am"; but, "I am who am." I am
Being! I am the essence of all life, I am the spirit that breathes
in everyone: the source that magnetizes every soul. I am the one
in whose image all human beings, male and female, Genesis
says clearly, are made. "I am" is, in other words, ungendered,
unsexed, pure spirit, pure energy, pure life. That assurance we
have, note well, on God's own word: "I am who am." Let there
be no mistake about it: woman or man, man or woman—the full
image of God is in you: masculine and feminine, feminine and
masculine godness. Hebrew scripture is clear, and the Christian
and Islamic scriptures, as well. God is neither male nor female—
God is of the essence of both and both are of the essence of God.

Actually, lest we be fooled by our own patriarchal incli-
nations to make God in our own small, puny, partial male
images, the Hebrew scriptures are full of the female attributes of God. In Isaiah (42:14) the Godhead, "cries out as a
woman in labor." To the psalmist, God is a nursing woman
on whose breast the psalmist leans "content as a child that
has been weaned" (Ps. 131:2). In Hosea (11:3–4) God claims
to be a cuddling mother who takes Israel in her arms. In
Genesis (3:21) God is a seamstress who makes clothes out of
skins for Adam and Eve. And in Proverbs, God-she, wisdom,
Sophia, "raises her voice in the streets," "is there with God
'in the beginning,'" (8:1–3, 22–31) "is the homemaker who
welcomes the world to her table" (9:5) shouting as she does,
"Enter here! Eat my food, drink my wine."

After centuries of suppressing the female imagery and the
feminine attributes given in scripture in order to establish the
patriarchy of lords and kings and priests and popes and power-
brokers as the last word and only word of every failing institution

in humankind—no wonder we are confused about who God is. But God is not! scripture is clear: God does not have—and clearly never has had—an identity problem. Our images of God must be inclusive because God is not mother, no, but God is not father either. God is neither male nor female. God is pure spirit, pure being, pure life—both of them. Male and female, in us all.

Clearly, women have been an essential part of God's economy of salvation from its foundation in religions in both West and East. What does all of this have to do with women of spirit and faith here and now? Why should we even consider the subject of the Divine Feminine at all? In the light of scriptural own images of God, in every religion everywhere, what kind of a life-denying, God-diminishing question is it to ask whether there is such a thing as a feminine dimension to God? On what grounds can we possibly deny the feminine face of God among us an equal place at every table: corporate boards, decision-making synods, ecclesiastical councils, Qur'anic academies and, shariah judge-ships? How can women be denied the chance to be listened to, the right perhaps even to be heard, the fullness of moral agency, and a public role to be reckoned with?

Lack of Consciousness

The social implications of ignoring or denying a topic such as this are enormous, life-changing, spiritually stunting. By cast-ing God in human form, in one human form only, we limit our knowledge of God. We ignore the feminine dimension of God in the world and God in women as well. We leave life to the war-riors, rather than to wisdom figures. We make masculinity the divine norm, ignoring and devaluing the feminine part of our-selves, in both women and men. We enthrone maleness, mascu-linity, the macho. God the father, God the avenging judge, God the warrior, God the lawgiver, and God the perfectionist over-whelm the fullness of the image of God. We create a distant and unemotional God that comes with the image of an exclusively masculine God—all rational and all-powerful—that affects our life at every stage and every moment. The model we have been given of the all-male God exercises power over everything, so we get confused trying to explain God's failure to use his power in order to save us from dangers.

Without a conscious awareness of the rest of the essence of God, of the Divine Feminine in God, we lose sight of God our mother, who forms us and influences us and encourages us to do good—not to be perfect but to do our best. We fail to remember God the mother who encourages us to repent and repair our mistakes, misjudgments, immaturities; God the mother who enables us to survive them. To understand God as Divine Feminine is to realize that all creation is co-creation. That creation is at least as much about what we do with creation to complete it, to lead it to new life once we have it, as it is about the notion that it was given to us in a fixed form. God, for instance, did not create nuclear bombs—humans did—and we can uncreate them anytime we want to, provided someone exercises leadership of the Divine Feminine to show us the way. The common response to attempts to reduce nuclear weapons is always seen as a loss of total power—the one attribute that is God's alone. Instead we pray for peace but do little or nothing to press politicians to practice it!

We must realize that God is the mother who carries us rather than lords it over us, who leads us to face the fact that the fate of earth is largely in our hands. The God who is both feminine and masculine energy, the God who in ourselves we all image—more of this or less of that—both feminine and masculine in each of us, not only raises standards for us to meet but helps us over the bar. This God—this Divine Mother God—feels compassion for us, as scripture says so clearly, "I have heard the cry of my people" (Exod. 3:7). This Mother God feels anger and pain when we suffer: "I am sending you to deliver them" (Exod. 3:10). This Mother God in us feels care and concern when we struggle: "Be not afraid, Abram, I am your shield" (Gen. 15:1). It is this God and we who go on now creating the world together, feeling together its pain, working together to recreate it. Leading other men and women to do the same.

Unity of God

This God is not only the Divine Masculine, medieval lord and master, father, warrior, and judge. This God is also the Divine Feminine—the one who feels, the one who cares, as well as prescribes, the one who is nursing mother, as well as protective father. The one who is also divine and feminine. This is the God who is completely other—and completely like us at the same time—in affection and care, in feeling and hope. This is the God who brings the world together—Hindu, Buddhist, Jewish, Christian, and Muslim—listening, learning, loving the other. If God is all being, all there is, masculine and feminine, then Plato's God of total power, total distance, total indifference, and total emotional detachment is deficient. A God like that lacks love, lacks the will to be co-creative in a co-creative world. A God like that lacks the compassion and the empathy it takes to love the imperfect perfectly well. That male God is the one we have fashioned at our peril. By ignoring the value of the feminine, we have made for ourselves a patriarchal God for a world in which feeling is the necessary glue that holds that world together. We have made for ourselves a God to keep everybody else under control.

It is in the name of the God made male that women have been suppressed and ignored and reviled, called lesser, called inferior, called irrational in every male-controlled religion. Why doesn't God fix such an obvious injustice? Because God didn't make the situation; humans did. It is humans who warp the theology, humans who ignore the scriptures, humans who create a world designed to make the powerful more powerful and to divinize themselves at the expense of every other religion on earth. It is humans who fail to lead us to a fuller image of God. Humans, to be true to their own image of God, must now undo that imbalance—for the sake of the entire world, for the humanity of women, and for authenticity of religion. No, God does not "fix" the world for us. But awareness of the fullness of God is the reality that requires us to fix it. God Divine Mother and God Divine Father is exactly what demands that being in all its glory—black and white, gay and straight, female and male—be respected and revered and embraced. Until all are, the fullness of the life that is God is only half alive in us, no matter how profusely we proclaim our rationality, no matter how confidently we argue our righteousness, no matter how sincerely we exalt our religiosity.

You see, it is not what sexism says about women that is sinful. It is what sexism says about God that is heresy, that corrupts the spirit. Doesn't sexism really imply that God is all-powerful—except when it comes to women; at which point the God who could draw water from a rock and raise the dead to life is totally powerless to work as fully through a woman as through a man? Is this the same God who also said, "Let us make humans in our own image; female and male let us make them"?

Feminine Leadership

What will women bring to churches in crisis and a planet in peril? What will women bring to the spirit of the times? Woman will bring womanhood to where only male lordship has been permitted to lead—distant, indifferent, and dictatorial. It is womanliness that is the invisible gift, the unseen presence, the continuing reminder of the Divine Feminine in and over all of humankind. Woman must bring the feminine to leadership—the missing dimension of the God-life in us all—enabling it in men and fulfilling it in women; the missing link of a theology everywhere, in every tradition, not only our own, that understands the nature of God but has yet to make it real so that we can all become what we are meant to become. So that we demonstrate, rather than simply profess, our respect for women, and women's insights, and women's values, and women's experiences. So that the women of our time everywhere may make the fullness of the love of God real for us all. Then we may all come to know ourselves, to be in the womb of our mother God. And right the images of God in every religion everywhere.

No doubt about it, women leaders like Miriam, prophet-esses like Huldah, judges like Deborah, liberators like Judith, keepers of the very line of David like Naomi and Ruth, the women at Jesus' tomb—all of them break through the patri-archal world of Hebrew scripture with earth-shaking regular-ity and clear recollection of the other face of God's presence and power. In a world in which a third live in abject poverty, two-thirds of those are women and girls—the poorest, hun-griest, most vulnerable, most threatened, least cared for, least listened to population in the world—patience is not enough. We need the courage now to lead us to a consciousness of the Divine Feminine in ways that make life changes for the world, for women in every religion everywhere. And, that will, at the same time, enrich the emotional, and spiritual develop-ment of men.

The Talmud reads, "If we had been holier people, we would have been angrier oftener." May God give us all the grace to feel a life-giving burst of holy anger!

—*Women, Spirituality, and Transformative Leadership*

The Place of Worship in Human Life

To be human is to struggle between two emotional magnets. On the one hand lies the temptation to give in to a sense of total abjection. After all, humanity is mortal, is limited, is feckless, is a history of disasters. On the other hand, there hovers in the unbounded awareness of what it means to be human, the prob-ability of sinking into unbounded arrogance. Humanity is, after all, also a bundle of beauty, a reservoir of ability, a possibility unlimited.

The moral question that arises from that dual awareness is clearly an important one, a real one. Just who are we? Are we, in our humanity, something glorious or are we, at base, actually nothing much at all? Of the two alternatives, neither is really adequate; both are dangerous.

The psalmist put it clearly and prayed, "What are we that you should care for us?" in one place and "We are little less than the angels" in another. Unsure which is which, we go through life torn between the two. Abjection threatens to turn our weary souls to dust. Arrogance promises to turn our world into nuclear dust and ecological devastation that stems from the human thirst for power and domination.

Only the awareness of a universe whose Creator is outside and above the boundaries of humanity can save us from either the curse of futility or the devastating consequences of self-satisfaction unfulfilled. It is God that humanity needs in order to complete itself. It is knowledge of God that defends us from despair and, at the same time, brings the saving grace of humility that comes with knowing our place in the universe.

It is this humility, this consciousness of God in our lives, this truth of who and what we are, this awareness of who and what God is, that can deliver us from ourselves for the sake of the rest of the human race.

To know our place in the universe is to recognize that God is God. We are not the masters of the world. We can make no demands on it. All we can do is to try to live our place in it well.

Knowing our limits while we stretch them to their fullest at the same time relieves us of the burden of striving for the perfection we can never reach. More than that, it lifts us to unimaginable heights of surety and trust, of calm and of faith. The God who made us what we are knows what we desire to be and waits with infinite patience while we become what we can. We, on the other hand, know that whatever we need to become all that we can be, this same great and loving God will supply. For all of that, we are thankful. From that gratitude grow love and commitment, faith and trust, wonder and worship.

Worship is the natural overflow of those who, with humble and grateful heart, understand their place in the universe and live in awe of the God who made it so. Worship is the heart of the liturgical year. —*The Liturgical Year*

The God of Many Tongues

Each great spiritual tradition, in its own way, suggests a model of what it means to be a holy person. Each of them shines a light on the human ideal. Each of them talks about what it takes to grow, to endure, to develop, to live a spiritual life in a world calculatingly material and sometimes maddeningly unclear.

Every major spiritual tradition—Hinduism, Judaism, Buddhism, Christianity, and Islam—brings a special gift to the art of living the spiritual life. Each of them refracts the light of its own spiritual wisdom texts in particularly sharp and distinct ways. Each of them strikes a different tone in giving the great truths of life that form a chord, a symphony of truth.

It is an enlightening excursion, this wandering into the spiritual insights of other whole cultures, other whole intuitions of the spiritual life. It depends for its fruitfulness on openness of heart and awareness of mind. But the journey is well worth the exertion it takes to see old ideas in new ways because it can bring us to the very height and depth of ourselves. It can even bring fresh hearing, new meaning to the stories that come down to us through our own tradition. A Sufi story defines the process clearly:

> *"Tell us what you got from enlightenment," the seeker said.*
> *"Did you become divine?"*
> *"No, not divine," the holy one said.*
> *"Did you become a saint?"*
> *"Oh dear, no," the holy one said.*
> *"Then what did you become?" the seeker asked.*
> *And the holy one answered, "I became awake."*

It is the task of becoming awake to our God, to our world, to the wisdom that even now lies within us, waiting only to be tapped, that is the real meaning of our questions. It is, more than that, the one great task of life.

May your journey through these questions bring you to a new moment of awareness. May it be an enlightening one. May you find embedded in the wisdom of the past, like all the students of life before you, the answers you yourself are seeking now. May they waken that in you which is deeper than fact, truer than fiction, full of faith. May you come to know that in every human event is a particle of the Divine to which we turn for meaning here, to which we tend for fullness of life hereafter.

—*Welcome to the Wisdom of the World*

God speaks in many tongues, glows in many colors, calls to us in many voices, is beyond any puny little parochial image we make of God. It is this great cosmic God we seek.

✻ ✻ ✻

Dogmas are signposts along the road of the soul on the way to God. They are meant to open our minds to mystery. They are not meant to keep us from learning about God in other places and ways.

✻ ✻ ✻

Religion is meant to lead us to the center and source of creation. The aberration of religion then lies in spending so much time as religious people claiming our truth and condemning everybody else's. When theology is used to condemn another person's path to God, it not only distracts us from the purpose of religion but it distorts it, as well.

✻ ✻ ✻

"What is the deepest meaning of Buddhism, Master?" the disciple asked. And in answer the Zen masters tell us, the teacher only bowed. It is in being able to find the sacred in everything that a person finally discovers God.

✻ ✻ ✻

"God is the East and the West and wherever you turn, there is God's face," the Koran teaches. "Behold I am with you all days," the evangelist Matthew says, "even to the end of time."

✻ ✻ ✻

The Hindus teach, "May peace and peace and peace be everywhere." Jesus says "Peace I leave with you, my peace I give to you." The overall message is clear: the abiding presence of God is a universal revelation.

✻ ✻ ✻

The Buddha said there is an Eightfold Path to inner peace: right view, right aim, right speech, right action, right living, right effort, right mindfulness, right contemplation. Jesus says there are eight beatitudes: mercy, poverty of spirit, mourning, meekness, hunger for righteousness, purity of heart, peacemaking, and witness." Do you think they decided on these together?

✻ ✻ ✻

In this world aspirants may find enlightenment by two different paths," we learn in the Bhagavad Gita. "For the contemplative is the path of knowledge; for the active is the path of selfless action." The Christian tradition teaches that both contemplation and a commitment to social justice are essential parts of the Christian life.

✻ ✻ ✻

"Hear O Israel: the Lord our God is One," we learn in Deuteronomy. And the Hindu prays, "He is the one God, hidden in all beings, all-pervading, the Self within all beings." And the Sikh says in the Mul Mantra, "He is the Sole Supreme Being, of eternal manifestation." Clearly, the whole world knows that our God is their God, too. So how can we be more loved than they?

✻ ✻ ✻

"I have breathed into humans My spirit," The Koran says. "Let us always consider ourselves as if the Holy One dwells within," the Talmud teaches. "It is no longer I who live, but Christ who lives in me," Christianity says. But if we are all vessels of the divine, how can we use religion to justify destruction of other human beings?

❊ ❊ ❊

"I have just three things to teach: simplicity, patience, and compassion," the Tao Te Ching teaches. "There are only three things that matter: faith, hope, and love. And the greatest of these is love." Wouldn't the world be different if we all loved what God loves—the other?

❊ ❊ ❊

How do I know if I'm finally becoming closer to God? It's when I see God in everyone I meet and touch God in everything that is.
                                              —*The Monastic Way*

TURNED INTO FIRE: RELIGIOUS LIFE

Since the late 1970s, Sister Joan has been a leading figure in the renewal of religious and monastic life. She has written extensively on both topics. We chose these two selections because they best represent her prophetic vision for religious and monastic communities as they face the future. Specifically, Fire in These Ashes *has been translated into seven languages.*

On the Way to a High Mountain

Mother Sylvester, my first prioress, made two trips to our novitiate yearly. In both of them, she came to ask us only one question. Patience was her hallmark; she tutored us with measured steps. In fact, she viewed with great benignity the fact that most novices failed the test rather routinely at the time of her first visit. At the same time, she was anything but complacent if we failed it at the time of her second one. "Why have you come to religious life?" she asked each of us in turn, arms folded under her scapular, head tilted down to scrutinize us over her glasses as she scanned us around the table. At first blush, we made up wonderful answers: "To give our lives to the church," the pious said; "To save our souls;" the cautious said; "To convert the world," the zealots said. But no, no, no, she signaled with a shake of the head. Not that. Not that. Not that. "You come to religious life, dear sisters," she said sadly, "only to seek God."

The fact is that the answer, simple as it may be, uncompromising as it is, cannot be improved upon, even today. Today most of all, perhaps. This generation above all, a generation in which all the foundations once considered immutable have shifted, ought to know the truth of that like few others ever have. When absolutes fail us and ministries falter and even the church, perhaps, becomes a distant and discomfiting place for those with new ideas or disturbing questions, the idea of seeking God and God alone takes on new power in life.

The Universal Human Quest

Seeking God is the universal human quest. It is common to all cultures. It is the fundamental human project. It is the common denominator of all the human enterprises. It is common to all human beings, necessary to all human endeavor, central to all human effort and ultimate to all human activity. What is more, it is the only reason that makes any sense whatsoever out of religious life. Religious life is not just another way of life. It is a way of life intentionally organized to pursue the human quest for God.

For the religious, immersion in God becomes the single, unmitigated and unnuanced reason for making every other plausible, worthy and determining motive in life—love, money, children, personal success—secondary to the life pursuit of Mystery among us. Immersion in God is the concept that brooks no other greater than itself. It is the question that undergirds every day, the longing for which any kind of loss, any amount of change, any degree of effort is acceptable.

We have too often, however, been seduced with greater intensity, by other explanations for religious life, all of them valuable and all of them true to a certain degree. We have sought to be "relevant." We have set out to be "incarnational." We have given ourselves untiringly to "the option for the poor." We have devoted ourselves to "the transformation of structures." We have evangelized and renewed and revised and reformed until we dropped from exhaustion. And all of those commitments are good and necessary, holy and worthy of attention, fundamental and imperative. But through it all, one thing and one thing only can sustain religious life, can nourish religious life, can justify religious life: The religious must be the person who first and foremost, always and forever, in whatever circumstance, seeks God and God alone, sees God and God alone in all of this confusion, in all of this uncertainty and, whatever the situation, speaks God—and God alone.

If religious life is to save a fire and fan a flame for whatever kind of religious life to come, the emphasis must then shift again. We must move from concentrating solely on what religious do to why they do it and what religious are to be. God-seekers, religious are to stand like beacons in the night so that others, too, may remember and never forget the only real reason to do anything in life, the final measure of everything we do. Religious must give as much conscious attention to the things of God as they do to the tiny, private, personal little worlds of the world in which we all live, however challenging, good and necessary those personal spaces may be. Otherwise, religious life is just one more social institution to be succeeded by social institutions after it rather than centers of contemplation where, we can hope, the mind of God can touch the mind of humanity.

Sign of Trouble

The first sign that something has gone wrong with religious life, then, is when work, any work, becomes more important than the quest itself and what it demands of us here and now. The work of teaching, the work of healing, the work of pastoring, even the work of being a religious itself is not as important as the seeking. Wherever we are, whatever we do, we must do it with the greater will of God in mind. That is, of course, the difference between being a religious and being a social worker. The social worker does a work that must be done and is worth doing. The religious falls so completely into the arms of Christ, the mind of God, that nothing will suffice except to become what one seeks: the merciful One, the loving One, the truth-telling One, the One who says, "Go you and do likewise." Point: it is not a particular work that captivates the religious, however good it is, however much it is needed. It is the God whom she holds in her heart and finds in prayer, in people, and in the transubstantiation of the planet into the reign of God that impels her life.

To seek God, then, is to be impelled to action. Separating search for God from doing God's work creates the very antithesis of the spiritual quest. The trick, of course, is to maintain the delicate balance between the two. In this century, religious life has suffered from both extremes. Religious dualism, taken to its outside limits, says one of two things—on the one hand, that prayer is enough and on the other hand that work is enough. The generation in which we find ourselves has said both. We have made public work the basis for evangelization and the defining characteristic of religious life. Having had those fail or falter, we have called religious life itself a failure as a result. We have also assumed that the cloistered life was closer to heaven because it was more distant from the world around it. Neither posture can be further from the truth if the prophets were really of God, if Jesus was really a contemplative. History confirms the fact that it is in the integration of the two—of action and contemplation, of contemplation with action—that religious life thrives. Our greatest contemplatives have been our most active people: Hildegard and Bernard and Teresa of Avila. Our most active people have been our most contemplative: Catherine of Siena, Charles de Foucauld, Ignatius Loyola. In our own time, the monk Thomas Merton did not operate a peace and justice center but he did make the question of peace and justice a burning question for the church. At the same time, the Jesuit priest and his married brother, Dan and

Phil Berrigan, did operate a peace and justice center but only out of an intensely public spiritual perspective.

The task of religious life is not a task at all, it is the application of the great questions of life to all of life's dimensions. The religious does not do charity without asking, "Why this injustice?" The religious does not teach without asking, "What must be learned that will change the world?" The real religious does not attempt to act before contemplating the reason for it, the consequences of it, the costs of it, and the contribution of it to the coming of the reign of God. The religious life makes contemplation a very active thing.

The purpose of religious life is the pursuit of the spiritual quest, the preservation of the spiritual questions, the articulation of the spiritual challenges from age to age, in whatever form and whatever season. But in that case, the current concern about the value of religious life is at least misguided, if not totally misunderstood. Is there any purpose left to religious life now that it no longer has as its hallmark the once great institutions raised to answer the major social questions of past generations? Indeed, and never more so. Now religious life has a chance to begin again, plumbing the Gospels and shouting the questions with which they confront a coming world. The question challenging society now is not "Is religious life valuable?" As long as the Gospel is valuable, religious life will be valuable. No, the real question is simply, is religious life viable? Is religious life itself religious enough to throw itself upon the Gospels again rather than upon the institutions which, though once they demonstrated it best, in this new age are now more mainstream, more of the culture than prophet to it?

But first of all, we ourselves must plumb the Gospels. Every day. Always. Without flagging. In every situation. We must live spiritual lives that flame for all to see, yes, but most of all we must live spiritual lives so deep, so regular, so clear that we cannot be surprised by opposition. We must create in ourselves spiritual reservoirs that take us past every barrier in church and state with peace in our hearts and calm in our lives, knowing without doubt that the questions we ask are not of our making only.

—The Fire in These Ashes

The Radical Christian Life

We are not meant to be long-distance observers of life. We are to give ourselves to the shaping of it, however difficult that may be in this day and age.

This commitment to co-creation is a great task, a noble task for which to give a life, but it is not a simple one. We are at a crossover moment in time—somewhere amid the certainty of the past, the demands of the present, and the possibility of the future. It is a moment again in human history that needs deep wisdom and requires holy struggle.

At the dawn of the twenty-first century, the world is shifting. In fact, the world is dizzyingly mobile now. As a culture, we are shifting away from being isolationist and independent to being global and interdependent.

It is a world where "Catholic and Protestant" have melted into simply being Christians together, and our new neighbors and their temples, monasteries, and mosques are Hindu, Buddhist, Jewish, and Muslim.

Our task now is to be radical Christian communities—in the here and now—not fossils of a bygone reality, not leftovers from an earlier golden age. Now we need new wisdom and a new kind of struggle to determine what we must be and do in the midst of these changing times.

Our choices are clear: We can go forward again and become something new in order to leaven the new or we can go backward in an attempt to maintain what we know better but which is already gone.

The question is then: What does it mean to be a radical Christian community in times such as these? And how do we do it?

The choice is ours. But, don't be fooled: not only is it not an easy choice; it is not an easy task.

Christians, serious seekers, now must choose either to retire from this fray into some paradise of marshmallow pieties, where they can massage away the questions of the time, the injustice of the age, with spiritual nosegays and protests of powerlessness— where they can live like pious moles in the heart of a twisted world and call that travesty peace and "religion"—or they can gather their strength for the struggle it will take to bring this world closer to the reign of God now.

But what can possibly be done in this runaway world of the powerful few by the rest of us who hold no malice and want no wars, who have no influence but hold high ideals, who call ourselves Christian and claim to mean it!

Who are we now? And who do we want to be?

Most of all, where can we possibly go for a model of how to begin to be a radical Christian witness in a society in which we are almost totally remote from its centers of power and totally outside its centers of influence?

My suggestion is that we stop drawing our sense of human effectiveness from the periods of exploration and their destruction of native peoples, or from the period of industrialization and its displacement of people, or from the periods of the world wars and their extermination of peoples.

My suggestion is that little people—people like you and me— begin to look again to the sixth century and to the spiritual imagination and wondrous wisdom that made it new. Because that is really the good news.

An Ancient Model

In the sixth century, Benedict of Nursia was an aspiring young student at the center of the empire with all the glitz and glamour, all the fading glory and dimming power, that implied.

Rome had overspent, overreached, and overlooked the immigrants on the border who were waiting—just waiting—to pour through the system like a sieve.

Rome—ROME!—the invincible, had been sacked. As in the book of Daniel, the handwriting was on the wall, but few, if anyone, read it. In our own world, the headlines are in our papers, too, and few, if any, are reading them.

But in the sixth century, one person, this young man, resolved to change the system not by confronting it, not by competing with it to be bigger, better, or more successful, but by eroding its incredible credibility.

This one single person in the sixth century—without the money, the technology, the kind of systemic support our age considers so essential to success and therefore uses to explain its failure to make a difference—simply refused to become what such a system modeled and came to have a major influence in our own time.

This one person simply decided to change people's opinions about what life had to be by himself living otherwise, by refusing to accept the moral standards around him, by forming other people into organized communities to do the same: to outlaw slavery where they were; to devote themselves to the sharing of goods as he was; to commit themselves to care for the earth; to teach and model a new perspective on our place in the universe.

And on his account—though numbers, history attests, were never his criteria for success—thousands more did the same age after age after age.

For over fifteen hundred years, popes and peoples across the centuries have called Benedict of Nursia the patron of Europe and credited the Benedictine lifestyle that he developed in the darkest period of Western history with the very preservation of European culture.

The values it modeled maintained the social order. And safeguarded learning. And gave refuge to travelers. And made rules for war that brought peace to chaos.

Those values turned a Europe devastated by invasion and neglect into a garden again. They modeled the equality of peoples. They provided a link between heaven and earth—between this life, chaotic as it was, and the will of God for all of life. Everywhere. Always.

But how was all of that done? And what does it have to do with us today? The answers upend everything our own society insists is essential to effectiveness.

The very model of life that Benedict of Nursia gave the world was exactly the opposite of what, in the end, was really destroying it.

To a world that valued bigness—big villas, big cities, big armies, big systems—Benedict gave a series of small and intense communities where people of one mind gathered to support one another, to find the strength for the fight. Their struggle was for survival, but their strength was community.

To an empire with a global reach—France, Britain, Egypt, Constantinople—Benedict gave an unending line of local groups whose solicitude for the people and understanding of the issues of the area from which they came was built into their very DNA. The struggle of such small groups was for survival, yes; but their strength was total engagement in the human condition.

To an empire intent on the centralization of all cultures into one, Benedict gave a model of autonomy, of agency, of individual self-development to a culture that accepted both submission and slavery far, far too easily. The struggle against such odds was for survival, yes; but their strength was a sense of human dignity and personal possibility—in an era that had neither.

To a world with a bent for monuments meant to mark the history and glory of an empire, Benedict abandoned the notion of a joint institutional history and built a common tradition out of many separate parts instead. The struggle was for survival of these autonomous small groups. Their strength was the singular commitment bred in each separate group to each carry the fullness of the tradition.

In a civic order strictly defined by specific roles and responsibilities, Benedict chose instead to create a lifestyle rather than to define a fixed work that the years could erode or the culture could abandon. The struggle was surely for survival; but the surety of that in every group was creativity and adaptation.

In a world made up of powerful institutions Benedict did not create an institution; instead, he started a movement—a loose collection of similarly serious and equal seekers who gave the world new ways of thinking about autocracy and narcissism, oppression and injustice, inequality and authoritarianism. The struggle was indeed survival. The strength was an energy and dynamism that affected the whole society.

And finally, in a world where the word of an emperor meant death, Benedict built a world where the word of God gave new life day after day after day to everyone it touched.

A Tradition That Transforms

And little by little, this little movement of serious seekers— bound together as equal adults in communities of heart and mind—crept up slowly on the culture around them, seduced its hardness of heart, converted its soul, and, in one small place after another, made the world whole again.

So why does it work? What can something so small, so fragile, possibly be able to give to a world like that? The fact is that Benedict left us a very simple structure, yes, but he left it standing on very deep pillars. He established it on values that spanned the whole human experience—not on rules or specific works that would crash and crumble with the crumbling of the time and cultures.

He based the life on human and spiritual insights that never go out of style: on foundational human needs, for instance, like community and work and service; on profound spiritual practices, like prayer and contemplation and humility; on major social issues, like stewardship and hospitality, equality and peace; on basic organizational givens, like leadership and communal decision-making, on mutual service and mutual obedience.

And so as every era grappled with its own agendas and issues, the importance or consciousness of each of these Benedictine values became the gift Benedictines gave to a culture out of sync with its own best interests.

Through it all, for centuries—centuries—Benedictine communities—small, local, and autonomous—worked in creative ways to meet the needs of the areas in which they grew, struggling always to shape and balance a deep and communal spiritual life with the great social needs around them.

They gifted every age out of the treasures of the heart that are the pillars of Benedictine spirituality. As a result, they grew and they concentrated and they specialized and they changed till there were as many slightly different but all basically the same Benedictine monasteries as there were stripes on a zebra.

If the twenty-first century needs anything at all, it may well be a return to the life-giving, radical vision of Benedict. Perhaps we need a new reverence for bold Benedictine wisdom if civilization is to be saved again—and this time the very planet preserved.

The Pillars of Benedictine Spirituality

Creative Work

This age needs to rethink work. Work in our time has either become something that defines us or something that oppresses us. We do it to make money, money, money or we decry it as an obstacle to life. We are a culture that too often stands between workaholism and pseudo-contemplation.

For years I watched Sophie, an old Polish lady across the street from the monastery, sweep the sidewalk in front of her house with a strong and steady hand and then move methodically to the front of the houses to her left and to her right.

She became, in fact, a kind of neighborhood joke, doing a fruitless task. After all, the street was spotless already, wasn't it? What was the use of this senseless monotony?

And then she died.

Newer, younger neighbors moved into her house who had no time, no interest, in sweeping sidewalks. And the street has never been clean since.

Sophie reminded me again of what Benedict's commitment to work was meant to teach us. I recognized in her that the work we do is not nearly so determining as why we do it.

Work—every kind of work: manual, intellectual, spiritual—is meant to be the human being's contribution to the development of the human race.

The Benedictine works to complete the work of God in the upbuilding of the world. We work, as well, to complete ourselves. We become more skilled, more creative, more effective. When we work we discover that we really are "good for something."

Work, the Benedictine sees, is an asceticism that is not contrived, not symbolic. It's real. It is a task that puts me in solidarity with the poor for whom the rewards of labor are few and far between while the rigors are constant and security is tenuous.

Work is our gift to the future, and if the work we do is a contribution to the order and the coming of the reign of God, and if we do it well, like Sophie, it will be needed, and when we are not there to do it, it will be missed.

Holy Leisure

This age needs to rethink leisure, as well. Play and holy leisure are not the same thing. Leisure is the Benedictine gift of regular reflection and continual consciousness of the presence of God. It is the gift of contemplation in a world of action. Holy leisure is a necessary respite from a wildly moving world that turns incessantly now on technology that grants neither the space nor the time it takes to think.

I remember the day some years ago when a reporter called to ask for an interview on some document that had just been released from Rome.

"I can't talk to you about that," I said. "I haven't seen it and I don't comment on anything I haven't had a chance to read and study."

"Well," he said, "if I send it to you, will you talk to me about it then?"

I calculated the time: This was Thursday. The document couldn't possibly arrive in the mail before Monday, so I figured I could meet the deadline I was working on now and get the new document read before he called.

"All right," I said, "You can send it."

A few minutes later I heard a clacking sound coming from an office down the hall.

"What is that?" I said to the sister in the office.

"It's the fax machine," she said. "It's something for you from New York and it's already over eighty pages long. There's a note on it about calling you back to talk about it this afternoon."

This is a world high on technology, short on time, starved for reflection.

Benedictine leisure is a life lived with a continuing commitment to the development of a culture with a Sabbath mind.

The rabbis teach that the purpose of Sabbath is threefold: First, to make everyone—slave and citizen alike—free for at least one day a week.

Second, to give us time to do what God did: To evaluate our work to see if it is good.

And finally, the rabbis say, the purpose of Sabbath is to reflect on life, to determine whether what we're doing and who we are is what we should be doing and who we want to be. Sabbath is meant to bring wisdom and action together. It provides the space we need to begin again.

If anything has brought the modern world to the brink of destruction it must surely be the loss of holy leisure. When people sleep in metro stations it is holy leisure that asks why.

When babies die for lack of medical care it is holy leisure that asks why.

When thousands of civilians die from "death by drones"—unmanned aerial predators that bomb their lands and lives unmercifully—it is holy leisure that asks, how can that possibly be of God?

To give people space to read and think and discuss the great issues of the time from the perspective of the Gospel may be one of Benedictinism's greatest gifts to a century in which the chaos of action is drying up humanity's deepest wells of wisdom.

Dom Cuthbert Butler wrote once: "It is not the presence of activity that destroys the contemplative life; it is absence of contemplation."

Holy leisure is the foundation of contemplation and contemplation is the ability to see the world as God sees the world. Indeed, the contemplative life will not be destroyed by activity but by the absence of contemplation.

In Benedictine spirituality, life is not divided into parts, one holy and the other mundane. To the Benedictine mind, all of life is holy. All of life's actions bear the scrutiny of all of life's ideals. All of life is to be held with anointed hands.

Who shall lead them into a contemplative life if not we?

Stewardship

The spirituality of stewardship, one of Benedictine spirituality's strongest, greatest gifts, must be rethought in our time.

The 401 pounds of garbage per U.S. citizen that the world cannot dispose of is made up of the Styrofoam cups we use and the tin cans we've discarded rather than recycled, while the rest of the world reuses three to five times as much material as we do. Humans today, are polluting earth, sea, and sky at a rate unheard of in any other period of history and we in the United States more than most.

But Benedictines before us brought order and organization, learning, scripture, and art, the tools of civilization and the sustenance of the soul.

They used every human form of education and skill to bring order out of chaos, equality to the masses, and healing to their world. Benedictines before us tilled dry land and made it green. They dried the swamps and made them grow. They seeded Europe with crops that fed entire populations, they raised the cattle that gave new life, they distilled liquors and brewed hops that brought joy to the heart and health to the body. It is not possible to live life with a Benedictine heart and fail to nurture the seeds of life for every living creature.

How, as Benedictines, if we are serious seekers, can we possibly build now what is not green? How can we soak our lands in chemicals and grow what is not organic? How can we possibly, as Benedictines, use what is not disposable and never even call a community meeting on the consequences to others of our doing so?

To allow ourselves to become chips in an electronic world, isolates in a cemented universe, women and men out of touch with the life pulse of a living God, indifferent to creation, concerned only with ourselves, and still call ourselves "good": is to mistake the rituals of religion for the sanctifying dimensions of spirituality.

The serious seeker knows that we are here to become the voices for life in everything everywhere—as have done our ancestors before us for over fifteen hundred years.

Benedictine spirituality, the spirituality that brought the world back from the edge before, asks us to spend our time well, to contemplate the divine in the human, to treat everything in the world as sacred. We need the wisdom of stewardship now.

Community

Community is a concept that our age must reexamine and renew. An old woman in my Pennsylvania hometown lived alone in her own home till the day she died. The problem is that she died eighteen months before her body was found, because no one ever came to visit her, no one called to see if she had gotten her prescriptions, no one checked when her water was turned off for lack of payment. And there are thousands like her in this world of ours.

And how are we reaching out to them? Benedictine community assumes by its very nature that we exist to be miracle workers to one another. It is in human community that we are called to grow. It is in human community that we come to see God in the other. It is in its commitment to build community that Benedictinism must be sign to a world on the verge of isolation.

But a Benedictine spirituality of community calls for more than togetherness—the very cheapest sort of community. Communal spirituality calls for an open mind and an open heart. It centers us on the Jesus who was an assault on every closed mind in Israel.

To those who thought that illness was punishment for sin, Jesus called for openness. To those who considered tax collectors incapable of salvation, Jesus called for openness. To those who believed that the Messiah—to be real—had to be a military figure, Jesus was a call to openness.

The Benedictine heart—the heart that saved Europe—is a place without boundaries, a place where the truth of the oneness of the human community shatters all barriers, opens all doors, refuses all prejudices, welcomes all strangers, and listens to all voices.

Community cannot be taken for granted. We must ask ourselves always who it is who is uncared for and unknown—dying from loneliness, prejudice, or pain—and waiting for your community and mine to knock on the door, to seek them out, to take them in, to hold them up till they can live again.

Real community requires mindfulness of the whole human condition—so that the spirit that is Benedictine may spread like a holy plague throughout the world.

Humility

Humility needs to be rediscovered if we are to take our rightful place in the world in this age. It was July 20, 1969, the night the United States landed the first man on the moon. I was standing next to a foreign exchange teacher who had come from Mexico to teach Spanish for us.

"Well," I laughed, looking up into the dark night sky, "There's the man in our moon." I could almost hear her bristle beside me. In a tight, terse voice she said back, "It is not your moon!"

At that moment I got a lesson in Benedictine humility, in international relations and racism and multiculturalism that springs from it, that no novice mistress had been able to articulate nearly as well.

Humility is about learning your place in the universe, about not making either yourselves or your nation anybody's god. It is about realizing that we are all equal players in a common project called life.

Learning like that can change your politics. It will certainly change your humanity—your soul.

In a culture that hoards money and titles and power and prestige like gold, Benedict makes the keystone value of his rule of life a chapter on humility that was written for Roman men in a society that valued machoism, power, and independence at least as much as ours.

It is the antidote to an achievement-driven, image-ridden, competitive society that is the hallmark of the modern age.

Humility, the acceptance of our earthiness, is also the antidote to the myth of perfectionism that, masking as holiness, can sink the soul in despair and lead it to abandon the very thought of a truly spiritual life in the face of the very failures we fear.

It makes us look again at our so-called patriotism, our sexism, our racism, and our narcissism, both personal and national.

It makes us look again even at our spiritual arrogance in the face of the world's other great spiritual traditions.

Most of all, it enables us to learn and to grow and never to be disappointed in what we don't get in life, because we come to realize it isn't ours to claim in the first place.

We need the wisdom of humility now. We need that quality of life that makes it possible for people to see beyond themselves, to value the other, to touch the world gently, and peacefully, and make it better as we go.

Peace

We must, most of all, in our time, rethink the meaning of peace. Over the archway of every medieval monastery were carved the words *Pax intrantibus*, "Peace to those who enter here."

The words were both a hope and a promise. In a culture struggling with social chaos, Benedict sketched out a blueprint for world peace. He laid a foundation for a new way of life, the ripples of which stretched far beyond the first monastery arch to every culture and continent from one generation to another, from that era to this one, from his time and now to ours. To us.

That is our legacy, our mandate, our mission—as alive today as ever, more in need in today's nuclear world than ever before.

Once we could teach that the major U.S. export was wheat. Now we have to admit that weapons are. We arm 250 different countries every year and provide almost half of all the arms sold in the world while we decry the selling of them.

Indeed, as Benedictines we must rethink our own commitment to Benedictine peace and our obligation to proclaim it in this world. Benedictine peace, however, is not simply a commitment to the absence of war. It is, as well, the presence of a lifestyle that makes war unacceptable and violence unnecessary.

Even if we dismantled all the war machines of the world tomorrow, it would be no guarantee that we would have peace. The armies of the world simply demonstrate the war that is going on in our souls, the restlessness of the enemy within us, the agitation of the human condition gone awry.

To all these things we need to bring a new spiritual imagination. Imagine a world where people choose their work according to the good it will do for the poorest of the poor—because they saw it in us.

Imagine a world where holy leisure, spiritual reflection rather than political expediency, began to determine everything we do as a nation—because they saw it in us.

Imagine a world where the care of the earth became a living, breathing, determining goal in every family, every company, every life we touch—because they saw it in us.

Imagine a world devoted to becoming a community of strangers that crosses every age level, every race, every tradition, every difference on the globe—because they saw it in us.

Imagine a world where humble listening to the other became more important than controlling them—because people saw it in us.

Imagine a world where what makes for peace becomes the foundation of every personal, corporate, and national decision—because they were called to it by us.

And now imagine what communities inspired by Benedict can do, should do, will do—consciously, corporately, conscientiously—to bring these things into being in every area, region, street, city, and institution, here and now.

Let us resolve again to follow the fiery-eyed radical Benedict of Nursia whose one life illuminated Western civilization. Let us, in other words, live Benedictine spirituality and illuminate our own darkening but beautiful world.

—*The Radical Christian Life*

CONTEMPLATIVE LIVING
Gratitude

> *If the only prayer you say in your life is "Thank you,"*
> *that would suffice.* —Meister Eckhart

Gratitude is not only the posture of praise but it is also the basic element of real belief in God.

When we bow our heads in gratitude, we acknowledge that the works of God are good. We recognize that we cannot, of ourselves, save ourselves. We proclaim that our existence and all its goods come not from our own devices but are part of the works of God. Gratitude is the alleluia to existence, the praise that thunders through the universe as tribute to the ongoing presence of God with us even now.

Thank you for the new day.
Thank you for this work.
Thank you for this family.
Thank you for our daily bread.
Thank you for this storm and the moisture it brings
        to a parched earth.

Thank you for the corrections that bring me to growth.

Thank you for the bank of crown vetch that brings color
to the hillside.

Thank you for the pets that bind us to nature.

Thank you for the necessities that keep me aware of your
bounty in my life.

Without doubt, unstinting gratitude saves us from the sense of self-sufficiency that leads to forgetfulness of God.

Praise is not an idle virtue in life. It says to us, "Remember to whom you are indebted. If you never know need, you will come to know neither who God is nor who you yourself are."

Need is what tests our trust. It gives us the opportunity to allow others to hold us up in our weakness, to realize that only God in the end is the measure of our fullness.

Once we know need, we are better human beings. For the first time we know solidarity with the poorest of the poor. We become owners of the pain of the world and devote ourselves to working on behalf of those who suffer.

Finally, it is need that shows us how little it takes to be happy.

Once we know all of those things, we have come face-to-face with both creation and the Creator. It is the alleluia moment that discovers both God and goodness for us.

Let us learn to come to prayer with an alleluia heart so that our prayer can be sincere. —*The Breath of the Soul*

Interiority

Living without speaking is better than speaking without living. For a person who lives rightly helps us by silence, while one who talks too much annoys us. If, however, words and life go hand in hand, it is the perfection of all philosophy. —Abba Isidore of Pelusia

It is a hurried and a noisy world in which we live. It is not an Egyptian desert of the third century. It is not a hermitage on a mountaintop. We are surrounded, most of us, at all times by the schedules and deadlines, the crowds and the distractions of a dense and demanding society.

We are an increasingly extroverted society, called away from our private selves on every level of life. Institutions even plan family events for us. They organize civic celebrations for us. They design financial plans for us. We spend the greater part of our lives meeting and satisfying the social requirements of institutions which, ironically, are supposedly designed to make personal expression possible, and end up consuming us instead.

Even the spiritual responses people make to the God who created us are determined in large part by religious bodies that carry within themselves the traditions of the denomination from which they spring. But the contemplative knows that ritual and rite are not enough to nourish the divine life within. They are, at best, the appurtenances of religion. Spirituality is not the system we follow; it is the personal search for the divine within us all.

Interiority, the making of interior space for the cultivation of the God-life, is of the essence of contemplation. Interiority is the entering into the self to be with God. My interior life is a walk through darkness with the God within who leads us beyond and out of ourselves to become a vessel of divine life let loose upon the world Going into the self, finding the motives that drive us, the feelings that block us, the desires that divert us, and the poisons that infect our souls brings us to the clarity that is God. We find the layers of the self. We face the fear, the self-centeredness, the ambitions, the addictions that stand between us and commitment to the presence of God. We confront the parts of the self that are too tired, too disinterested, too distracted, to make the effort to nurture the spiritual life. We make space for reflection. We remind ourselves of what life is really all about. We tend to the substance of our souls.

No life can afford to be too busy to close the doors on chaos regularly: twenty minutes a day, two hours a week, a morning a month. Otherwise, we find in the middle of some long, lonely night when all of life seems unraveled and disoriented that somewhere along the line we lost sight of the self, became fodder in the social whirl and never even noticed, until psychic darkness descended, that it had happened to us.

The contemplative examines the self, as well as God, so that God can invade every part of life. We are an insulated society. We are surrounded by noise and awash in talk. We are smothered by a sense of powerlessness. And frustrated by it all, we suffer temper tantrums of the soul. The contemplative refuses to allow the noise that engulfs us to deafen us to our own smallness or blind us to our own glory. Interiority is the practice of dialogue with the God who inhabits our hearts. It is also the practice of quiet waiting for the fullness of God to take up our emptiness. God lies in wait for us to seek the Life that gives meaning to all the little deaths that consume us day by day.

Interiority brings us the awareness of the Life that sustains our life. The cultivation of the interior life makes religion real. Contemplation is not about going to church, though going to church ought certainly to nourish the contemplative life. Contemplation is about finding God within, about making sacred space in a heart saturated with advertisements and promotions and jealousies and ambitions, so that God, whose spirit we breathe, can come fully to life in us.

To be a contemplative it is necessary to spend time every day stilling the raging inner voice that drowns out the voice of God in us. When the heart is free to give volume to the call of God that fills every minute of time, the chains snap and the soul is at home everywhere in the universe. Then the psyche comes to health and life comes to wholeness.

The fact is that God is not beyond us. God is within us and we must go inside ourselves to nourish the Breath that sustains our spirits.   — *Illuminated Life*

Listening: The Key to Spiritual Growth

> *Let us open our eyes to the light that comes from God, and our ears to the voice from heaven that every day calls out this charge: "If you hear God's voice today, do not harden your hearts." —Rule of Benedict, Prologue: 9–13*

The bells that ring over every Benedictine monastery are an archaic way to get a group's attention to the order of the day, and, if that were their only purpose, there are surely better ways to do it. Buzzers and clocks and public-address announcements and blinking lights, for a few, would certainly do a better, more efficient job. But Benedictine bell towers are about more than the schedule of the day. Benedictine bell towers are designed to call the attention of the world to the fragility of the axis on which it turns. Benedictine bell towers require us to listen even when we would not hear. . . . And listening is what Benedictine spirituality is all about in a culture that watches but very seldom hears.

Benedictine spirituality is about listening to four realities: the Gospels, the Rule, one another, and the world around us. Most of us listen easily to one or two of these realities, but only with difficulty do we listen to all four. We read the scriptures faithfully but fail to apply them. We listen to the needs of the poor but forget the reading of the Gospel entirely. We go to spiritual directors regularly but ignore or overlook the insights of the people with whom we live. We prefer to hear ourselves than to listen to wiser hearts for fear they might call us beyond ourselves. Benedictine spirituality requires a medley. . . .

But the Benedictine spirituality of listening puts us in dangerous territory. If we really listened to the Gospels, we would question a lifestyle that endlessly consumes and hoards, is blind to the homeless, and unconcerned about the unprepared. How is it possible to listen to the scripture about the rich young man, or the blind leper, or the grieving widow, and not know that in this century all the miracles for today's poor and outcast and crippled depend on us? If we really listened to the people with whom we lived, could we bear to see children neglected or partners ignored or neighbors rejected? If we really took the thoughts of our hearts and the hopes of our lives to those wiser and holier than we for examination, how could we tolerate situations that could have and should have been ended before they began to eat away at our best selves?

The Rule teaches us to listen to the circumstances of our own lives. We have to begin to face what our own life patterns might be saying to us. When we are afraid, what message lurks under the fear: a horror of failure, a rejection of weakness, panic at the thought of public embarrassment, a sense of valuelessness that comes with loss of approval? When we find ourselves in the same struggles over and over again, what does that pattern say: That I always begin a thing with great enthusiasm only to abandon it before it is finished? That I am always reluctant to change, no matter how good the changes might be for me? That I keep imposing unsatisfactory relationships with people from my past on every new person I meet? That down deep I have never given myself to anything except myself? Not to my friends. Not to my work. Not to my vocation.

Until I learn to listen—to the scriptures, to those around me, to my own underlying life messages, to the wisdom of those who have already maneuvered successfully around the dangers of a life that is unmotivated and unmeaningful—I will really have nothing whatever to say about life myself. To live without listening is not to live at all; it is simply to drift in my own backwater.

Listening is, indeed, a fundamental value of Benedictine spirituality. More than that, Benedictine listening is life lived in stereo. The simple fact is that everybody lives listening to something. But few live a life attuned on every level. Benedictine spirituality doesn't allow for selective perception; it insists on breadth, on a full range of hearing, on total alert. We have to learn to hear on every level at once if we are really to become whole. . . .

There is no quick and easy way to make the life of God the life we lead. It takes years of sacred reading, years of listening to all of life, years of learning to listen through the filter of what we have read. A generation of Pop Tarts and instant cocoa and TV dinners and computer calculations and Xerox copies does not prepare us for the slow and tedious task of listening and learning, over and over, day after day, until we can finally hear the people we love and love the people we've learned to dislike, and grow to understand how holiness is here and now for us. But someday, in thirty years and thirty days perhaps, we may have listened enough to be ready to gather the yield that comes from years of learning Christ in time, or at least, in the words of the *Rule of Benedict*, to have made "a good beginning." Until then, the monastery bells ring out patiently, patiently to remind us to listen. Just listen. Keep listening.

—*Wisdom Distilled from the Daily*

A Time for Peace

The question is, what is the way to the beginning of peace?

The philosopher Blaise Pascal wrote, "The unhappiness of a person resides in one thing, to be unable to remain peacefully in a room." It is silence and solitude that bring us face-to-face with ourselves and the inner wars we must win if we are ever to become truly whole, truly at peace. Silence gives us the opportunity we need to raise our hearts and minds to something above ourselves, to be aware of a spiritual life in us that is being starved out by noise pollution, to still the raging of our limitless desires. It is a call to the Cave of the Heart, where the vision is clear and the heart is centered on something worthy of it.

There are some things in life that deserve to be nourished simply for their own sake. Art is one, music is another, good reading is a third, but the power of the contemplative vision is the greatest of them all. Only those who come to see the world as God sees the world, only those who see through the eyes of God, ever really see the glory of the world, ever really approach the peaceable kingdom, ever find peace in themselves.

Silence is the beginning of peace. It is in silence that we learn that there is more to life than life seems to offer. There is beauty and truth and vision wider than the present and deeper than the past that only silence can discover. Going into ourselves we see the whole world at war within us and begin to end the conflict. To understand ourselves, then, is to understand everyone else as well.

There are two major obstacles, however, to a development of a spirituality of peace. The fear of silence and solitude loom like cliffs in the human psyche. Noise protects us from confronting ourselves, but silence speaks the language of the heart. Silence and solitude are what really bring us into contact both with ourselves and with others. Deep down inside of us reside, in microcosm, all the human hopes and fears, the struggles to control them, the hope to set them free, and the peace that comes when we have confronted both the best and the worst in ourselves and found them acceptable.

Silence requires a respect for solitude, however, and solitude is even more frightening than quiet. One of life's greatest lessons is that solitude and loneliness are not the same thing. Loneliness is the sign that something is lacking. The purpose of solitude, on the other hand, is to bring us home to the center of ourselves with such serenity that we could lose everything and, in the end, lose nothing of the fullness of life at all.

Quiet has become a phantom memory in this culture. Some generations among us have had no experience of it at all. It has been driven out by noise pollution that is endemic, invasive, clamorous. Everywhere. Everyplace. Not simply in New York City. In Small Town, USA, it is blaring every hour of the day. There is Muzak in the elevators and public address systems in the halls and people standing next to you in the hardware store talking loudly on cellular phones and everywhere, everywhere—in offices and restaurants and kitchens and bedrooms—the ubiquitous television spewing talk devoid of thought while people pay no attention at all and shout above it about other things. There are loudspeakers in boats now so the lake is not safe. There are rock concerts in the countryside now so the mountains are not safe. There are telephones in bathrooms now so the shower is not safe. Corporate offices are now beehives of cubicles, cheek by jowl. We don't think anymore; we simply listen. The problem is that we are so deluged with sound that we are accustomed to listening only to things outside of ourselves, however vacuous the message, however pointless the talk.

Silence is the lost art of this society. Clamor and struggle have replaced it. Silence, of course, was once a thing to be dealt with in the human condition. Silence was a given. Men went with the flocks up a lonely mountain for weeks and had to learn to be at peace with themselves. Women worked in the kitchens of the world grinding corn and plucking chickens, deep in thought, attuned to the things around them. Children picked in the fields in long, separated rows, learning young to hear birds and wind and water, weaving their fancies from the materials of the earth. Silence was a friendly part of life, not a deprivation, not a fearsome place to be.

People knew that the silence in which they lived as a matter of course was anything but empty. On the contrary. It was full of the self and all its clamor. Silence had things to teach, and silence was a stern taskmaster, full of angels to be wrestled with and demons to be mollified.

Silence stood demanding and somber, waiting for attention. The substance of silence, you see, is the awakening soul and that, all the great spiritual writers knew, is something that shallow hearts assiduously avoid. It is one thing to arm wrestle the demons outside of us. It is entirely another to brave the adversaries within. But dare them we must or die only half finished, only partially human, only somewhat grown.

The desert monastics of the third century were very clear about the role of silence in the development of a mature spirituality.

"Elder, give me a word," the seeker begged for direction.

And the holy one said, "My word to you is to go into your cell and your cell will teach you everything."

The answers are within you, in other words. And so are the questions. Your questions. The questions no one can ask of you but you. Everything else in the spiritual life is mere formula, mere exercise. It is the questions and answers that rant within each of us that, in the end, are all that matter. Then we get to know ourselves as no one else knows us. Then we blush at what we see. And lose our righteousness. And come to peace.

For those who cringe from silence like the plague, fearful of its weight, cautious of its emptiness, the shock that comes with the revelations of silence goes deep. The heaviness and emptiness we feared give way very quickly to turmoil and internal pressure. Silence enables us to hear the cacophony inside ourselves. Being alone with ourselves is a demanding presence. We find very quickly that either we must change or we shall surely crumble under the weight of our own dissatisfaction with ourselves, under the awareness of what we could be but are not, under the impulse of what we want to be but have failed to become. Under the din is the raw material of the soul. Under the din is self-knowledge, is self-acceptance, is peace.

Silence does more than confront us with ourselves, however. Silence makes us wise. Face-to-face with ourselves we come very quickly, if we listen to the undercurrents that are in contention within us, to respect the struggles of others. Silence teaches us how much we have yet to learn. Or, as we get older, silence perhaps reminds us too that there are qualities that we may never with confidence attain and that will war for our souls till the day we die. Then face-to-face with our struggles and our inadequacies, there is no room in us for mean judgments and narrow evaluations of others. Suddenly, out of silence, comes the honesty that tempers arrogance and makes us kind.

Because we have come to know ourselves better, we can only deal more gently with others.

Knowing our own struggles, we reverence theirs. Knowing our own failures, we are in awe of their successes, less quick to condemn, less likely to boast, less intent on punishing, less certain of our certainties, less committed to our heady, vacuous, and untried convictions. Then silence becomes a social virtue.

Make no doubt about it, the ability to listen to another, to sit silently in the presence of God, to give sober heed and to ponder is the nucleus of the spirituality of peace. It may, in fact, be what is most missing in a century saturated with information, sated with noise, smothered in struggle, but short on reflection. The Word we seek is speaking in the silence within us. Blocking it out with the static of nonsense day in and day out, relinquishing the spirit of silence, anesthetizes the heart in a noise-numbed world and destroys our peace.

An ancient wrote: Once upon a time, a disciple asked the elder, "How shall I experience my oneness with creation?"

And the elder answered, "By listening."

The disciple pressed the point: "But how am I to listen?"

And the elder taught, "Become an ear that pays attention to every single thing the universe is saying. The moment you hear something you yourself are saying, stop."

Peace will come when we stretch our minds to listen to the noise within us that needs quieting and the wisdom from outside ourselves that needs to be learned. Then we will have something of value to leave the children besides hate, besides war, besides turmoil. Then peace will come. Then we will be able to say with Kazantzakis, "I fear nothing; I hope for nothing; I am free."

—*For Everything a Season*

Become a Prayer

The flight from Manila to Tokyo had been, to all appearances, totally routine. We were about an hour from touchdown when the captain came on the intercom: "When we left Manila," the voice said, "we got a signal from the on-board computer telling us that there is something wrong with the plane's landing gear. We have no idea what that is or how serious it may be. Your cabin crew will instruct you how to prepare for a crash landing. Emergency vehicles will meet us on the runway. Please listen carefully now to your flight attendant. . . ." The schoolboy next to me said, "How do I tell them to call my sister first. I don't want my mother to hear about this on a phone." Then, the noise in the cabin stopped. The entire planeload of tourists and business people, of whole families and solitary travelers like me went dead, cold, silent. For almost an hour we packed up our gear, removed glasses and shoes and jewelry. Then, we simply sat and waited, frozen in silence. "Did you say a prayer," someone asked me later when I was telling the story. "No," I said. "I didn't say a prayer; I became a prayer."

Prayer comes at many levels, shapes, and moments in life. None of them are really predictable. All of them are real.

There are books aplenty written on the subject of prayer, of course, but I have come to the point where I doubt that anybody can really "teach" anybody how to pray. That, I figure, is what life does. We can learn prayer forms, of course, but we do not learn either the function or the purpose of prayer until life drags us to it, naked and in pain.

Theologians of the late nineteenth and early twentieth centuries were very good at dissecting prayer. There was spoken prayer, silent prayer, prayer of the mind, prayer of the heart and union with God, they told us. And approximately in that order, if I remember correctly all the manuals I read on the subject. It all seems pretty amusing to me now. I was trying to learn to pray exactly the same way I learned to run a printing press. By the book. In both cases I discovered that the only way to learn to do it was to do it for a long, long time.

They also taught us that there were four purposes of prayer: "adoration, contrition, thanksgiving, and supplication." Now there was something useful. Boring for years, not at all inspiring, perhaps, but more and more useful as life went on, not because it said much about prayer, but because it said so much about life.

Most important of all though, at least for me, was the line in the *Rule of Benedict* that instructs the monastic community to keep prayer brief and the monastics to leave chapel quietly so that anybody who wants to stay behind for private prayer can do so without interruption. In those two simple statements I learned enough about prayer to last me for a lifetime: first, that in order to learn to pray we need to do it regularly. And second, that real contemplative prayer starts where formal prayer ends.

Point: prayer is not a technique. It is an attitude of mind, a quality of soul and a dimension of the daily.   —*Gospel Days*

Spirituality for the Long Haul

Vision, sacrifice, and hope are the caretakers of the future. Without them tomorrow is impossible and today is straw.

What is needed then is not short-term effort. What is needed then is a spirituality for the long haul, a constant, unyielding commitment to keep on critiquing what is beyond critique. What is needed then is an internal energy for justice that comes unbidden and simply will not die, even in the face of defeat. That kind of spirituality, I think, is based on four realities: It demands a memory of church that is above institution. It requires an enterprise worthy enough to merit the waste of a life. It depends on an unquenchable sense of gospel truth. It assumes an unremitting dedication to personal authenticity.

A Life-Size Question

"If you expect to see the final results of your work," an Arab proverb teaches, "you have simply not asked a big enough question." To sustain a stay in a dry and barren desert, it is necessary to be about something great enough to be worth a lifetime of unrewarded effort. The great questions of life are questions that do not admit of cheap and easy answers. They are rooted in the bedrock of the culture and demand the emptying out of souls before they can really be answered. The women's issue is an obvious one, for instance, but it is not an easy one. That women must soon be seen as equals in the church, adults in the world, artists and thinkers in society is clear. The amount of education and analysis and protest and courage that it will take, on the other hand, to reshape centuries of warped and distorted and heretical thought patterns that have been theologized and institutionalized in the name of God staggers the mind.

No single capital campaign will do the trick. No one speech will change the climate. No single law will undo eons of damage. It will take a million lives heaped on top of one another in the rotundas of congress and on the marble stairways of the Vatican to burst the bonds of arrogance and superiority that make God male and males more favored by God. For women and men everywhere who realize that they are about the fulfillment of Genesis, no amount of time, no expenditure of life will be too much to ask for the lives of women and men yet to come.

We have, Genesis teaches us, been put into the Garden "to till it and to keep it." Co-creation is a human responsibility that carries with it grave implications. There are simply some divine cravings in life—the liberation of the poor, the equality of women, the humanity of the entire human race—that are worth striving for, living for, dying for, finished or unfinished, for as long as it takes to achieve them.

A Sense of the Gospel

The inexorable tide of the gospel message is simply too strong to resist. Teresa of Avila in *The Interior Castle* writes, "This is the reason for prayer, my daughters, the purpose of this spiritual marriage: the birth always of good works, of good works."

The person immersed in the spiritual life finds out all too soon that prayer is not a massage. Prayer is an opening of the self so that the Word of God can break in and make us new. We do not pray in order to change God. God is not a magic act we use to save us from the human condition. No, we pray so that God can change us. God is the One, the All, the Best in whose image we have all been made and to whom we must aspire, all lesser images to the contrary.

The problem is that once we see the Jesus who cured lepers despite the thinking of the institution that sickness was the result of sin, we can no longer stand quietly by in our own time while AIDS patients are ignored or worse. Once the way that Jesus treated women begins to puncture the hard wall around our hearts, no amount of "tradition" can blur or justify the aborted vision with which we live today. Once we see the Jesus who questioned Herod and challenged the Pharisees and contested with the High Priest, there is simply no way that we can stand by mute and satisfied while systems rest heavy on the backs of nonunion laborers in Mexican maquiladoras or on scavengers in the Philippines or on welfare mothers in rat-infested apartments in New York slum hotels. Prayer unmasks. Prayer converts. Prayer impels. Prayer sustains the journey to justice. A spirituality without a prayer life is no spirituality at all and it will not last beyond the first defeat. For those who have tasted contemplation, the thirst for justice burns the heart out and will not be damped, whatever the wait, however dear the cost.

A Memory of Church

The eye of God and a soul of prayer are not enough, however, if we lose sight of the struggle that has brought us to the point on which we stand. An asceticism of the present demands a lover's heart. It is always easy to criticize the church and sometimes hard to transform it. At the same time, there will be no tomorrow for the church, if we forfeit its fragile present or fail to understand the beauty of the yesterdays that have brought us to this needy, but growing, place.

It is after all the church that is the reservoir of the unfinished truth which fires us. It is the church that is keeper of the sacraments that nourish us. It is the image of those who bore the church on their backs before this age—Francis, Teresa of Avila, Martin Luther, Catherine of Siena, Ignatius of Loyola—who feed the hope that lies in us. Without those moments of revelation and grace, everything else is useless. But with them, anything is possible and the insanity of the long haul becomes the only kind of sanity worth having.

A Commitment to Personal Integrity

Finally, a spirituality for the long haul is based on a commitment to personal authenticity. If the vision has value and the prayer has depth, then a person cannot do otherwise than struggle and strive for the coming of the will of God, however slow its dawning. There is always the need to be true to oneself. When a person of prayer, a person of vision, begins to work in behalf of the poor, it is impossible to do otherwise. When a person of heart, a person of soul, begins to contest with the forces of patriarchy, it is impossible to do otherwise. When a person of hope and a person of faith start down the long path of prophetic action, it is impossible to turn aside to lesser things. That's why prophets are so dangerous: they cry in season and out of season, politely and impolitely, loud and long. And they do it because, having prayed the vision, they cannot live with themselves and do otherwise.

"It is not your obligation to complete your work, but you are not at liberty to quit it," the Talmud teaches. The person who sees the world as God sees the world, whose prayer life is more converting than comforting, who walks in the footsteps of those who loved the church to life in hard times past, whose sense of personal integrity is deeper than the need for social approval, is in for the long haul. —*Compass Magazine and New Designs*

Universalism

We must move from asking God to take care of the things that are breaking our hearts to praying about the things that are breaking God's heart. —Margaret Gibb

The person who learns to pray with the heart of God has no patience for injustice anywhere. They see with the prophet's eye. They break down national boundaries. They transcend gender roles. They have no sense of color or caste, of wealthy or poor. They see only humanity in all its glory, all its pain.

The person of prayer is not a person of private agendas. The more we become like God, the greater-hearted we become as well. We have no sense anymore of "we and they" or "them and us" or "me and mine." Now our hearts open to take in the heart of the world.

When, in prayer, we come to discover God's universal love, we suddenly realize that God does not take sides, that we have no priority on God alone. We finally understand that the God we seek is the God of the world and so, to seek that God, we must develop hearts as big as the world ourselves.

Then, racism makes no sense and sexism is as much a sin as any other kind of discrimination, and war is blasphemy against humanity. Then we become bigger than our single nation, broader than any one religion, truly catholic—universal—in our cares and beliefs and commitments.

To develop a cosmic heart is a moment of profound transformation. We can never be the same again. We are beyond the boundaries we have created to separate the human race into my race and theirs.

Then prayer becomes truly co-creative.

Otherwise prayer is nothing more than some kind of spiritual spa designed to make me feel good. It is reduced to an exercise the intent of which is to assure me of my own value. It swaddles me in self-righteousness and self-serving. It makes God an icon, a tribal God whose concerns are no bigger than our own. Then God carries a flag, becomes a male potentate, excludes females and passes out personal gifts.

Then we make ourselves God and our God a poor, miserable creature indeed—a national patriot, maybe; a great male warrior, perhaps, but certainly not the God of all creation. Then we are simply worshipping ourselves and calling it prayer.

—*Breath of the Soul*

FAITH

I Believe: "Yes" to the Mystery of Life

Everybody believes in something. There is no such thing as an age of "unbelievers." Some believe in self-determination and some believe in God the puppeteer. Some believe that reality is a mirage and some believe that reality is all there is. Some people believe in a God of wrath, others in a God of love. But underneath all of them there is one constant: Whatever we believe at the deepest center of our being determines what we ourselves become, even when we say we believe in something else.

No one goes through life empty of belief. Each of us draws from a well of ideas that guides us from choice to choice to choice until our life becomes the sum total of each mitered one of them. Some of those ideas are borrowed. They come from authorities and stand fast, at least until tested. Borrowed ideas are somebody else's interpretation of the human story. The ideas that shape the final us, however, come the hard way. They are the attitudes, the assumptions, the concepts which, even if handed down, will, if we are lucky, have been tried by fire. Distilled from experience, these ideas burn themselves into our souls as life works its will on us until, at the end, we find ourselves to be believers pared to the core. The fringes don't matter anymore once we come to understand the big things in life: love, commitment, God, justice, Jesus.

Ideas from authority we treat with respect. Ideas from experience we regard as pearls of great price. These are the beliefs that illuminate for us our own human story in the light of the universal one. The best beliefs, surely, are those that have been tried and found consistent with the instincts of the rest of the universe who down the long corridors of time have come back again and again to the truisms of life: There is something beyond us; there is something bigger than we are that calls us on; there is a purpose to life. It is my story flashed against the screen of the human story. It is, for the Christian, my story seen in the light of the Jesus story. It is belief tested and found to be true, not scientifically but spiritually. It is not statistical, not measurable, not historical, not scientifically verifiable. It is much better than that. It is the spiritual insight that erupts out of a community tempered by tradition and in concert with the consciousness of streams of witnesses before it, even while acknowledging that within the context of the created universe the Jesus story occupies but a millisecond.

Belief is not contrary to fact. It simply transcends it. To believe something is to know its truth not so much in our minds but in the center of our souls. We believe in goodness, for instance, because, however effective evil seems to be, it contradicts the highest aspirations of humanity. We believe in love rather than hate, because love draws out the best in us, while hate feeds on our smallnesses. We believe in the people whose hearts we hold in our hands, whatever the situations that challenge that certainty, because we ourselves are nourished by that relationship. We believe in the spiritual because the material is simply not enough to justify the sense of the unfinishedness of life that lurks in every human heart. In sum, belief is the ability to know what we cannot see. None of our beliefs, if they are really "belief," are sure in the way that chemicals in scales are sure. Belief is sure in the way that truth is sure. It rings in our hearts like tines on crystal.

But belief is not supernatural sleight of hand designed to save us from the exigencies of life. "There are those who say in winter," the Sufi story teaches, 'I shall not wear warm clothes. I will trust in God to keep me warm.' But they forget," the story says, "that the God who made winter gave human beings the power to protect themselves from it." Belief is not fantasy. Belief is not an excuse for irrationality. Faith is not what gives us the tricks it takes to control God. Belief is a basis for personal development and a topographical map of life that signals a way through the valleys and plains, raging rivers and vast oceans, of experience in which we grow. Belief makes of life more a quest than a place. Belief is not what makes it possible for us to settle down complacent in our goodness, certain that if we keep the rules we will have life without having to live it. "I went to church every week, I did everything I was told to do, I believed in God," people say. "How could this divorce have happened?" As if belief were some kind of insurance policy against life. On the contrary. Belief is what enables us to weigh our options in the light of what is really real, what is really important in life and, in the end, stay the course.

To be without belief is to lose sight not only of where we're going but why we're going there. We become confused not only about where we are now but about where, as one more human heartbeat in a sea of life, we've been. Unbelief becomes the ground of confusion, fosters a sense of meaninglessness in life, and leaves us with a feeling of bone-weary loneliness in the universe. Without belief in something greater than ourselves, answers to the questions of why we're here, what we're doing, and how we are to live fade like gray ghosts on a white horizon. Then life shrinks to the dimensions of our own petty little world. Then we become prisoners of our own small selves, captured and trapped in an even smaller box. Then life becomes just one more anthill in space. Belief in God may not be provable, true, but it is hard to imagine anything more senseless than unbelief.

There is, nevertheless, a senseless kind of belief, too. There is a dependency that masks as faith. This kind of belief thrives on absolute answers to the absolutely unanswerable, demands proofs for the unprovable, traffics in magic rather than mystery, and calls it Christianity. This is the kind of religion that sets out to control God. Masked as virtue, it conjures up rules and regulations, admissions policies, and trials by fire to measure a person's right to heaven. It binds God to our laws and confuses being correct with being holy. It makes God as small as we are. It copes by convincing itself that it is possible to achieve perfect security by manipulating the cosmos. It uses God as a crutch for living. I know that kind of faith. I've been there. I collected indulgences, too.

The weakness in a spiritual life that rides on rules and regulations, definitions and doctrines, is that it knows only as much of God as authority defines for it. People who rely only on predigested answers know the rituals and canons of the faith, perhaps, but they may know far too little of the God who dwells within them. They look outside themselves for answers to the spiritual life and bind God to bargains that God never made. They miss the God who is everywhere. They do not really believe, protest as they might. They simply seek to exchange compulsive compliance for perfect collateral. It is a kind of spiritual insurance plan. They may practice religion, but they run the risk of ignoring the God who does not exist to be bound into therapeutic service.

The truth of life is that life is not a given. We are its co-creators. The globe is in our hands. Life is at our mercy. We must be impelled by the vision that inspired it, committed to the glory that created it, and confident in the beauty that sustains it. To say "I believe" is to say that my heart is in what I know but do not know, what I feel but cannot see, what I want and do not have, however much I have. To say "I believe" is to say "yes" to the mystery of life.   —*In Search of Belief*

Doubt

The letter in my hand was written on pink flowered stationery and had a poignant ring. This was not a business-as-usual order, I realized, as much as it strove to sound that way. No, this letter broke life open to the core, and all under the guise of the mundane. "I would like to order thirty copies . . ." the letter began.

For a moment I had almost put the note down to mark it for transfer to the order department, sure that it had simply gotten to my desk by mistake. But on second thought I realized that the letter was simply too long, too personal, to be nothing but a purchase form.

I went on reading.

Here was a woman, the writer said of herself, who organized book discussions for women in the area. They go to church, she went on, "but they find no one in any of them who will honor their questions." They are afraid even to ask questions, she said, because "when they ask a question they're treated as if they're heretics or have already lost their faith. Especially if they point out that the answer they get doesn't answer anything for them." Reading circles were the only way she knew, she wrote, "to help women find their voices."

Then she added what was not routine, even in letters of that sort. "I, myself, don't go to church. I'd like to be part of a praying community, but I don't believe all the things they taught me anymore so I think it is more honest just to stay away."

I paused for a moment. No doubt about it: as a class, churches have been far better at giving answers than they have been at receiving questions. Catechism classes and Sunday School sessions, well-taught as they may have been, have been churning out routine answers to routine questions at regular age levels for eons. Unfortunately, the very age at which most people outgrow catechism class is exactly when they begin to grow into the spiritual confusions that are the essence of adulthood. Then the old answers begin to thin a bit.

For those for whom the questions persist, the choice is a bitter one: We can allow our spiritual lives to be capped in adolescence, assuming that faith has something to do with accepting childish answers to complex issues. Or we can follow our questions to the center of the mystery that stretches far beyond the theological politics of historical documentation. We can search to the point where only wonder will do or we can turn the spiritual life into some kind of corporate strategy aimed at storing up rituals in return for heaven. The one answer leads to the awesome undefinability of God. The other one reduces God to the exercises of a theological athletic field.

The fact is that all the great spiritual models of the ages before us found themselves, at one point or another, plunged into doubt, into darkness, into the certainty of uncertainty: Augustine, John of the Cross, Teresa of Avila, Meister Eckhart, John the Baptist, Thomas, Peter, one after another of them all wondered, and wavered, and believed beyond belief.

Surely, then, doubt is something to be grateful for, something about which to sing an alleluia. Unlike answers that presume the static nature of God and the spiritual life, doubt stretches us beyond ourselves to the guidance of a God whose face is not always in books. Doubt is what leaves us open to truth, wherever it is, however difficult it may be to accept.

But most of all, doubt requires us to reconfirm everything we've ever been made to believe is unassailable. Without doubt, life would simply be a series of packaged assumptions, none of them tested, none of them sure, and all of them belonging not to us, but to someone else whose truth we have made our own.

The problem with accepting truth as it comes to us, rather than truth as we divine it for ourselves, is that it's not worth dying for—and we don't. It becomes a patina of ideas inside of which we live our lives without passion, without care. This kind of faith happens around us but not in us—we go through the motions. The first crack in the edifice and we're gone. The first chink in the wall of the castle keep and we're off to less demanding fields.

Doubt, on the other hand, is the mother of conviction. Once we have pursued our doubts to the dust, we forge a stronger, not a weaker, belief system. These truths are true, we know, because they are now true for us rather than simply for someone else. To suppress doubt, then, to discourage thinking, to try to stop a person from questioning the unquestionable is simply to make them more and more susceptible to the cynical, more unaccepting of naive belief.

It is doubt that is the beginning of real faith.

The only real corrective for passive disbelief is passionate doubt. Our institutions are filled with people who never question whether or not the government and the Constitution are of a piece, whether our churches and the Gospel are compatible. So we produce unpatriotic patriots and corporate believers, people more committed to the system than they are to the following of Jesus. And we produce them at an alarming rate.

"Life is doubt, and faith without doubt is nothing but death," Miguel de Unamuno wrote. But in this case it is not the body that is dead, it is the mind, it is the soul. Worse, there is a complacency in untested faith that makes us vulnerable to the vagaries of change and disciples of a thousand idols. If God is still an old man in the sky for us, then to find not a hint of him in space exploration can be a real challenge to faith. If we never put our own beliefs to the test of inner truth, we are susceptible to every seller of intellectual schemes who stops us along the way. We become consumers of multiple falsehoods in our very desire for truth.

But doubt reduces complacency and leaves us open to larger, better explanations than the mythical ones we give to children until they are old enough to absorb the fact that God really is "pure spirit," however much we cannot imagine what that is, or how it can be, or what it means to the place of God in a material world.

The faith that demands explanations and "proofs" is not faith at all, of course. Faith is "things hoped for but not seen." But fortunately there is a bit of Thomas—the one who would not believe that Jesus was among them still without being able to touch his wounds—in all of us. There is a bit of the doubter in each of us who will not believe without seeing for ourselves that what is said to be true does indeed have some kind of truth to it, no matter how illogical, no matter how obscure.

Did this world make itself? Maybe—but hardly. Did I go through this illness alone? Perhaps—but in the midst of the depression of it, something outside myself sustained me, nevertheless. Has my hard life been without joy? Not completely—and sometimes, in the midst of the worst of it, I have known peace and strength greater than my own making. Have I never known the presence of God? No, in fact I have sometimes known it with consuming awareness.

It is at the point where we desire to see, because down deep our hearts believe what our minds cannot explain, that faith sets in. But the path to that kind of faith is only through the darkness of doubt.

There is simply a point in life when reason fails to satisfy our awareness of what is clearly unreasonable and clearly real at the same time—like love and self-sacrifice and trust and good. Data does not exist to explain these unexplainable things. Then only the doubt that opens our hearts to what we cannot comprehend, only the doubt that makes us rabidly pursue the truth, only the doubt that moves us beyond complacency, only the doubt that corrects mythologies not worthy of faith can lead us to the purer air of spiritual truth. Then we are ready to move beyond the senses into the mystical, where faith shows us those penetrating truths the eye cannot see.   —*Uncommon Gratitude*

In a Dark Wood

I believe that God is and that God wills our good—and that is enough. The rest is simply a matter of learning to see the sacred in the mundane. I see God very differently now from what I was taught to believe was an adequate image of God. "God our loving Father with a stopwatch" has become for me the God of light, truth, energy, and life.

God is the ground of our being. God is the air I breathe. My life and my spiritual life, my life and the life of God are one and the same thing. A church is a vehicle for consciousness of God. It is also a storehouse of the spiritual tradition. For that I'm grateful, because it enables us to trace the history of spiritual development back through the ages. It confirms the fact of continual development and continual effort in need of reform. It frees us to grow. Having said all that, I do not see the church itself as essential to spiritual development but the cycle of liturgical seasons; the constant call to the incarnational and the sacramental gives me life. It's when the best ideals of the church come in conflict with its structures—in regard to women, for instance—that I see the church as an obstacle to the Christian gospel and a scandal to the tradition.

Needless to say, my lifelong determination to enter the monastery was rooted in faith and the desire to live a deeply spiritual life. I entered the monastery at the age of sixteen, but as I got older and began to understand the role of religious life in church and society, I knew that the purpose of our lives was not to create a monastic cocoon for ourselves but to live and work in such a way that we left the world better for other people than we had found it. The Benedictine commitment to immersion in the scriptures and the rooting of the life in equality, peace, stewardship, hospitality, and a 1,500-year history of autonomous monasteries of women, as well as of men, made it perfectly clear to me what kind of things I should be attending to in this century.

It has not always been easy—I went through a terrible period as a young sister—to the point that I thought I would have to leave religious life because I doubted the divinity of Jesus. Only when I realized that I did believe deeply and profoundly in God could I come to peace with the fact that faith in God would have to be enough. It was a dark, empty time. It threw me back on the barest of beliefs but the deepest of beliefs. I hung on in hope like a spider on a thread. But the thread was enough for me. As a result, my faith actually deepened over the years. The humanity of Jesus gave promise to my own. Jesus ceased to be distant and ethereal and "perfect." Jesus let no system, no matter how revered, keep him from a relationship with God. And that union with God, I came to understand, was divine. Then I understand also that questions are of the essence of a mature faith. I don't fear my questions anymore. I know that they are all part of the process of coming to union with God and refusing to make an idol of anything less. The point is that during that difficult time I didn't try to force anything. I simply lived in the desert believing that whatever life I found there was enough for me. I believed that God was in the darkness. It is all part of the purification process and should be revered. It takes away from us our paltry little definitions of God and brings us face-to-face with the Transcendent. It is not to be feared. It is simply to be experienced. Then, God begins to live in us without benefit of recipes and rituals, laws and "answers"—of which there are, in the final analysis, none at all.   — *In a Dark Wood*

Who Are the People Who Were Waiting for Pope Francis?

Sister Joan began writing for the National Catholic Reporter *in 1983. She was a member of the team NCR sent to Rome in April 2005 for the funeral of Pope John Paul II, the conclave, and subsequent election of Pope Benedict XVI. In this article she comments on a column published in her hometown newspaper about the "weariness" many Catholics have felt during the pontificates of both John Paul II and Benedict XVI. Pope Francis, she suggests, symbolizes for them a potential seed of hope for positive change.*

Pat Howard, columnist and managing editor of the *Erie Times-News*, my hometown newspaper, brought his own experience of church-watching to this second papal election in eight years. His description of having been disappointed in the way the church has responded to the questions of the time in the last two papacies gave me a new way to understand what I have been hearing from so many people in so many places these last three weeks.

The importance of Howard's opinion piece as a bellwether comment lies in the fact that Erie, Pennsylvania, is not a hotbed of dissent against anything. On the contrary: This is the kind of small city Americans call "a great place to raise a family." There are churches in every neighborhood of every stripe in the Christian catalog. There are some longtime Jewish synagogues with their congregations deeply embedded in the life of the city. There is a growing Muslim social center and a strong core of new refugees. We are, that is, a mixed population, and we live together well. There is nothing either New Age or critically atheistic about the area's social climate. On the contrary: This is a place that registers "average" on just about every social index. Obviously, then, opinion here can be thought to cover a great deal of ground.

So while reams are being written about what kind of man this new pope should be—scholar, saint, administrator, reformer, whatever—Howard puts his finger on what kind of people are waiting for this pope, whoever and whatever he is. He describes his own growing disillusion with the character of the church and his reasons for it in ways that are eerily reminiscent of similar conversations across the country and from one group to another.

Howard is clear about the issue: "Pope Benedict's Vatican labeled . . . as part of the problem (those who were) too willing to entertain questions and views the hierarchy has declared to be verboten . . . too open to engaging the real lives, moral qualms, and evolving understanding of people in the modern world. . . ." I still believe the church will change in due course," he concludes. "What I underestimated was the weariness that comes with the waiting."

That's it exactly, I said to myself. It is weariness that is palpable in so many groups now. "I have very little hope in this election," I hear over and over again. "It will all simply go on business as usual," they say, and you can almost hear the sigh in the voices.

The problem is that weariness is far worse than anger. Far more stultifying than mere indifference. Weariness comes from a soul whose hope has been disappointed one time too many. To be weary is not a condition of the body—that's tiredness. No, weariness is a condition of the heart that has lost the energy to care anymore.

People are weary of hearing more about the laws of the church than the love of the Jesus who says whatever a person's struggles, "Remember, I am with you always" (Matt. 28:20).

People are weary of seeing whole classes of people—women, gays and even other faith communities again—rejected, labeled, seen as "deficient," crossed off the list of the acceptable.

They are weary of asking questions that get no answers, no attention whatsoever, except derision.

They suffer from the lassitude that sets in waiting for apologies that do not come.

There's an ennui that sets in when people get nothing but old answers to new questions.

There's even worse fatigue that comes from knowing answers to questions for which, as laypersons, they are never even asked.

More false news of a priest shortage drains the energy of the soul when you know that issue could easily be resolved by the numbers of married men and women who are standing in line waiting to serve if for some reason or other, some baptisms weren't worth less than others.

They get tired watching Anglican converts and their children take their place at the altar.

It gets spiritually exhausting to go on waiting for a pastor again, and instead getting a scolding, reactionary church whose idea of perfection is from the century before the last one rather than the century after this one.

They're weary of seeing contraception being treated as more sinful than the sexual abuse of children.

All in all, they're weary of being told, "Don't even think about it." They're weary of being treated as if they are bodies and souls without a brain.

It's weariness, weariness, weariness. It's not an angry, violent, revolutionary response. It's much worse than that. It's a weary one, and weariness is a very dangerous thing. When people are weary, they cease to care; they cease to listen; they cease to wait.

These are the kind of people who waited for a new pope, whatever kind of man he might be.

At first sight, Jorge Mario Bergoglio—Pope Francis—is a quiet and humble man, a pastoral man, and as a Latin American, a leader of 51 million Catholics, or the largest concentration of Catholics on the planet, which is not business-as-usual as far as papal history goes.

But perhaps the most profound and memorable moment of his introduction is that he presented himself on the balcony in front of thousands of people from all parts of the world not in the brocaded fashion of a pope, but in a simple white cassock.

And then came the real shock: He bowed to the people. Bowed. And asked them to pray a blessing down on him before he blessed them. Francis, I remembered, was the Christian who reached out to Muslims. Francis, the one who listened to every creature in the universe and dialogued with it.

Indeed, if this Francis, too, is a listener, there is hope for reconciliation, hope for healing, hope for the development of the church.

No doubt about it: We know who the people are who have been waiting for a pope and why they are weary. The question now is, does he know how weary they are? And does he care? Really?

From where I stand, something has to change. Maybe, just maybe, this time. . . .

—*National Catholic Reporter*, March 14, 2013

Why I Stay

First published in Lutheran Women Today *in 1996, "Why I Stay" has become the number one requested and reprinted of Sister Joan's seven hundred articles.*

"It is good to have an end to journey toward," Ursula Le Guin writes, "but it is the journey that matters in the end." The truth of that statement explains how it is possible, necessary even, for me as a Roman Catholic to stay in a church that is riddled with inconsistencies, closed to discussion about the implications of them, and sympathetic only to invisible women. The fact is that over the years I have come to realize that church is not a place, it is a process. To leave the church may, in fact, be leaving part of the process of my own development. And so, intent on the process of grappling with truth, I stay in it, even when staying in it for a woman is full of pain, frustration, disillusionment, and far too often, even humiliation. Both of us—this church and I— have need to grow. The church needs to grow in its under-standing of the Gospel, and I need to grow in my understanding of myself as I strive to live it. It is, in other words, a journey of conversion for both of us.

There is, also, a model for the staying that lurks within me, prodding me in hard times to trust my questions, accusing me on dark days of prizing weakness more than truth, consoling me in hard times with the courage of endurance, and inspiring me always to keep the faith whatever the weakness of the system that heralds it. What haunts me are the memories of Jesus con-testing with the Pharisees, weeping over Jerusalem, teaching in the synagogue, and presiding over the Seder on Holy Thursday. My models are clear: Jesus proclaiming his truth whatever the situation, whatever the cost; Jesus grappling with the depression that comes from failure, from rejection; Jesus trusting the truth, living the faith and hoping to the end.

Those are the models that make the rest of the journey. When the church has little time for women's presence, takes little notice of women's questions, holds little respect for women's insights, devotes itself to preaching the gospel of equality for women but preserves a male theology and a male system, this demands a purpose far beyond ourselves.

I stay in the church, a restless pilgrim, not because I don't believe what the church has taught me but precisely because I do. I believed when they taught us that God made us equal and Jesus came for us all. I believed in the Jesus they showed me who listened to women and taught theology to women and sent women to teach theology and raised women from the dead. And so today, I believe that the church, if it is ever to be true to that same Gospel, must someday do the same—it must commission women as Jesus did the Samaritan woman, listen to women as Jesus did the Canaanite women, raise women to new life as Jesus did the daughter of Jairus. I stay in the church because there is nowhere else I know that satisfies in me what the church itself teaches us to seek: a sacramental life that makes all life sacred, a community of faith that celebrates life together, the proclamation of the image of God alive in each of us, the contemplation of truth that makes life meaningful. I know clubs and societies and congregations of deep sincerity who do great good. The problem is that I need sacrament and common faith and a sense of the divine in the core of my humanity, as well as I need good talk, good works, and good intentions.

I stay in the church because, though the lights have gone out in parts of the house, I know myself to be at home. I realize now with penetrating anger how sexist the church itself really is, whatever its professions of faith in Jesus and love for women. But I also realize that this is the family I was raised in. This is the family that gave me my first images of God, my first feeling of human worth, my first sense of holiness, my first invitation to a goodness measured by more than "success." Just because a family is dysfunctional, as this one is, does not make it less the family. If anything, we must work all the harder to bring all of us to health in it.

I stay in the church because I have the support from other women, from feminist men, from a women's community that enables me to worship with human dignity and a sense of theological inclusion. Otherwise, I do not know how possible it would be to stay. At the same time, because I know my own need for the strength of a conscious and understanding community, I have come to understand and honor those who, lacking that kind of support, choose to leave it. For many, churchgoing has become more an experience of systemic devaluation than spiritual growth. After years of waiting for change, then, they have chosen to try to find God by themselves rather than being excluded by the community from the common search. These are the women in whom beats a Catholic heart but, like many another abused or belittled woman, they get to the point where, for their mental health, say with pain and still with love, "I will not divorce you but until this changes, I cannot live under the same roof."

I stay in the church for the simple reason that because it has come through so much already, I know it can come through more. This is the church that finally repented the Inquisition, that eventually accepted Galileo, that at length stopped selling relics, and that, in the end, caught up with Luther and at long last embraced an ecumenical movement. Among other things. This is a church that has known sin and regretted it. This is a church that has the potential, the credentials, to understand mine, as well.

I stay in the church, wiser now, less idealistic, more balanced in my hope for instant change, more spiritually mature myself, perhaps. In the first two weeks of my initial trip to Rome in 1972, I was appalled by what I saw there—the pomp, the posturing, the oppressive and arrogant sense of power that seeped out of every office, hung over every meeting, colored every ritual. I was young and intense. I had, I thought, lost my faith. I wanted never to go back there. "Patientia, patientia," an old monastic counseled. "You will come back and you will grow to understand. . . ." The sentence trailed off into irritating nothingness. Understand what? But by the end of the next two weeks and the next fifteen years of meetings there, I came to understand its meaning for myself. I grew to realize that for those whose faith is mature, only God is God. Not the institution. Not the system. Not the history. Not the pope. God is in the church, not in the chancery. The church is a vehicle for the faith, not the end of it.

Finally, I stay in the church because the sexist church I love needs women for its own salvation. The truth it holds, women test for authenticity.

We are sanctifying one another, this church and the women who refuse to be silent, refuse to be suppressed. What each of us sets out to convert will in the end convert us as well. Women will call the church to truth. The church will call women to faith. Together, God willing, we will persist, women despite the madness of authoritarianism, and the church regardless of the irritation of unrelenting challenge. We will perdure together. We will propel ourselves to the edges of our potentials for holiness.

"Why does a woman like you stay in the church?" a woman asked me from the depths of a dark audience years ago. "Because," I answered, "every time I thought about leaving, I found myself thinking of oysters." "Oysters?" she said. "What do oysters have to do with it?" "Well," I answered her in the darkness of the huge auditorium, "I realized that an oyster is an organism that defends itself by excreting a substance to protect itself against the sand of its spawning bed. The more sand in the oyster, the more chemical the oyster produces, until finally, after layer upon layer of gel, the sand turns into a pearl. And the oyster itself becomes more valuable in the process. At that moment, I discovered the ministry of irritation."

I stay in the church with all my challenge and despite its resistance knowing that before this is over, both it and I will have become what we have the capacity to be—followers of the Christ who listened to women, taught them theology, and raised them from the dead.   —*In the Heart of the Temple*

The Spirit of God Is a Wild Thing

The Holy Spirit, God's energizing presence among us, the life force that drives us beyond ourselves, that whispers us into the great quest within, that makes life alive with a purpose not seen but deeply, consciously, stubbornly felt even in the midst of chaos, even at the edge of despair, sounds the truth in us that we are more than we seem to be. Life does not begin and end with us. There is more than we know, there is an electric charge animating the world at every level and, most of all, within. Holy Spirit suffuses all of life, calls us into the mystery that is God, reminds us of the model that is Jesus, brings us to the fullness of ourselves. Holy Spirit is the great anti-gravitational force that calls us out of somewhere into everywhere, that keeps us moving toward, through, the black holes of life, certain that on the other side of them is light, waiting and wishing us on.

Do I believe in the Holy Spirit? You bet I do. Nothing else makes sense. Either the Spirit of God who created us is with us still, either the presence of Christ who is the Way abides in us in spirit, or the God of Creation and the Redeemer of souls have never been with us at all. God's spirit does not abandon us, cannot abandon us, if God is really God.

If we are to understand emerging consciousness as a manifestation of the Spirit of God alive in the land, then never has an age seen revelation, consciousness, and wisdom working more clearly than in this one. The signs of new awareness of the human relationship to God are everywhere, in all nations, in all peoples. The Holy Spirit has spoken through married couples and professional personnel about birth control, for instance. The Holy Spirit has spoken through women—and other eminent theologians, theological societies, and male scripture scholars as well—about the ordination of women. The Holy Spirit has spoken through laity and bishops and multiple other rites of the church alike about the ordination of married men. But no one listens. The Holy Spirit in people of good will is a voice crying in the wilderness, rejected, ignored, and reviled. One element of the church determines the voice of the Spirit and does so, it seems, by refusing to listen to its other manifestations.

God the Creator and Jesus the Way—always with us on the one hand, but never with us on the other—would move humanity, the early church was now sure, by means of the promptings and presence of the Spirit of God who created us and who lives among us and is in us still. Holy Spirit was not a disembodied ghost, not an immaterial being. On the contrary. The Spirit embodied the life force of the universe, the power of God, the animating energy present in all things and captured by none. Because of the Spirit, Jesus was not gone and God was not distant, and the life force around us bore it proof. The Spirit was the restless urge to life in us leading life on to its ultimate.

The Spirit of God moves us to new heights of understanding, to new types of witness, to new dimensions of life needed in the here and now. The static dies under the impulse of the Spirit of a creating God. We do not live in the past. We are not blind beggars on a dark road groping our separate ways toward God. There is a magnet in each of us, a gift for God, that repels deceit and impels us toward good. The gifts are mutual, mitered to fit into one another for strength and surety.

We are, in other words, in the most refreshingly trite, most obviously astounding way, all in this together—equally adult, equally full members, equally responsible for the church. Nor does any one dimension of the church, then, have a monopoly on insight, on grace, on the promptings of God in this place at this time. The Spirit of God is a wild thing, breathing where it will, moving as it pleases, settling on women and men alike.

—*In Search of Belief*

A Creed

> I believe in one God
> who made us all
> and whose divinity infuses all of life
> with the sacred.
> I believe in the multiple revelations
> of that God

alive in every human heart,
expressed in every culture,
and found in all the wisdoms
of the world.

I believe
that Jesus Christ,
the unique son of God,
is the face of God
on earth
in whom we see best
the divine justice,
divine mercy,
and divine compassion
to which we are all called.
I believe in the Christ
who is One in being with the Creator
and who shows us the presence of God
in everything that is
and calls out the sacred in ourselves.
I believe in Jesus, the Christ,
who leads us to the fullness
of human stature,
to what we were meant to become
before all time
and for all other things that were made.
Through Christ
we become new people,
called beyond the consequences
of our brokenness
and lifted to the fullness of life.

By the power of the Holy Spirit
he was born of the woman Mary,
pure in soul
and single-hearted—
a sign to the ages
of the exalted place

of womankind
in the divine plan
of human salvation.
He grew as we grow
through all the stages of life.
He lived as we live
prey to the pressures of evil
and intent on the good.
He broke no bonds with the world
to which he was bound,
He sinned not.
He never strayed from the mind of God.
He showed us the Way,
lived it for us,
suffered from it,
and died because of it
so that we might live
with new heart,
new mind,
and new strength
despite all the death
to which we are daily subjected.

For our sake
and for the sake of eternal Truth
he was hounded
harassed
and executed
by those
who were their own gods
and who valued the sacred
in no other.
He suffered so that we might realize
that the spirit in us
can never be killed
whatever price we have to pay

for staying true to the mind of God.
He died
but did not die
because he lives in us
still.
"On the third day" in the tomb
he rose again
in those he left behind
and in each of us as well
to live in hearts
that will not succumb
to the enemies of life.
He changed all of life
for all of us thereafter.
He ascended into the life of God
and waits there
for our own ascension
to the life beyond life.

He waits there,
judging what has gone before
and what is yet to come
against unending values
and, in behalf of eternal virtue,
for the time when all of life
will be gathered into God,
full of life and light,
steeped in truth.
I believe in the Holy Spirit,
the breath of God
on earth,
who keeps the Christ vision present
to souls yet in darkness,
gives life
even to hearts now blind.
Infuses energy

into spirits yet weary, isolated,
searching and confused.
The spirit has spoken
to the human heart
through the prophets
and gives new meaning
to the Word
throughout time.
I believe in one
holy and universal church.
Bound together by the holiness of creation
and the holiness of hearts forever true.

I acknowledge the need
to be freed from the compulsions
of my disordered life
and my need for forgiveness
in face of frailty.
I look for life eternal
in ways I cannot dream
and trust
that creation goes on creating
in this world
and in us
forever.
Amen.

Amen to creation, to the God who is life, to courage,
and to hope, to the spirit of truth, to nature, to happiness,
to wholeness, to the place of women in the plan of God,
to the Christ who calls us
beyond the boundaries of ourselves,
to forgiveness, and to everything that streches our hearts
to the dimensions of God. Amen. Amen. Amen.
In all of this we can surely believe. As God has.
                                        —*In Search of Belief*

2

PASSION FOR LIFE

There is a greater purpose to life than simply making a living.
—Joan Chittister

For Sister Joan, life is a sacred adventure. It is a gift from the Holy One and not to be squandered. Like the poet Stanley Kunitz, she counsels us to "Live in the layers not on the litter," or surface of our lives. We are to cultivate our humanity—consciously. Yet Sister Joan acknowledges that doing so is a lifelong process. It requires a willingness to recognize our wounds, our personal and social dysfunctional patterns of behavior. These darker dimensions of our personalities can dwarf our capacity to be fully human. Moreover, Sister Joan cautions in these pages: pay attention! We live not for ourselves alone. We are our neighbors' keeper. All we must do is commit to "waking up" each day, to "listening with the ear of our heart," each day, to becoming, then, the best lovers we can possibly be—each and every day of our lives.

BECOMING FULLY HUMAN

What Does It Mean to Be Human?

To ask what it means to be human strikes at the fabric of the soul.

But I have seen humanity. I know its face even when I cannot define it. It is emblazoned in my mind. It measures my character and condemns my disregard. Anything less than these images disappoint me to the core.

I have a picture in my mind of nuns putting flowers in the gun barrels of Filipino soldiers in Manila who then refused to shoot into the crowd. I still hold in my heart the sight of a young man in Tiananmen Square standing in front of a moving tank that

117

then turned back. I carry the image of men carrying a lone sur-
vivor out of a tangle of earthquake wreckage on a swaying over-
pass that then collapsed. Every time these images flash before my
mind I remember that to be human is to give yourself for things
far greater than yourself.

I have a memory, too, as a twelve-year-old of crying silently
but bitterly face-down into a pillow on the living room floor.
That day, my bird, my only life companion, had disappeared
up an open flue in our apartment wall. There were visiting rela-
tives in the house, in my bedroom, whom I knew were not to be
disturbed. The needs of the guest came first, I had been taught.
But when the house was safely dark, I let the pain pour out, not
simply for the loss of my dearest possession but also in sorrow
for my own carelessness in his regard. Then, suddenly, I felt the
covers around me tighten. My mother had gotten in on one side
of the mattress, my father on the other, and together they held
me all the long and empty night. I learned then that being human
meant to enter into someone else's pain.

And that is what we have lost. We "defend" ourselves by threat-
ening the globe and our own level of civilized humanness with it.
We have chosen technological progress and financial profits over
the needs of human beings. We have bartered the quality of our
own souls; we live the denial of Reverence for Life.

But we have become a society of machines and business
degrees, of stocks and bonds, of world power and world devastation, of what works and what makes money. We train our young
to get ahead, our middle-aged to consume, and our elderly to
be silent. We are sophisticated now. We talk about our ideas for
getting ahead rather than about our ideas for touching God. We
are miles from our roots and light-years away from our upbring-
ings. We have abandoned the concerns of the civilizations before
us. We have forsaken the good, the true, and the beautiful for
the effective, the powerful, and the opulent. We have abandoned
enoughness for the sake of consumption. We are modern. We are
progressive. And we are lost.

So what do I believe in? What do I define as human? I believe in the pursuit of the spiritual, in the presence to pain, and the sacredness of life. Without these, life is useless and humanity a farce.

To be human it is necessary, perhaps, to think again about what matters in life, to ask always why what is, is. To be human is to listen to the rest of the world with a tender heart, and learn to live life with our arms open and our souls seared with a sense of responsibility for everything that is.

Without a doubt, given those criteria, we may indeed not live the "better life," but we may, at the end, at least have lived a fully human one.   —*What Does It Mean to Be Human?*

What's Important in Life?

Once upon a time, there was an elder who was respected for his piety and virtue. Whenever anyone asked him how he had become so holy, he always answered, "I know what is in the Qur'an."

So when the old man died, they raced one another to his hut to find out for themselves what was in his Qur'an. "Well, what is it?" they shouted.

The disciple holding the book looked up from it amazed and said with wonder in his voice, "What is in this Qur'an are notes on every page, two pressed flowers and a letter from a friend."

There are some things in life, whatever its burdens, however it is spent, which if we cultivate them will never die, will be the source of our joy forever, will sustain us through everything.

"Two pressed flowers," beauty of the bloom, memories of past good days, remain in memory and heart long after the event has ended. Beauty scatters seeds of hope in us. It reminds us of time that was good for its innocence. It brings us face-to-face with the natural. It reminds us that, like the seasons, whether we want this present moment or not, it has a place in our growth that in the end will flower forth in ways we cannot now see.

"Two pressed flowers" become the treasury of those moments in time when spontaneous laughter made a moment rich and

unforgettable. They echo on in life long after the moment ends
and ring a reminder to us of the incessant, bedrock beauty of
life, however long or many its sad days. They remind us that
there is in life, down deep, and unexpectedly, an essential basic
and beautiful goodness that redeems all the moments we ourselves overlay with greed or hatred or anger or self-centeredness.

The holy life cultivates those moments. They are the heartbeat
of the universe. They make us glad to be alive. They hold us up
in hope when everything around us seeks to drown us in despair.

They remind us, whatever the tenor of today, that we have
known beauty once and can find it again.

"Notes in the margins of our scriptures" lift us above the
mundane and make us look again at what we are, at what we are
called to be. They require us to be reflective about what we do
and why we do it. They remind us that there is a greater purpose
to life than simply making a living. Reflection—this conscious
comparison of the goals and hope of my life with all the possible purposes of life—gives us a new sense of the nobility of life.
It stretches us to be everything we can be, in even the worst of
circumstances. It refuses to remain mired in the search for power
and security that isolate us from the rest of humankind.

Reflection on the great questions of life puts everything else
into perspective. We are meant to be about more than money
and social craftiness. We are called to be more than simply pass-
ersby in life. We are here to strive for the best in us, to reach into
the center of us, to remember that we are decidedly human and
decidedly more than that at the same time. We have within us
the stardust of the universe, and we are on our way home.

Nothing smaller than the cosmos is meant to distract us from
a God's-eye view of life.

Finally, friendship—love —"letters from our friends," touch
us so that we might eventually learn to touch others. We come to
this world from the moment of birth unable to function without
the help of others. We grow, then, into that purpose ourselves: to
care for those around us so that, caring for one another, we may

all live secure in the knowledge that we are safe and wanted, necessary and loved.

Our letters remind us that it is what and whom we have loved which, in the end, shapes the quality of our lives.

When all the stages of life have passed us by, these things alone remain: the spiritual treasure that stretches our souls to see what our eyes cannot, the remembrance of how beautiful life really is under all its ugliness, and the love of those around us who make the journey gentle as we go.

If the question is, what things are really important in life? the answer depends on what is in the Qur'an that is your heart.

To make the journey of life and cultivate none of those things is to squander our years. Anything less is pure chimera. We grasp for mercury and morass when we concentrate only on cosmetic beauty and transient power, for social connections and uncertain security. Those things are all real, of course, even necessary. They are part of all our lives at one time or another. But they deceive. They only come and go. They are running through our fingers like water through a strainer, even as we speak.

If the question is, what is really important in life?—the answer is only life itself, living it well, immersing it in beauty, love, and reflection. —*Welcome to the Wisdom of the World*

The Search for Happiness

In folktales of the East written thousands of years ago, there is a story which, in the annals of contemporary happiness research, is still as fresh as yesterday. OSnce upon a time, an angel appeared to a seeker hard at work in the field of life and said, "I have been instructed by the gods to inform you that you will have ten thousand more lives." The wanderer, who had been pursuing the dream of eternal life for years, slumped to the ground in despair. "Oh, no," the seeker cried. "Ten thousand more lives; ten thousand more lives!" and the seeker wailed and rolled in the dust.

Then the angel moved on to another seeker bent over in the heat of the day and repeated the same message. "I have been told to tell you," the angel said, "that you will have ten thousand more lives." "Really?" the seeker exclaimed. "Ten thousand more lives?" Then the seeker straightened up, arms flung toward heaven, head up, face beaming, and began to dance and prance and shout with joy. "Only ten thousand more lives!" the seeker cried ecstatically. "Only ten thousand more lives!"

There is, I've come to understand as the years go by, a bit of both those seekers in all of us. Certainly in me.

One part of me, like the seeker promised ten thousand more lives, goes in and out of phases at the very thought of it, moaning with the Hebrew psalmist as I go, "O woe is me that my journey is prolonged." With the poet, "I all alone between my outcaste state" when life takes one of its erratic swings and turns on me, deprives me, I think, or rejects me, or, most of all, denies me what I want. I mourn the lack of something, someone, sometime, somewhere, which, I'm certain, must surely make me happy again.

There is another part of us, though, that has a thirst for life that simply cannot be slaked. The more of its surprises, the greater its challenges, the broader its scope, the faster our hearts beat, the more deeply our soul breathes in the very thought of tomorrow. We get up every morning ready for whatever life brings and intent on shaping it to our own ends. We are alive with life.

I have loved life. Like the second seeker I have loved every moment of it, however deep the difficulty of living in a family that was never really a family. I lusted after every breath of it. I always thought of it as getting better, getting fuller, even while I lived a life that by nature limited the things others used to mark their security or their success or their lifetime records of happiness. I got older and loved it even more. There wasn't much left of its memorabilia in my drawers and cupboards, but I found a great deal of what it meant to me inside. Whatever the struggles of it—the deaths, the life changes, the polio, the wrenching attempts to make better the parts of it crushed under the weight of inertia—I would take more of it if I could. And I am convinced that I am not alone.

I look back on a life that has, it seems, had its share of what the world could call unhappiness: early deaths that changed the course of my life but which I cannot claim destroyed it; debilitating illnesses that never really managed to debilitate me; sharp shifts in the hopes and plans of a lifetime that leave me a bit wistful yet but not at all defeated; and the continuing struggles to be fully human in a man's world and fully adult in a religious culture whose history has belied its theology, whose practice has been to be more comfortable with martinets and minions, "help mates" and male overlords, than with its thinking women.

But real as all those things are, they are the stuff of challenge, not of unhappiness. Unless, of course, I fail to make the distinction between what it is to be challenged by life and what it is to be fulfilled by it. Happiness, I have learned, is a work in progress.

Happiness is what outlasts all the suffering in the world. It is the by-product of learning to live well, to choose well, to become whole, and to be everything we are meant to be—for our sake and for the sake of the rest of the world, as well.

We become happy by learning to appreciate what we have as well as to achieve what we want.

We become happy by cultivating the highest levels of human response in ourselves—in the arts, culture, creativity, understanding, productivity, and purpose.

We become happy by concentrating on the gifts of life rather than obsessing over its possible pitfalls. As Ezra Taft Benson said, "The more we express our gratitude to God for our blessings, the more God will give to our mind other blessings. The more we are aware to be grateful for, the happier we will become."

We become happy by refusing to allow externals to be the measure of the acme of our souls. "Those who have cattle," the Kenyans teach us, "have care."

We become happy by refusing to be beguiled by accumulation or power or pure utilitarianism, by power or excess or withdrawal from the great encounters with life. For it is the happy life that asks more of us than we realize we have and then surprises us by enabling it in us.

We become happy by defining a purpose in life and pursuing it with all the heart that is in us, with all the energy we have. Then we, all of us—those around me and I myself—may know ourselves at the end to have lived well and done well, to have known the tide of a general, pervasive, deep, and overwhelming sense of well-being, to have been born for a purpose and to have achieved it.

Finally, we must learn to keep our eye on happiness rather than simply on pleasure. It is the confusion of the two that endangers the goal.

The process of redefining happiness for ourselves lies in learning to keep our eyes on the real thing. Once you know what that really is, you will never stop pursuing it.   —*Happiness*

God's Will for Us

There are three clues and three cautions about what it means to discern what we are meant to do in life if we really want to do the will of God.

The clues are clear: the will of God for us is that we fulfill what we have been given, what we were born with, what we are in the raw.

First, to do what we are meant to do in life we must have whatever natural potential it takes to do it. And more than that, we must be willing to pay the price to succeed at it. Perhaps the saddest, most damning words in the lexicon of life are: "She never lived up to her potential." Nothing comes from nothing attempted. The greatest geniuses practice before they play in public.

Second, to do what we are meant to do in life, we must have great passion for it. What we do with our life is our gift to the human race. To do it well, we must give it everything we have so that the work of God on earth can be done through us. The effort we fail to give to what must be done will only delay its coming to life. To say that we are committed to doing peace work but do it poorly or seldom or carelessly or irresponsibly only means that many will go on suffering even longer from the effects of violence.

Third, to do what we are really meant to do in life, we must see what we are doing not only as the real purpose of our life but also the ultimate legacy of our life. It is what we will leave behind us for future generations to build on. God did not finish creation; God started it. Its ongoing development God leaves to us. What we do in life makes us the hands of God in living flesh and blood.

God is not a vending machine that prints fortunes or a global positioning system that tells us where to go. We have been created with everything in us that we need in order to determine what we are meant to do in life. That is where God wants us to be, that is what God wants us to be doing, that is the will of God for us.

It is coming to the completion of our best selves, it is in following the magnet in our hearts, that we become our whole selves. Then we will have come to fullness of life, to the flowering of our best gifts, to being what we were meant to be, to finding the reason for which we were born. Then, having followed the deepest inclination of our hearts, we will have discovered what life is really all about. And that is surely the will of God for us.

—Following the Path

Sanctity

What the world calls saints says something to the rest of us about what our own lives can be. All of them bring to consciousness the notion that there may be far more to life than we are seeing. There may be far more in life than what we have managed to acquire. There may be far more that life demands of us than we are willing to give. Christian sanctity is clearly more a communal than a private concept, more a social than a personal process. What I am, the rest of the world has the right to be. What I am becomes benchmark for the rest of society as well. I carry on my back the obligation to be what the world needs me to be and I look in hope for those who have carried that same obligation before me. The Christian life requires a commitment to the life of the Christ who consorted with sinners, cured lepers, raised women from the dead, contested with the officials and challenged the state. It is a life of prophetic presence and selfless service in a world whose soul has gone dry.

Saints, as a result, have always been a part of Christian history. They are those who, clear of soul and straight of eye, chart their lives by remembering its meaning. Saints mark the way for those who come after them. They are the pathfinders, the models, the stars in the darkness of every generation who enable us to remember the glory of humanity as well as the magnetism of divinity. They give us promise of possibility in the depths of despair and hope in the midst of the mundane. They bring new light to those parts of life grown dull from neglect. They remind us at our worst of what humanity can be at its best. They give us new insight into old truths, a new look at the God in our midst who goes among us so that the blind may see and the deaf may hear and the poor may have proof of liberation.

For those who ask, then, Why have saints? the answer is, Why not have saints? Every generation needs heroes. It is not that saints are humans who have become divine. It is that saints are humans who have become fully human, fully the best that a human can be, fully attuned to life at its most meaningful. The saints are those around us in tiny neighborhoods and spacious offices who confront us daily with the great questions of life and bring to them the answer of themselves.

We search for the signs of the best in ourselves at all times and in all places. We measure ourselves by the measure of those who have wrestled with the same angels, lived in the same darkness, borne the same heat of the day and come to triumph, come to light, come to a new consciousness of the truth of life despite the pressures around them and the struggles within. We look for those around us who make life's great Jesus-story real and true. We watch for those who have touched Jesus and become new because of it so that we ourselves can find purpose in stretching to touch it.

Clearly not everyone who points the way to God for us may themselves be perfect. There are figures gleaming in their holy causes who are awkward in their personal lives. They are sometimes in confusion, as we are. They are often in conflict with themselves, as we are. They are virtuous beyond telling in one dimension and weak to the point of sin in others. At the same time, they hold a fire in their hearts bright enough to light a way for many. They are impelled by the will of God for humankind and they will brook no less. They stand on gilded stilts above the rest of their generation, their comrades, their kind and become a sign for all generations. They are a proof of possibility from ages past and a symbol of hope for ages yet to come. They stand in mute conviction of the age in which they live and challenge us to do the same. Most of all, they are important to us now. "One does not help only one's own generation," the Hasidim teach. "Generation after generation, David pours enthusiasm into somber souls; generation after generation, Samson arms weak souls with the strength of heroes."

Sanctity in the Christian tradition requires far more than personal piety, then. It assumes a life so rooted in the will of God, so committed to others, and so large in the scope of its concerns that it raises questions in the hearts of the rest of us about the quality of our own souls, the depth of our own lives, the value of our own choices.

The saint sees the world as God sees the world and responds wherever they are, however they must, so that the Jesus who lives in them may live through them.

It is a dark and dangerous journey and means more than a fidelity to dogma, more than the preservation of doctrine, more than the keeping of the law. It demands high valor and great faith. It lives hidden sometimes as Charles de Foucauld did with the Arabs simply to build a private bridge between Islam and Christianity. It becomes hugely public sometimes as did Bartolomé de Las Casas in his defense of the humanity of the American Indians. It goes where it may not go and does what it may not do as did Catherine of Siena in her involvement in church politics and her criticism of the pope. It lives a fiercely abandoned life sometimes as did Franz Jägerstätter who alone of all his village refused induction into Hitler's army and was executed because of it. But always, always, it lives more out of principle than it does out of piety. It goes above and beyond the normal norms to show again God's glory waiting in the normal. It lives the daily in a way that challenges us all. And it is in no way amenable to the official standards of the day. Francis of Assisi stretched the mind of the church about wealth. Teresa of Avila expanded the vision of the church about the nature of private spirituality. Harriet Tubman taught the church in her courageous deceit what it could be in the face of fear. Monsignor Hugh O'Flaherty, Vatican official in World War II Rome, proved in his protection of Jewish refugees that the church was still capable of sanctity in a world full of sin.

We must begin once again to walk the roads of Galilee with the One who brings us into ourselves to wrestle with the demons designed to keep us there, beyond ourselves to a world in need, and above ourselves to see the world as God sees the world. We must become what we all think we cannot be if we are ever to become what we are all called to be: "icons," "rebels," "stars," and" "saints."   —*In the Heart of the Temple*

New Story about Jesus

The story charms me. The person who sent it to me swears it's true, of course. But it really doesn't make much difference to me if it actually happened or is delightfully apocryphal. It's hard to forget, because its real truth has something very important to say about the core, the essence, of liturgical spirituality.

It was a normal rush-hour day in a New York City airport. Commuters raced down concourses to make quick connections between major incoming flights and local helicopters or business jets that would take them from one small airport to another in time for supper. Men in heavy coats swinging heavy briefcases, and women in high heels loaded down with cumbersome shoulder bags skidded around vendors and carts, corners and counters in a mad rush to reach gates where the doors were already closing. There wouldn't be another flight for at least an hour. They pushed and jostled, bumped and pounded their way through a jumble of people dashing down the same corridor but in the opposite direction.

Suddenly, everyone heard the crash. The fruit stand teetered for a moment and then tilted the fruit baskets off the counter-top to the floor. Apples and oranges rolled helter-skelter up and down the concourse. Then the girl behind the counter burst into tears, fell to her knees, and began to sweep her hands across the floor, searching for the fruit. "What am I going to do?" she cried. "It's all ruined. It's all bruised. I can't sell this!" One man, seeing her distress as he ran by, stopped and came back. "Go on," he called to the others still running ahead of him down the corridor. "I'll catch you later."

Seeing how frantic she was, he got down on the floor with the girl and began putting apples and oranges back into baskets. And it was then, as he watched her sweep the space with her hands, randomly, frantically, that he realized that she was blind. "They're all ruined," she kept saying.

The man took forty dollars out of his wallet, pressed it into her hand. "Here," he said as he prepared to go, "here is forty dollars to pay for the damage we've done." The girl straightened up. She began to grope the air, looking for him now. "Mister," the bewildered blind girl called out to him, "Mister, wait. . . ." He paused and turned to look back into those blind eyes. "Mister," she said, "are you Jesus?"

For those of us who live in the rhythm of the liturgy week upon week all our lives, the question must be, so what? What has happened to us as a result? Who have we become? Who are we on all the rest of the weekdays of our lives?

Indeed, there is in this story of a blind fruit seller the echo of a gospel story about a blind beggar. Those who have been immersed in the liturgical year all their lives would well be the kind of people who would stop to help pick up apples and oranges in the midst of an agenda that could seem much bigger than those things at any given moment. "Jesus, Son of David," the blind Bartimaeus cried out as Jesus came down the dusty road, "have mercy on me!" (Mark 10:47).

The liturgical year sets out to form in us the spirit of the One who stopped and listened and gave new sight to the beggar's eyes just as the salesman in the story gave insight as well as money to the blind fruit seller. Are you Jesus? people ask us silently every day. And the answer liturgical spirituality forms in us if we live it with constancy, with regularity, with fidelity, is surely, yes.

—The Liturgical Year

Healing and Forgiveness

In the Parable of the Good Samaritan, Jesus tells of a traveler who, having been mugged by robbers, was left stripped, beaten, and bleeding on a public road. First, a Levite, an official of the temple, and then a priest, the agent of temple sacrifice—holy men both we are led to think—pass by the broken one. The scripture says they pass "on the other side." They go as far away from the violence, the need, the pain as possible.

Then a Samaritan—the national and religious outcast of that Jewish society—comes by. And the healing begins. The Samaritan, having suffered himself, recognizes the suffering of the other. He understands pain and rejection. He knows how misery feels. He knows what a sense of abandonment can do for a person. So, he reaches out beyond himself.

The Samaritan pours oil, costly medicines for those times, on the beaten one's wounds. He carried him to an inn on the "back of his own beast." He pays for his care. He simply ignores the assumptions and the prejudices of the society around him and then the healing begins.

Healing does not begin with the moralizing of the righteous who avoided the unclean one—as this society, for instance, avoids AIDS sufferers or alcoholics, welfare mothers or gay neighbors. Healing does not begin with the piety of the pious who say that such things are not what religion is all about.

No, healing only begins when the one who understood suffering, who had wept himself, then wept over the suffering of another. The story of the Samaritan makes obvious for us the fundamental elements of the healing process—the ones beyond technique or politics, civic charity or public niceties.

First, the Samaritan simply faces the pain. He admits it. He honors it. The Samaritan does not ignore suffering or recoil from it or try to minimize it or explain it away. He knows calamity when he sees it—anywhere and in anyone. Without the Good Samaritans in life who enable us all to face our woundedness, to attend to the wounds in ourselves, we have no capacity for the pain of others. And healing is not possible.

Second, the Samaritan shows us, too, that healing requires us to risk old attitudes, to explore new values and even to change some of our petrified beliefs. The model of the Samaritan is very clear: Healing depends on our own resolve to transcend our canonical confines, to go out of our way to be, to think, to do what we would not, under any standard circumstances, choose to do otherwise.

Third, the Samaritan shows us that when I heal the other, I heal something in myself as well. The Parable of the Good Samaritan, you see, is not about the curing of one person, a wounded stranger. No, this story is about the healing of two people—the stranger and the Samaritan—both of whom carry the scars of abuse as do all of us at all times.

In this case one has been beaten in body, the other in soul. One has been wounded by the physical brutality of people around him; the other has been wounded by ideas that cripple and limit and bind a person to small, small worlds.

But the Samaritan and the stranger are not the only ones in the story who bear wounds. The priest and the Levite are maimed too—whether they know it or not. The priest, the professional religious, has been taught to ignore the wounds of those who do not meet with religious approval and thinks himself virtuous for ignoring them. His wound is a spiritual one.

The Levite, the relentless custodian of temple rituals and a pillar of his community, simply forgives himself the obligation to be a full human being and so hurries on too busy to stop, too narcissistic to care. Being "religious" is enough for him. His wound is a communal one.

One posture teaches us fear and loathing. The other perspective teaches us the kind of indifference and insensitivity that can come with idol worship. Whatever the situation, the end result is pain. Those who fail to transcend their own inner boundaries in order to heal the wounded, go on living in their own wounds forever.

The Samaritan, the priest, and the Levite, models of the healing process and our part in it, give us clear warning that we cannot heal ourselves of our wounds by clinging to them.

1. To be healed we need to want to be healed, to be larger than our pain, stronger than our woundedness.

I must choose not to imprison myself in my own pain, in the creeds and jingoisms, in the biases and prejudices that cut me off from the pain of the rest of the world. There is more to life than that.

2. Healing, the Samaritan shows us, requires that we set out to find whatever new life we can find to tide us through the terror of the abandonment, the degradation of the abuse. It is time to get a life instead of to mourn one.

Healing is a process of refusing to be wounded unto death, of beginning to be bigger of mind and soul than we ever thought we could be.

3. Healing, we see in both the Samaritan and the stranger, requires us to trust the process of growing. Healing comes for both the beaten and the intellectually bound when they step across the lines in their minds and hope that this time—in this person, in this situation—they will find the acceptance and the understanding, the care and the security they need to join the human community one more time.

4. Finally, I need to become a Samaritan myself. The whole world needs Samaritans, healers, who understand pain themselves and who are therefore most qualified to take the wounded

into the arms of their hearts, listen to the pain of the other, enable them to talk, allow them to cry.

Samaritans transcend their own small lives and learn about the human condition, something they could never have come to without having become healers themselves. The whole world— its poor and lonely; its displaced and angry; its deprived and robbed of the resources of life—needs Samaritans who listen and understand, tend to their wounds, and get them help. At that point, we rise from our graves of pain—persons and peoples alike—a new creation, a sign of hope to generations to come.

Clearly, weeping and healing are one and the same thing. Our only real questions then are: Over what do we ourselves weep? And, because of our tears: What are we reaching out to heal?

I urge you to listen to the Samaritans of our own time and to ask yourself where you yourselves fit in the great, the ultimate, the most humane human enterprise of the healing of the world. Only together can we possibly do the great works of healing, which in our time are waiting to be done by those "who cross the street," who do not "stay at a distance" from the pain of the world but whose hearts are great enough, human enough to weep for it.   —*God's Tender Mercy*

Spirituality of Aging

If we learn anything at all as time goes by and the changing seasons become fewer and fewer, it is that there are some things in life that cannot be fixed. It is more than possible that we will go to our graves with a great deal of personal concerns, of life agendas, left unresolved. That becomes clearer and clearer by the year. Some of the family fractures will not yet have healed. Some of the words spoken in heat and haste will not have been redeemed. Some of the friendships will not have been renewed. Some of the dreams will never be realized. So has life been wasted? Has it all been for nothing?

Only if we mistake the meaning of the last period of life. This time of life is not meant to solidify us in our inadequacies. It is meant to free us to mature even more.

To hope that in the end all the ruptures will have been repaired, however, is at best unreal. People are long gone and even longer out of touch. Nothing can be done at this late stage to reopen the conversations, let alone fix the rifts or heal the lingering wounds.

Many of the things for which we still feel responsible, even feel guilty about, we couldn't do anything to undo now—even if we wish we could. We can't put back together a failed marriage.

We can't cancel the years of neglect, a lifetime of indifference, a history of disregard for the people who had a right to expect our concern. There is nothing we can do now about a lifetime of lack of contact with our children, the tension we felt with our mother, the distance we felt from our father, the jealousies and outbursts and petty irritations that marked years long past, that call up still all our own defenses. That time, those situations, are simply gone. Out of our hands. Beyond our control.

Inside the scars still smart, though. We have been hurt. We have done the hurting. We made the mistakes. We created the mess that came from them. And there is not now and never was, as far as we could see, any way to put Humpty-Dumpty back together again. So now what?

If we cannot deal directly with all the unfinished struggles of our lives, how can we possibly face the end of life with any kind of serenity?

The fact is that the unrest that accumulates over the years is the very grace reserved for the end time, the last years, the pinnacle of life. Only now can the consciousness of these wrongs really make a difference in us. Only now can this pain be made productive. Why? Because now we must deal with it all ourselves. There is no one here to forgive us anymore, no one to tell us we were right, no one to surrender to our insistence, no one left for us to refuse to consort with. Instead, it is all alive within us. Now we must go down into the deepest part of ourselves and come to peace, not with our old antagonists but, more importantly than that, with ourselves, with the conscience we have been refusing to reconcile with for years.

There are issues far more germane to what happened in our life than simply the questions of who did what to whom and why and what happened to us as a result. Instead, what must be addressed now is what we became as a result of them. Did we become a fuller human being or did we only go through life proclaiming our innocence despite the soul song within that told us how guilty we really were?

This is the period of life when we must begin to look inside our own hearts and souls rather than outside ourselves for the answers to our problems, for the fixing of the problems. This is the time for facing ourselves, for bringing ourselves into the light.

This is the period of spiritual reflection, of spiritual renewal in life. Now is the time to ask ourselves what kind of person we have been becoming all these years. And do we like that person? Did we become more honest, more decent, more caring, more merciful as we went along because of all these things? And if not, what must we be doing about it now?

Whatever caused the rifts in our life, we had some part in the making of them. What of that demanding, narcissistic, spoiled child yet remains in us? And are we willing now to deal with the dross of it?

As the body begins to go to air, as we begin to melt into the beyond, are we able to put down those things in us that have been an obstacle between us and the rest of creation all our lives?

Can we come eye to eye with our own souls and admit who we are? If we have been selfish, can we bring ourselves to the daily discipline of caring for others? If we have been dishonest about ourselves, can we take care now to tell the real truth about ourselves? If we have been godless, are we able to trust that the Creator of Life must therefore also be the home of our souls, and can we bow before the Life that has claim on our own?

Can we begin to see ourselves as only part of the universe, just a fragment of it, not its center? Can we give ourselves to accepting the heat and the rain, the pain and the limitations, the inconveniences and discomforts of life, without setting out to passively punish the rest of the human race for the daily exigencies that come with being human?

Can we smile at what we have not smiled at for years? Can we give ourselves away to those who need us? Can we speak our truth without needing to be right and accept the vagaries of life now without needing the entire rest of the world to swaddle us beyond any human justification for expecting it? Can we talk to people decently and allow them to talk to us?

Old people, we're told, become more difficult as they get older. No. Not at all. They simply become less interested in maintaining their masks, more likely to accept the effort of being human, human beings. They no longer pretend. They face the fact that now, this period, this aging process, is the last time we're given to be more than all the small things we have allowed ourselves to be over the years. But first, we must face what the smallness is, and rejoice in the time we have left to turn sweet instead of more sour than ever.

A burden of these years is the danger of giving in to our most selfish selves.

A blessing of these years is the opportunity to face what it is in us that has been enslaving us, and to let our spirit fly free of whatever has been tying it to the earth all these years.

—*The Gift of Years*

THE ART OF LIVING

Relationships

Life goes through a good many more stages, I think, than the ones most commonly identified—childhood, youth, adulthood, middle age, old age. I don't think that life's stages have much to do with age, with the number of years we've spent breathing, at all. I think the parts of life are best described by the kinds of relationships most commonly made in each.

The years and phases of life call for different levels of relationship. We talk, for instance, about playmates, buddies, gangs, schoolmates, friends, acquaintances, colleagues, lovers, soul mates, and then, at the end, friends again. Each of these various types of relationships represents a stage in our own maturity and development. They teach us, a level of the soul at a time, what it means to discover that we are not alone in life, not the center of life, not the standard of value for anyone else's journey through life.

We learn something valuable from each and every one of them about what it means to be alive, a social being, a companion on the journey.

Playmates provide companionship; buddies give us a sense of security as we begin to learn our way through life; gangs give us a feeling of belonging; schoolmates bring a feeling of camaraderie in the face of the crowd; friends provide the beginning of intimacy; acquaintances become a lifeline in strange places; colleagues provide professional identity; lovers teach us the otherness of life; soul mates bring us home to the self; friends put cement under our feet again just when we begin to realize that our own legs are not as strong as they used to be. It is a lifelong series of coming to understand ourselves through our feelings.

The relationships we form at each stage make every stage that follows both easier to negotiate and more meaningful. It is a precious thing, relationship, meant to be savored and certain to be demanding. It is our relationships that teach us how to be a human being rather than a prima donna, a useful member of the human race rather than a spoiled diva.

Our relationships grow us up and make life possible—all the way to the grave. It is incumbent upon us to make them possible, both for the other's sake and for our own.

—*The Monastic Way*

Dailiness

Crises we're good at. It's dailiness that gets us down.

Dailiness tests the mettle of the self. The ability to go back to the same task, day after day after day—taking care of the children, doing the shopping, hawking a product, stacking the shelves—with new attention to the task, with new concern for the outcome, takes a special kind of faith, another kind of trust.

Having worked in a counseling relationship with people for almost thirty years, I know the problem. It's not long before a good counselor knows the rest of the story after the first paragraph of the first interview. A great counselor, on the other hand, isn't listening for the scenario; there are only so many of those in the world. A great counselor goes beyond the facts to listen keenly for the way this very mundane situation affected this particular person and why. And there are no two alike of those in the world. It's learning to bring your whole self to something that makes the difference between a happy life and a dull life, a holy life and an empty one.

Life is not made up of crises; life is made up of little things we love to ignore in order to get on to the exciting things in life. But God is in the details. God is in what it takes in us to be faithful to them. God is in the routines that make us what we are. The way we do the little things in life is the mark of the bigness of our souls.

The "mundane" is certainly dull, I agree, and may even limit us—not only our perceptions but even the breadth of our questions. At the same time, there is something very freeing, very humanizing about the mundane. Doing dishes and buying vegetables get us back in touch with ourselves, give us time to smell the earth of our lives, give us time just to be. We will go on long after the big ideas fade and the profession ends. The question is, will there be anything in me then? Will there be a me in me? It all depends on how I deal with the mundane.

The problem with dailiness is that it's not nearly as routine as it's supposed to be. It takes patience and persistence. It takes a willingness to give of ourselves beyond what our role descriptions demand. It requires us to pour ourselves out, not to store ourselves up for our own satisfaction.

I lived in a residence hall once where the accountant doubled as receptionist. Except that she would never look up at anyone at the desk. And when you did cough enough to annoy her into action, she punished you for it by refusing to find the forms you needed so you wouldn't ask again. It happens everywhere—and we know it. I have watched parents relegate their children to a set of TV cartoons rather than talk to them. And I have felt the irritation of having all my own grand plans consumed by someone else's agenda for me.

Then I read Katherine Paterson's entry in the journal one day. Paterson wrote, "As I look back on what I have written, I can see that the very persons who have taken away my time and space are those who have given me something to say." Having been so irritated by interruptions so often, I could feel the back of my neck get hot as I read.

To think of your interruptions as your education is a wonderful attitude to have. I must come to see in my own life that the mail that comes, the people who call, the meetings that happen, the children who erupt in the center of our lives are all grist for my mill.

But perhaps the hardest part of the spirituality of dailiness is having faith enough to deal with the discouragement that comes with finding ourselves trapped in a moment that never ends. In that one long, drawn-out moment of sadness, disquietude, frustration, rejection that comes into every life and has a way of staying, sometimes for years, can lie the most arduous moments of the spiritual life. "Who will roll away the stone for us from the entrance to the tomb?" Janet Ross-Heiner wrote, as if in memory only of one tomb long gone and not mine. But I've seen people in tombs called marriages, called failure, called depression, called ennui. And I have known a few tombs myself.

It's the dailiness of the tomb that really calls for faith, for trust, for perseverance and persistence. We want to live in resurrection all our lives, but it is the waiting time that makes us worthy of it.

It's when we go on in the heat of the noonday sun that we know what it is like to walk the dusty roads of Galilee. It's when we go on without firecrackers or music that we understand what the desert is like. It's when we go on despite the fact that quitting would be more satisfying that we know that God has taken control of our lives. Then, we are being used for something greater than ourselves. Then, we are being used to bring the world around us to fullness. It's licking the stamps and taking down the chairs and making the callbacks that finally, finally change the world. And that is the spirituality of dailiness.

Dailiness is the great deep pit out of which the character of our lives takes its most lasting shape. It is the repository of our greatest graces and site of our worst losses. It is the treasure house of all our yesterdays and the reserve out of which we draw strength for all our tomorrows.

Dailiness is what makes us fully and finally what we really are.

—Called to Question

Conversion

The first gift of struggle is the call to conversion—the call to think differently about who God is and about who I am as an individual. It calls us to think again about what life really means and how I go about being in the world. These are deeply spiritual questions that touch on our notions of God as well as on our ideas of ourselves.

To live bent on conversion is to live welcoming of the tomorrow that is already in embryo, rather than to attempt to cement today into eternity. Conversion does not expect to settle down, it expects only to become new over and over again. It sees change as the impetus to explore the other part of the self, demanding as that may be to do, difficult as that may be to begin, unwanted as that may be at this time.

The kind of change that shocks us into new beginnings is the kind of change that gives us new life. Yes, it forces us down unwanted paths, leads us stumbling through the Mephistophelean rills and recesses of the dark sides of the soul—angry, fearful, resistant, and unbelieving. But it also prods us from task to task in life until, at the end, we find ourselves full-statured and full of grace. It is a moment of great freedom. It is a moment made for open arms and wild-eyed explorers of a cosmos filled with red nebulae and black holes.

Conversion is the opening of the heart to the grace of new possibilities. It does not blame God for plotting nefarious plans to test and try and torment us. It recognizes in the glory of new life that God simply companions us, simply stands by ready to receive our tattered, restless selves, as we are tested, tried, and tormented by the machinations of life itself. God guides us to new life by allowing us to open our eyes to possibility and find it for ourselves.

The important thing to understand is that conversion is not always immediate. It can even be impossible, sometimes for years. But the longer we put it off, the longer we resist change, the longer it takes for us to become more than we were when the struggle began.

Change is an invitation to see life differently now than I did before. It stretches my vision and opens my heart to what I could not see in life before life picked me up and put me down in the middle of it: I go to Africa and begin to see black people differently. I work with a Muslim and begin to see Islam differently. I lose what I have clung to for my security for years and begin to see myself differently. Change converts me from the narrowness of perspective that trapped me in the small confines of my former self to a more expansive, more flexible citizen of the world. It calls me to imagination.

And so when conversion comes, I finally discover that there is more than one way to be in the world. I learn, perhaps with some chagrin, that there is more than "the American way," more than "a man's way," more than "my way" of doing things. I open my arms to the rest of the world and it reaches down and takes me in.   —*Scarred by Struggle, Transformed by Hope*

Commitment

In order to understand the nature of commitment, there are two questions that need to be asked about it. The first is, when does it happen? The second is, what is it about? The answers are more obvious than we have been given to believe.

First, commitment happens on a daily basis, not once and forever. It is something we grow into, not something we come to full-blown. And second, it is not a call to some sort of static state of life. It is a call to move always toward the best self we can possibly be.

The prompt in my idea-journal read one day, "But Jesus came and touched them, saying, 'Rise and have no fear.'" Reading it a few years later, my response surprised even me. I wrote, I wonder what it takes to really "rise and have no fear." I have a great deal of fear sometimes. I fear that I will do poorly what I want to do well. I fear that I have done all the wrong things in life, made all the wrong choices. I fear being trapped by other people's expectations. I fear grinding my life away in the great institutional sacrifice—for which there is no final sense, and even little present purpose. I watch religious life and fear that it was the wrong thing to have done in the first place and yet—even knowing how poorly I've done it—I know it was not. And in the core of me, as a result, I really do "have no fear."

Commitment, I had finally come to understand, drives us on past the pursuit of perfection to a sense of being at home within ourselves.

Commitment is what we have at the end of a hectic day, after the children have finally gone to sleep, and we know that, hard as it is, staying here, loving these children, paying these bills, is still what we must do if we are to be who we really want to be. When we revisit an old decision and know, whatever the scars of it, that this way of life is still the best thing we could have done for ourselves to become the spiritual fullness of what we are capable of being, we are at last "committed."

At the same time, commitment has its problems—and its distortions. One kind of spiritual culture says that once you've begun a thing, you must complete it, no matter the cost. The other culture says that once a thing begins to get difficult, happiness—fulfillment—demands that we leave it and start over somewhere else, whatever the effect on everyone around us. One posture glorifies masochism; the other, license. I understand both positions, but I have come to deny both of them.

More people stay in marriages out of a sense of responsibility than of intimacy, I'm sure. And isn't that why I stay where I stay, too? The more intimate I have become with God, the less dependent I feel on the community for personal satisfaction or security, as if the dailiness of personal connections are now secondary to the Center of the life. So I am not here because I so much need these particular people but because I must meet the responsibilities of the years.

There is a point of personal growth, in other words, at which I become myself, become free, become open to the world. Then commitment has done its thing. Then I do not stay where I am because I must. I stay where I am because where I am has brought me to a point of concern beyond the self.

There are "the responsibilities of the years," those obligations that emerge from the awareness of my place in the world. Then I know that it is not only right for me, but it is also right for others, that I am there. I am where I am supposed to be, not only for my own development, but for the sake of the development of the world around me.

But "right" as a thing may be for me, the temptation to abandon it tests our inner direction every day. Test is the price of commitment. "Looking, listening, and learning offer the modern equivalent of moving through life as a pilgrimage," Mary Catherine Bateson wrote.

My "pilgrimage" has been a different one. For me, it has been listening, learning, and saying. The end of this compulsion to truth is unclear to me. Will it be silence, alienation, or abandonment? Will I remain in this holy vessel of endless sin and sexism called the church? Or will I choose to follow my own sins instead? It is a more profound question than first meets the eye.

Commitment has something to do with seeing a good thing through—even when it goes bad in places. It lies in working out my own weaknesses, even as I work out the weaknesses around me. It unmasks me to myself. Commitment gives me the chance to stay in place and grow. It is not about staying in place and going to seed.

Commitment does not end at its beginning. It is the vehicle by which we unfold before ourselves and the world into something worth being at the end of it: a loving father, a good mother, a faithful religious, a deeply spirit-filled human being whose presence is a gift to the world. But getting there may take a lot of changing until we come to that place that does not bind the spirit and serves to unleash the energy of the soul.

To find in ourselves our deepest aspirations is to discover whether the path to God is either still before us to be seized or yet behind us, prodding us on.   —*Called to Question*

Simplicity

When Abba Macarius was in Egypt, he found a man with a mule stealing his belongings. Then, as though he were a stranger, he helped the robber to load the animal, and peacefully sent him off, saying, "We have brought nothing into the world, and we cannot take anything with us. Blessed be God in all things."

—*Tales of the Desert Mothers and Fathers*

Simplicity is the art of seeing things as they are and making no attempt to argue that they are more than that, are other than that, can be dealt with in other ways and still be as pure, as honest as they are in themselves. We can make complicated claims that seek to justify another reading of Abba Macarius's attitude toward the robber but in the end what is right, is right. The fact is that we do come into the world empty-handed and we go out the same way, so—as Macarius implies simply—why do we spend so much of life trying to acquire things? Simplicity is honesty, about life, about ourselves.

The simple person puts on no airs, requires no special attention, dominates no conversations, lives quietly and responsibly, seldom seeks the services of others and, even more so, seldom requires the best of anything, let alone everything.

They're a rare breed, these simple people. In fact, the higher you go in the system, any system—finance, government, business, church—the harder they are to come by. Protocol takes over. But then, all the more refreshing they are when found. And they do exist. I know because I have known some.

I have known what the world would call "a socialite" who came from a working-class family and married into a world she had never experienced or could possibly be expected to know. There are, after all, strict rules for such things—but she never kept them. She answered her own door, cooked her own meals, did the dishes after her own dinner parties. She could have hired a platoon of people to do those things for her but she preferred to do them herself. She refused to forget what it felt like to clean up after people. Or do something for them personally, with her own hands, rather than have the secretary come up with something at the last minute.

The proof of her simplicity? Everyone—from groundskeeper to governor—felt comfortable in her presence. Thanks to her, they all learned to be a little more comfortable with themselves.

I have known a bishop who functioned as a pastor in a small, neighborhood, African-American church. He moved around the world with the elite of the elite but he did so in a worn pair of black trousers and an old black shirt. Politicians, who did not think it necessary to enhance their own standing by being seen among the gold-and-purple-silk set of ecclesiastical royalty, loved him. And so did the peasants and the children and the prisoners he talked to everywhere. None of them, in fact, could do enough for him, but he never seemed to notice, and he never, never asked for it.

I have known nuns who spend every minute of every day preparing for the next meal in a soup kitchen. They haul and tug and stir and serve—and call every guest by name. Like Jesus before them, they do not think that status and privilege, titles and honors are "things to be clung to."

I knew a billionaire who lived in a single-story home in a quiet neighborhood on the edge of town. He owned no planes or yachts or exotic summer homes, but when he died, he left a hundred million dollars in gifts to all the neediest charities in town labeled "From an Anonymous Friend."

That's simplicity. No fanfare. No processions. No acknowledgments. Just the deep down conviction that we are who we are. And, depending on what we do with it, that is enough for anybody.

People like that are proof to the rest of us that there is no amount of things or images that can possibly improve on what we really are.   —*The Monastic Way*

Success

We get instructed in the meaning of success even while we are very young, which makes it so much more difficult to enjoy life as we get older.

We talk about teaching our children to be successful, but we really mean that we teach them to be competitive. All our lives we compete, in fact, and call it success.

We compete for jobs and positions and promotions and salary increases. We compete with our neighbors to get a bigger house. We compete with other parents by prodding our children on to even more competition. We compete with the rest of the family to plan bigger, more exotic trips. We run every life course, we jump every hurdle, we display every ribbon and trophy and plaque the world has to give. And in the end, we're exhausted.

But it is not so much the striving that is the problem as it is the sacrifice of all the other dimensions of life in order to achieve it. We sacrifice our own opinions, our own desires, our own interests, our own personal goals to meet the needs of people around us, and in the end, we sacrifice the burgeoning of the self for the brass rings of the social system—his better job; their family pride; the world's expectations.

Did we succeed? At what? And who knows? It all depends on what we've always thought success must be about.

The only good thing about the whole system, if we're lucky, is that the role will end before we do. And probably sooner than we think. Then, we will begin the task of rethinking everything we ever thought success was all about.

Retirement is the counterculture of the culture. It says that just being alive and learning to live well is sign in itself to the rest of humanity of the quintessential goodness of life. The purpose of a job is to make a living, not to make a life. Making a life is something we're meant to do beyond the role. This is the part of life in which we work at succeeding at all the other dimensions of what it means to be alive.

The questions with which we are faced at retirement are not the questions this society instructs us to answer as we seek societal "success."

Did we succeed at making the family a "family"? If not, there are still years left to do it. We can call the kids instead of waiting for them to come to us. We can send cards and offer our car and take the grandchildren to the zoo now.

Did we succeed at being a good neighbor? If not, there are people on the block who need someone to pick up things at the store for them, people down the hall who would love to go out for a drive, people who would love to have someone to play cards with, to go to the show with, to share simple food and long conversation.

Did we succeed at developing a genuine spiritual life, the kind in which the presence of God dominates our whole existence, above and beyond worship attendance on holy days and at liturgical events? If not, we can join a prayer group now or a reading group or a social action group and do what needs to be done to leave the earth a better place than when we arrived on it.

Did we succeed in living gently on earth, on creating a balance in our lives of time with nature, time with people, time with God, time for reflection, time for a new kind of personal development? If not, it's time to plan our days rather than simply have them slip by unnoticed.

Did we succeed in learning how to be happy ourselves by walking the dog, making jewelry, learning to fish, restoring wood—doing something that we do only because we love doing it?

Did we succeed at developing the kind of interior life it takes to weather the external demands of life?

Did we succeed at becoming a real person? A person who is real!

In the end, it becomes so clear: success is a much simpler thing than they ever told us. It has to do with having the basics, with learning to be happy, with getting in touch with our spiritual selves, with living a balanced life, doing no harm, doing nothing but good. The only test of the good life here is happiness.

—*The Gift of Years*

Beauty

It was the kind of thing philosophers love to write about and people love to talk about and students love to theorize about but which most of us never really see. Beauty, we're told, is a basic human instinct, the kind of thing that separates us from the animals, an intrinsic quality of the human soul, the irrepressible expression of contemplative insight. It has something to do with what it means to be alive.

Beauty— however primitive our circumstances, however limited a people's resources may be, we're told, will live on. Humans are made for beauty. The soul seeks it out. The mind wrestles with its meaning. The artist creates it in the midst of squalor. The philosopher dissects its properties. The human community makes beauty its bulwark against despair. As long as beauty exists, life is worth living. When beauty gives way to kitsch, to ostentation, to vulgarity, to the demeaning of great art in plastic replicas, beware the chaos in the human spirit. But is this true? And how do we know that?

I remember the shock that went through my system long after I had left that kind of question behind with all the other term papers I'd written early in my student days that had also long been gathering dust. It happened in two unlikely places, the first in Mexico, the second in Cité Soleil in Haiti.

In the gold museum in Mexico City, I got my first real glimpse into the truth of what I'd read in philosophy books. There, displayed with all the finesse of locked jewelry stores on Rodeo Drive or the Champs-Élysées in Paris, were dangling gold earrings and gleaming gold bracelets and shining gold pendants and amber stones set in gold rings. And all of this by one of the oldest cultures on earth, known for human sacrifice, and high learning, and a warrior society, and great architecture. And under it all, breathtaking beauty—the sign of a soul in search for the sublime.

I remember stopping in front of display cases simply to try to put all those aspects of life in a primitive society into some framework I could understand. And suddenly I realized that a society that could make such beauty was capable of endless human potential, however much struggle it takes to come to fullness. The inferior savage was clearly a myth of our own limited imaginations.

The second time that beauty shocked me into a new sense of what it means to be human in an inhuman environment happened in the slum of all slums in Haiti. Here people live in one-room hovels made of corrugated steel over mud floors. They bear and raise one child after another here. They eat the leftovers of society. They scrounge for wood to cook. They sleep in filth and live in rags and barely smile and cannot read. But in the middle of such human degradation they paint bright colors and brilliant scenes of a laughing, loving, wholesome community. They carve faces. They paint strident colors on bowls made out of coconuts. They play singing drums across the bare mountains that raise the cry of the human heart. They manufacture beauty in defiance of what it means to live an ugly forgotten life on the fringe of the wealthiest nation the world has ever known. They are a sign of possibility and aspiration and humanity no amount of huts or guns or poverty or starvation can ever squelch. Beauty, art, literature, contemplation of the human spirit drive the human race beyond, above, despite the inhumanity that tugs at our heels as we try to move beyond it. —*The Monastic Way*

Mercy

Thomas Ann Hines, a divorced mother of an only child, learned mercy the hard way. When her son, a freshman at college, lay murdered by a seventeen-year-old drifter who first solicited a ride from him and then, when he got in the car, turned a gun on the young driver, Thomas Ann descended into a pit of anger and vengeance.

The murder was a random, groundless, indefensible act. And her son was not the only person who died that night—Thomas Ann was alone, distraught, full of the kind of pain and hate that paralyzes the heart and stops life in its tracks, even for the living. Her son, a good boy, a successful student, the hope of her life was gone. She herself was completely alone now, without a future, without hope, without any reason, it seemed, to live.

But thirteen years later, Thomas Ann Hines visited her son's killer in prison, intent only on getting information about the night of the killing. But when, in the course of the conversation, the young man put his face down on the small table at which they sat and began to sob, she touched the man. And she got to know him.

The story shocked the country. "How could she do such a thing?" people asked. Or, more to the point, perhaps, they asked themselves the question, "Could I ever do such a thing? Could I possibly show mercy to someone who had done something so senseless, so heinous, so destructive to me?" Thomas Ann's answer to the question was a simple one: "If my son was sitting in this room," she said, "I'd want someone to reach out a hand and lift him up."

The story is not only a moving one, it is an enlightening one for all of us. It teaches us something very important about mercy.

Mercy is what God does for us. Mercy discounts the economic sense of love and faith and care for a person and lives out of a divine sense of love instead. Mercy gives a human being who does not "deserve" love, love. And why? Because, the scriptures answer, God knows of what we are made.

The fact is that we are all made of the same thing: clay, the dust of the earth, the frail, fragile, shapeless thing from which we come and to which we will all return someday. We are all capable of the same things. Our only hope is that when we are all sitting somewhere bereft, exposed, outcast, humiliated and rejected by the rest of society, someone, somewhere will "reach out a hand and lift us up."

Every one of us is capable of every sinful thing. Most of us have simply never had the opportunity or the anger or the sense of desolation it takes to do it. While we're being grateful for that, it behooves us to be merciful to those who have.

—*God's Tender Mercy*

Hospitality

> *Let every guest be received as Christ.*
>
> —*Rule of Benedict,* chapter 53

Hospitality in a culture of violence, and strangers and anonymity has become the art of making good connections at good cocktail parties. We don't talk in elevators, we don't know the security guard's name, we don't invite even the neighbors into the sanctuary of our selves. Their children get sick and their parents die and all we do is watch the comings and goings from behind heavy blinds. Benedict wants us to let down the barriers of our hearts so that this generation does not miss accompanying the innocent to Calvary as the last one did. Benedict wants us to let down the barriers of our souls so that the God of the unexpected can come in.

"In India," Ram Dass writes, "when people meet and part they often say, 'Namaste,' which means: I honor the place in you where the entire universe resides; I honor the place in you of love, of light, of truth, of peace. I honor the place within you where if you are in that place in you and I am in that place in me, there is only one of us . . . 'Namaste.'" In Benedictine spirituality, too, hospitality is clearly meant to be more than an open door. It is an acknowledgment of the gifts the stranger brings. "By a bow of the head or by a complete prostration . . . Christ is to be adored and welcomed in them."

But Benedictine hospitality is also a return of gifts. The stranger is shown both presence and service. After a trip through hard terrain and hot sun, the guest is given physical comfort and a good meal, spiritual instruction and human support. Not even a fast day is counted as important as eating with a guest. Not even asceticism is counted as holy as care for the other. Obviously, from the point of view of the *Rule of Benedict*, it isn't so much what we do for those curious others in our lives, the strange, the needy, the unscrubbed, as it is the way we do it. We can give people charity or we can give them attention. We can give them the necessities of life or we can give them its joys. Benedictine hospitality is the gift of one human being to another. Benedictine hospitality is not simply bed and bath; it is home and family.

"It's a barren prayer," St. Cyprian wrote, "that does not go hand-in-hand with alms." For the Benedictine heart the reception of the poor is an essential part of going to God. We cannot be too busy, too professional, too removed from the world of the poor to receive the poor and sustain the poor. Anything else, Benedict warns in a society that is by nature class-structured, is not hospitality. It is at best more protocol than piety. Those who can buy their comforts or demand their rights are simply receiving what they can get, with us or without us. Those who have been thrown upon the mercy of the world are the gauge of our open hearts.

It is an important distinction in a culture in which strangers are ignored and self-sufficiency is considered a sign of virtue and poverty is a synonym for failure. Hospitality for us may as much involve a change of attitudes and perspectives as it does a handout. To practice hospitality in our world, it may be necessary to evaluate all the laws and all the promotions and all the invitation lists of corporate and political society from the point of view of the people who never make the lists. Then hospitality may demand that we work to change things.

—*The Rule of Benedict: A Spirituality for the 21st Century*

Laughter and Humor

> *. . . a time to weep, and a time to laugh*
>
> —Ecclesiastes 3:4

Laughter liberates and laughter uplifts. When laughter comes into a life, nothing is impossible, nothing is too difficult, nothing can defeat us. We can survive the noonday sun and the darkness of death and the grinding boredom of dailiness and still find life exhilarating. Other things in life change character like chameleons on plaid, but laughter is always ornament, always grace.

There are obstacles to laughter, however, that pass as virtues in the people who possess them. One is negative spirituality, an acerbic approach to life in the name of righteousness. These people are the dangerous kind. Not only do they intimidate small children in church, but they pass judgment on good parties as well. They make themselves harbingers of the God of Wrath. These types brook no nonsense in the pursuit of holiness. These types make holiness a plague rather than a passion.

These people take as their truth that laughter diminishes the sacredness of life. I (and God, too, if we take the Bible in earnest) think otherwise. Sarah laughed, God laughed, and the Book of Proverbs laughs. That is pretty important laughing.

The second obstacle to the presence of laughter in life comes from preoccupation with perfectionism. The need to surpass ourselves drains every ounce of energy from the human psyche. Nothing funny, nothing fun, can seep into the soul of a person on the way to pseudo-perfection. These are brittle types who cannot afford to take anything lightly for fear they find themselves more human than marble. These people play Bach, never chopsticks. They dance the Tango, never the Chicken.

These people have forgotten, if they ever knew, that there are some things that must always be laughed at in life:

1. Laugh when people tell a joke. Otherwise you might make them feel bad.

2. Laugh when you look into a mirror. Otherwise you might feel bad.

3. Laugh when you make a mistake. If you don't, you're liable to forget how ultimately unimportant the whole thing really is, whatever it is.

4. Laugh with small children. They laugh at mashed bananas on their faces; mud in their hair; a dog nuzzling their ears; the sight of their bottoms as bare as silk. It renews your perspective. Clearly, nothing is as bad as it could be.

5. Laugh at situations that are out of your control. When the best man comes to the altar without the wedding ring, laugh. When the dog jumps through the window screen at the dinner guests on your doorstep, sit down and laugh awhile.

6. Laugh at anything pompous, at anything that needs to puff its way through life in robes and titles. Will Rogers laughed at all the public institutions of modern life. For instance, "You can't say civilization isn't advancing," he wrote. "In every war they kill you in a new way." And thanks to his laughter, we began to see what was going on around us in fresh and shocking perspective.

7. Laugh when all your carefully laid plans get changed: when the plane is late and the restaurant is closed and the last day's screening of the movie of the year was yesterday. You're free now to do something else, to be spontaneous for a change, to take a piece of life and treat it with outrageous abandon.

There are some things, of course, that do not qualify for laughter, that do not refresh the human heart, that set out to hurt whole classes of people, in fact, and that should never, under any conditions, be tolerated under the pretense of humor. Ridicule passed off as wit only reinforces determining stereotypes that justify the ongoing oppression of a people. More to the point, it measures the stature of those who stoop to it. Johann Wolfgang von Goethe wrote, "People show their character in nothing more clearly than by what they think laughable." Ethnic jokes and sexist sneers and racial slurs and jeering at physical limitations do not empty the human soul of debris. They simply fill it with a venom disguised as humor.

In the final analysis, we should laugh at anything that is not a matter of life and death. Laughter is the atrium to wisdom. "Never try to teach a pig to sing," the Sufi say. "It only frustrates the teacher and irritates the pig." Life will never be flawless, but laughter makes of the flaws a gratifying and gracious patchwork piece.

Finally, laughter gives us the freedom of Jesus, who foolishly questioned the authority of the state and smilingly stretched the imagination of the church. "The poor shall inherit the Kingdom," he laughed. "The Kingdom of Heaven is like a woman," he smiled. "God is daddy," he chuckled. He danced from town to town, healing, making people smile with new hope, bringing invitations to people in trees and light-footedness to lepers. He fished where there were no fish. He invited guests to eat with him when he had no food. He taught babies and poked fun at Pharisees and told winsome stories, and spiritual jokes about women who would not let pretentious judges alone.

Day after day he smiled his way from one theological absolute to another and left the world with enough to smile about till the end of time.

Once we learn to laugh and play, we will have come closer to understanding our laughing, playing God. The God of ridiculous promises is a God who laughs, a God to be laughed at and laughed with, until that moment when all pain washes away and only the laughter of God is left to be heard in the heavens.

—*For Everything a Season*

Transformation

Meridel Le Sueur, who lived to be ninety-six, wrote, "I am luminous with age." Luminous. Not painted. Not masked. Luminous! They are the women and men who see with wider eyes, hear with tuned ears, speak with a more knowing tongue. These are people with soul.

There is an important part of the aging process that lies in simply getting accustomed to being older. Part of being a vigorous older person demands, first of all, that we learn to accept it for what it is, a new and wonderful but different stage of life. We must admit, even in our own minds, to being older in a culture that is so youth-centered that age is something to be hidden, rather than celebrated.

Me? we say. Seventy? Impossible. One can almost hear the tone of shame that goes with it. It burrows into the center of us, and an alarm sounds in the heart. How could life be almost over, we worry, when we were just beginning to understand it, to enjoy it, to love it? And with the fear of age, if we succumb to the notion that being older is some kind of obstacle to life, comes the loss of one of life's most profound periods.

The problem is that preparation for aging in our modern world seems to be concentrated almost entirely on buying anti-wrinkle creams and joining a health club when the truth is that what must be transformed now is not so much the way we look to other people, as it is the way we look at life. Age is the moment we come to terms with ourselves. We begin to look inside ourselves. We begin to find more strength in the spirit than in the flesh.

The way we view ourselves changes from period to period in life. It is not a steady-state experience, and its most impacting definition comes in middle age. Then, we all get some kind of power, however limited it may be, just by virtue of seniority, if nothing else. We find ourselves in charge somewhere: in charge of the children, in a position of control on the job, in a position of preferment in the family, at a higher social level in the group. We have arrived.

But all of a sudden it seems, as quietly as I arrived, I am now just as quietly dismissed. Power and control cannot be my definition of self anymore. I must now find in myself whatever it is that gives me a personal place in the world around me: I'm fun to be with; I care about other people; I have begun to live for deeper, richer, more important things than I have ever done before. I am caretaker, public watchdog, social advocate, companion now. I begin to see myself differently now. I begin to discover that, in many ways, I am far more important now than I have been all my previous life.

I begin to see the world differently, too. It is to be treasured, to be explored, to be enjoyed. An evening on the beach as the sun goes down is worth all the cocktail parties I've ever attended.

Other people begin to look different to me, too. They are as transformed as I am. I no longer see them as roles. They are people now, individuals not problems, not connections, not a measure of my own value. My value now rests entirely in me, in what kind of person I am with others.

I find, too, that the number of absolutes in my life is precipitously reduced. I'm a lot less dogmatic now about the nature of God. I'm not as sure as I once was about what is gravely damning and what is not. Most important of all, I am happy to put that decision in the hands of the God whose nature seems far more compassionate now—as I have gotten more compassionate myself.

Finally, I now see life newly, too. Once I thought of it as a kind of major-league competition for money and status and things. Now I see it as something to value for itself. I begin to realize that it is not about having much—it is about having enough. I begin to understand that the tragedy of life is that so many have so little that even just having enough to live on is beyond them. I begin to understand that there's something wrong with that. I have had more than enough help in life. And what about these others? What is my responsibility to them now?

It is the moment of final and full transformation. I have become the fullness of myself, but only once I was able to put down the cosmetics of the self, like the titles, the privileges, the symbols, and the signs of being something more than I was and at the same time less than I was.   —*The Gift of Years*

Life Fulfilled

The sunflowers seemed to go to seed early this year. Thomas— potter to the world, brother to us—died in the quiet way he'd always lived and will be buried soon in the urn he made for himself after the surgery proved futile. And in the midst of it, another friend struggles with a diagnosis that defies itself at every turn. No doubt about it. The signs are clear everywhere: The shadows of life are longer now. Even the grass has seared a bit. And with the changing of the climate and the dulling of the sun and the lengthening of the nights, something inside ourselves slows and changes and turns, as well. With the turning of the seasons of our lives, life takes on a far more precious hue.

It is the season of memories now. It is the time of year that piques hope and prods it to doubt. It is, then, the time of the year in which resurrection takes on a new kind of meaning. Yes, things die and no, nothing ever dies because yes, it goes on living again in us.

Death seems so cruel, so purposeless at times. But it's not. Death is what alerts the rest of us to life—just when we have grown tired of it ourselves, perhaps, or worse yet, simply unaware of it at all.

Death is the call to look again at life—this time with a wiser eye. Life, for the likes of us, is not a series of struggles and irritations. That, it seems, is reserved for refugees and farm families on hard soil and peasant types on mountaintops and peons in barrios. Our life, on the other hand, is a panoply of opportunities. It does not depend on "luck." It depends on what we do with it, how we approach it, what we make of what we have, how we distinguish between wants and needs—and, most of all, how much of ourselves we put into making it better, not only for ourselves, but for those who lack the resources even to begin to make it better for themselves.

Death, the awareness of its coming, the sounds of it around us, is what calls us to a life beyond apathy, beyond indifference, beyond unconcern. Death reminds us to live.

This is the period when the parts of us that died with the death of those we loved rise again in the recollection of past moments and the tears of past tendernesses. This is when we know for certain that every deed we ever do lives on somewhere in someone who remembers it. This is when we are made to see death as a prod to life.

The death of the year, the death of the past begins to bloom again in old memories and the lessons we learned from them, in long known truths and newly realized loves, in new perceptions of past obscurities.

The time is short for all those things. The time is now. The time is for reflection on what we've lost in life, yes, but for what we have left in life, too. It's time to begin to live life fuller rather than faster.

Death gives us all the gift of time. Our own and the time of those around us. It calls us to stop and look at sunflowers next time, to care for the grass always, to embrace the planet forever, to pay attention to our friends, to take comfort in the dark, to remember that the daffodils will unfold again. It is time to plant spring in our own hearts, to remember "the light that no darkness can take away."

Then, when death comes for us, as it surely will, we will know that it is only prelude. "I don't know what's there," the dying old woman said to her grieving friend. "I only know that God is there. So, don't worry. That is enough."   —*The Monastic Way*

3

PASSION FOR JUSTICE

Since God lives in us all, the destruction of the other has got to be a sin against God. —Joan Chittister

The issues explored in this section should engage every genuine Seeker, every person who desires to live a fully human life. They include but do not exhaust the injustices that have been of growing concern to Sister Joan for over fifty years, namely, dualistic worldviews and anthropologies, patriarchal domination (religious and secular) and women's oppression, religious imperialism, unjust wars, nuclearization, poverty, blind obedience, avarice and arrogance. She has brought clarity, depth and breadth to bear on these injustices.

To any who would listen, she has pleaded we become conscious of the unjust suffering in our midst and across the globe. Like the prophets before her, she has engaged in her own "ministry of irritation" by speaking truth to power across institutions. Like them she has passionately urged us to hear the cry of the widow, the orphan, and the stranger, along with every excluded "Other" who, theologian José Sols has written, "complicates our identity . . . makes us uncomfortable . . . [and] alters our life like the man who 'fell among robbers' in the parable of the Good Samaritan" (José Sols in Jesus of Galilee: Contextual Christology for the 21st Century (Orbis, 2011). *Sister Joan continues to expose evil with courage and illuminate the darkness in our church and world with inexhaustible light.*

SPEAKING OUT

Prophets of a Future Not Our Own

At a crossroad, remember, there are three possible options to choose from: the first choice is simply to quit a road that is going nowhere. We can move out, and move on, we can move away from it all, and leave the unfinished mission undone.

The second choice is to give in to the fatigue of the journey that comes from years of being ignored—or worse—of being ridiculed or excommunicated and so go silently into oblivion. The second choice, in other words, is to crawl into a comfortable cave with nice people and wait for the storm to go by.

The third choice is to refuse to accept a decadent present and insist on celebrating the coming of an unknown but surely holy future. The third choice is to go steadfastly on following the path of the prophets, of those who spoke before us but were also not heard until long after the fact. The third choice is a choice that demands great courage.

Prophets are those who take life as it is and expand it. They simply refuse to shrink a vision of tomorrow to the boundaries of yesterday.

But never forget as well, that the prophets, like you and I—discouraged by the present, weary from trying—also toyed with all three options. But in the end chose to go on following the spiritual magnet of their lives rather than allow it to wither.

The prophets—every one of them—when they came to the crossroads, when they came to a chance to settle down there, to quit, to accept what was, chose instead to keep on going.

Despite it all—if not with a sense of total and immediate success, then as sirens in the night, as seeders of far-flung seeds, as eternal agitators in the soul of the nation, as torches in the murk of confusion, they chose to go on, illuminating to others down century after century the eternal Word of God.

They chose to go on shouting the message upon which the future rested and the people depended if they were to find their way out of the darkness to which a failed leadership had con-demned them.

These prophetic people—people just like us: simple and sin-cere, eager and inspired—these fruit growers like Amos and small business people like Hosea, these priests and sheep mas-ters, these theologians and writers and dreamers like Isaiah and Ezekiel, these struggling lovers and suffering witnesses made no small choices indeed.

They chose courage; they chose the expansion of the soul; they chose to stake their lives on what must be rather than stake their comfort on what was.

And what happened to them because they cared more about these things than they did about the preservation of the past?

They were exiled, publicly condemned, persecuted, ridiculed and ignored. That's what happened.

And what did they do about it? They went on.

And how could that be? Easy: they were more committed to the Word of God than they were to acceptance by those who claimed to be the guardians of the Word of God, but betrayed its meaning.

They were more committed to commitment than they were to social approval.

They were more given to faith in God than they were to fidel-ity to the system. They were more full of hope in the future than they were afraid of pain in the present. They were more commit-ted to the Word of God than they were to the fear of those who spoke for the institution but claimed to speak for God.

They were more committed to new questions than they were to old questions.

They were people of their times. And they preferred to stand alone with God alone.

They believed beyond institutional theology to the God whose will for the institution was that it not only preserves the word but lives it.

They lived very much in the present for the sake of a future that they knew would not be their own.

And they call us to do the same.

—*Call to Action*, keynote address
November 7, 2010

Prophet or Critic

When we think of prophets, we conjure up images of howling hurts and eyes of steel. What we fail to see in the prophet's eyes and hear in the prophet's howl is the rage that comes when, seeing pain, a person stands helpless in its wake. The prophet's wail is the cry of despair that comes from those who stand in front of a burning building but are powerless to put out the flame. The prophet's shriek rises out of the angst of helplessness that stops the breath of the living at the bedside of the dying. The prophet does not cry against us; the prophet cries for us.

Judgment, you see, comes from compassion. Compassion, in fact, demands judgment so that the sufferer may be liberated and the suffering itself may be scourged. The prophet in society carries the burden of both judgment and compassion. To have one without the other is not to prophesy at al at all. "There is nothing heavier than compassion," Milan Kundera writes. "Not even one's own pain weighs so heavy as the pain one feels with someone, for someone, a pain intensified by the imagination and prolonged by a hundred echoes." It is compassion, then, that is the textile of prophecy, the raw material that compels us to get it right, to get it straight, to get it true.

Avengers without love are not prophets. At the same time, lovers without a sense of accountability are not prophets either. The prophetic figure brings to a situation full of despair the face of feeling and the face of hope. The prophet is one who suffers because of us and yet believes in us at the same time. The prophet drags us by hair of the head, if necessary, to the heights of our potential, against our own worst will. The prophet comes with a father's zeal and a mother's love, breathing the Word of God and saying, "I love you" at the same time.

But in that case, who is not called to be a prophet? Who can stand by, watch a world go sour, and yawn?

There is a major difference between a critic and a prophet. Critics stand outside a system and mock it. Prophets remain clear-eyed and conscientious, inside a sinful system, and love it anyway. It is easy to condemn the country, for instance. It is possible to criticize the church. But it is prophetic to love both church and country enough to want them to be everything they claim to be—just, honest, free, equal—and then to stay with them in their faltering attempts to do so, even if it is you yourself against whom both church and state turn in their attempts to evade the prophetic truth of the time.

The French papacy at Avignon did not want to hear the call of Catherine of Siena but, in the end, she prevailed and they returned the Holy See to Rome. The powers that be did not want to hear Joan of Arc and killed her to silence her, but in the end, her prophetic word outlasted them all. Neither church nor state wanted to hear Dorothy Day and Thomas Merton in their pleas for the poor and their prophetic cries for peace, but in the end, it is their messages that expose the secularization of the church, that haunt it at the turn of every gospel page, that challenge it to this day and that have marked its best presence in these times.

The function of the prophet is not to destroy. The function of the prophet is to expose whatever cancers fester beneath the surface so that what is loved can be saved while there is yet time.

To claim, then, that to criticize the government is treason, to insist that to criticize the church is disunity, may be the greatest perfidy and the deepest infidelity of them all. It is a prophet's lot to risk the two so that what is worth loving can be lovable again.   —*The Cry of the Prophet*

The Church and Women:
Speaking in the Name of God

Rome sweats in August, as the sirocco, the hot wind that blows through the city from Africa, whips dust into your eyes as you push against it, cooling nothing. So, on this particular day, the cool of the marble, the high ceilings, and dark halls and shuttered windows of the Vatican felt more humane than intimidating. Most of all, I admired the man with whom I was to meet. Cardinal Eduardo Pironio, Argentinean spokesperson for the poor, had been brought to Rome because there had been death threats made against his life. Like Jeremiah, whom King Ahab called "that troublemaker of Israel" and Jesus, whom both Romans and high priests considered a rabble-rouser, Pironio spoke a truth the Argentinean government did not want to know. He was a man who could hear the poor of the world. So, he could hear women, too. And I told him our truth. I told him about our frustration over documents that defined women's lives, but never asked for either our input or our response. I told him what it felt like to be invisible in the church, of all places. I told him about the increasing alienation of women in the church.

His deep dark eyes were sad. There was no doubt he understood. But then he dropped his shoulders, clasped his hands between his knees and began to shake his head slowly from side to side. "Jhoan, Jhoan, Jhoan," he said. "What you say is true but you must never say it any place but here. For the sake of the church," he said, "you must never say these things in public. Only here"—he gestured around the room—"only here behind closed doors, between ourselves."

I understood his concerns. I know as well as he did that unity is a fragile strength. But I also knew what he didn't. For the sake of the church, what women wanted had to be said in public because there was nowhere else for a woman to say it. Other than a few token women whose presence is designed to deceive us as to who really has the power, no women ever get behind the closed doors where the final draft of church documents are written, or the pronouns are determined, or the committees are chosen, or the boards are set up. But if the best of them, if a Pironio, couldn't see that, then I knew that to stay in this church was going to take a special kind of spiritual strength. Years later, I saw that conversation and that conclusion mirrored over and over again in the journal. Nothing had changed.

The spirituality demanded at a time of tension in the church itself requires more than patience. "Time changes nothing," the proverb teaches. "People do." But while we work for change, we need a spirituality of conviction, honesty, awareness, endurance, and faith in the God whose time is not our time.

—*Called to Question*

Divided Loyalties: An Incredible Situation

The pedophile scandal has exposed the curse of blind obedience. It has warped the hearts and minds of many otherwise good Catholics, bishops in particular. Sister Joan challenges the church to examine its teaching in this regard, eschewing another false dualism: blind fidelity to the church or fidelity to one's conscience.

For all the certainty about the facts of the case, there is still an aura of discontent everywhere about the situation surrounding clerical sex abuse in the church. No one disputes the data now; everyone disputes the nature of the problem. And worse than that, the data simply keeps piling up on all sides.

First, the world called it an "American problem." As in, "Those Americans are a wild bunch anyway, what else can you expect?" The Vatican went so far as to dismiss the issue as simply another demonstration of American exaggeration—what the Irish call the American tendency to be "over the top."

Then Ireland found itself engulfed in the problem and suddenly the outrage was no longer seen as "over the top." On the contrary, it became a display of integrity. Nor were the numbers seen as being exaggerated by the media. On the contrary, the numbers of child victims, the world began to understand, had, if anything, been minimized.

Now, the boil has broken in Europe, too: in the Netherlands, in Austria, in Germany, and, oh yes, in the Vatican, as well.

Now, the United States is no longer seen as being hysterical about a nonproblem but early in its confrontation of it, also a decidedly American trait.

But what, precisely, is "it?" What is the real problem?

Note well: After stories of the first few high-profile cases of serial rapes and molestations and their unheard of numbers died down, the focus shifted away from individual clerical rapists to the unmasking of what was now obviously a systemic problem. This prevailing practice of episcopal cover-ups, of moving offenders from one parish to another, rather than expose them either to legal accountability or to moral censure in the public arena, occupied the spotlight. It was a practice that saved the reputation of the church at the expense of children. It traded innocence for image.

But we know all of that. So why doesn't all of this just settle down and go away? Why won't these people—these survivors— "just forget about it," some people said.

The answers to that question are both personal and social.

For some, of course, the need to expose their experiences comes out of the need to heal themselves by reclaiming a sense of control over their lives. To stop living in the shadow of victim-hood and powerlessness. For others of them, it was because, having had their secret shame exposed, they now found the courage themselves to speak out about the unspeakable ghost that had for so long haunted their lives.

But it is also possible that the survivors go on drawing our attention to the situation because, this time, consciously or unconsciously, they are trying to warn us of a second aspect of the problem, still largely undefined, that is at least as serious— even the incubator, in fact—of the obvious issues of cover-up and concealment.

The dilemma that really threatens the future of the church is a distorted notion of the vow of obedience and the tension it creates between loyalty to the Gospel and loyalty to the institution—translate: "system."

In this case, the problem swirls around Ireland's Primate, Cardinal Sean Brady, a good man with a good heart and a good reputation. Until now. In 1975, then Father Sean Brady, a newly certified canon lawyer and secretary to then Bishop Francis McKiernan, now deceased, in the diocese of Kilmore, took testimony from two young boys abused by the serial rapist Father Brendan Smyth. At the end of those interviews, Brady exacted a vow of silence from the boys which effectively protected Smyth from public censure and enabled him to go on abusing children—including in the United States—for another eighteen years. Brady, too, said nothing to anyone about the case, other than to his bishop, ever again. Not to the *gardai*, not to the courts, not even to the bishops to whose dioceses Smyth had then been sent.

Challenged now to resign because of that failure to give evidence of a crime, Brady's answer is the Nuremberg defense: He was only following orders; he did not have the responsibility to make any reports other than to his bishop; he was only a notetaker. All of these elements of the situation are now in hot dispute.

But the question is deeper than the simple ones of role and organizational responsibility.

The question is, Why would a good man with a good heart, as he surely is, think twice about his responsibility to take moral and legal steps to stop a child predator from preying on more children everywhere, some of them for years at a time?

The answer to that question is a simple one: It is that the kind of "blind obedience," once theologized as the ultimate step to holiness, is itself blind. It blinds a person to the insights and foresight and moral perspective of anyone other than an authority figure.

Blind obedience is itself an abuse of human morality. It is a misuse of the human soul in the name of religious commitment. It is a sin against individual conscience. It makes moral children of the adults from whom moral agency is required. It makes a vow, which is meant to require religious figures to listen always to the law of God, beholden first to the laws of very human organizations in the person of very human authorities. It is a law that isn't even working in the military and can never substitute for personal morality.

From where I stand, if there are any in whom we should be able to presume a strong conscience and an even stronger commitment to the public welfare, it is surely the priests and religious of the church. But if that is the case, then the church must also review its theology of obedience so that those of good heart can become real moral leaders rather than simply agents of the institution.

A bifurcation of loyalties that requires religious to put canon law above civil law and moral law puts us in a situation where the keepers of religion may themselves become one of the greatest dangers to the credibility—and the morality—of the church itself. —*National Catholic Reporter*, March 17, 2010

Amos: The Prophet in the Mirror

The prophet is not a mentally deranged psychotic gone amuck in the streets. In fact, the wild-eyed and unbalanced need not apply. Some of the finest, most stable and least extroverted people in salvation history have been called to prophecy and witness. Moses, for instance, had great misgivings about finding himself stripped psychologically naked and alone in the political snake pit of the times. Mary of Nazareth had no preparation whatsoever for the task of confronting an entire system with the presence of Jesus. Martin Luther King, Jr., a young, newly ordained minister, felt very ill-prepared to defy a racist nation. No doubt about it, if prophecy takes anything at all, it takes great emotional balance, rugged mental health. If anything, the people God sends to call us to our spiritual senses completely obliterate whatever image of the mangy and berserk we have carried in our souls and called "prophet."

Most of the prophets, what's more, are certainly not mystics; many of them are not even unusually pious people. They claim a "word" but seldom a vision. None of them have been religious fanatics. On the contrary, all of them have been rather average types, who kept their hand to the plow and their souls on course. They were hardworking and spiritually steady, seekers of the first degree. Nowhere does scripture say that they themselves were privately or personally perfect, at least not according to the religious standards around them. But two things are certain: they knew clearly what God wanted for their world, and they never forgot what God expected of them.

The prophet Amos was Mr. Normalcy. He was the man down the street in the modest little house with the awnings, the garden, and the wrought iron fence. Self-employed. Financially secure. Politically independent. And very, very aware of what was going on around him. He was a simple man with a powerful, God-given insight. He owned his own vineyards; he tended his own sheep. He was just like everybody else, except that he wasn't. Amos thought very differently from others. And he said so. That was his first mistake. He was just like the people around him. What right did he have to tell anybody anything? The fact is that Amos prophesied to a world that was totally satisfied with itself.

In the time of Amos, Israel flourished. The country engorged itself on the goods of the world. Israel stood at its most powerful and prosperous peak since the time of King David, Israel's greatest most charismatic leader. Life was good. The boundaries of the nation extended farther than they ever had before. Production and profits were up. As far as the merchants and the military and the monarch were concerned, Yahweh was blessing Israel.

Amos, in other words, found himself completely akin but totally out of step with his times. Amos saw the wealth, of course, but Amos had the effrontery to question where the power and prosperity had come from and what the Israelites had done to gain it. In answer, Amos cited war crimes and tax foreclosures and "failures at the gate," where the elders of the city met to mete out justice but all too often decided against the poor in favor of the rich and powerful.

It's a hard lesson, this awareness that what we know in our hearts to be the will of God we must speak in the light. It is a lesson we try consistently to avoid. We don't rock boats. We don't talk politics. We don't mind other people's business. We go along.

We are not the prophetic type. Neither are the people in the neighborhood. Nor are the people in the parish. Nor are the people in our family. Nor are we. And yet it is to our "normal little worlds" that each of us is called to be prophet now as Amos was then.

Indeed, just when we convince ourselves that disturbing dinner parties is not what we're about, there in front of us stands Amos. He was a private person, not a professional religious. He was uneducated in a sophisticated world. He was well-to-do in a society of have-nots. He was a global visionary in a nationalistic world. And with those gifts he did what he could to make the world a better place. He demanded justice from the judges. He preached in the temple what the priest, to curry favor, would not say about the policies of the king. He spared nothing and no one from the heat of God's light. He knew what it meant to be told that such things were not his business; yet, driven by the Word of God, he made them the stuff of the spiritual life.

As long as the work of God on earth is yet undone, Amos' prophetic cry is to the prophet in each of us, muted for years now, perhaps, but forever on call. Who knows? It may be precisely you and your insights, your very average voice, and your clear-hearted vision for which the world now waits.

—*The Cry of the Prophet*

Wanted: Women of Spirit in Our Own Time

In 2012, the Vatican, under the aegis of the Congregation of the Doctrine for the Faith, accused the Leadership Conference of Women Religious, in the United States, of radical feminist views that undermined church teaching. Having been a leading voice on religious life since Vatican II, as well as a past president of LCWR, Sister Joan offers her perspective on this historic situation.

The Leadership Conference of Women Religious is meeting in Dallas under scrutiny from Rome and with a cloud hanging over its head. What shall we think about this: The women religious who built and staffed every work of the church from this nation's earliest days to the present are accused of being unorthodox, unfaithful, and unfit to make adult decisions about what they need to hear and who they want to have say it.

The problem is that in the face of opposition they have also been unafraid.

What shall we think about that? Think David, maybe, who confronted the giant Goliath; think Moses, perhaps, who faced the Red Sea with an Egyptian army at his back; think Judith and her handmaiden, certainly, who routed Holofernes and saved the city; think Shifra and Puah, without doubt, who refused the order to murder Jewish newborns and so saved the nation. Think Mary of Nazareth and Mary of Magdala, who stood as independent women alone and unblinking. Think moment of decision.

Then think of the foundresses of every religious order you have ever known, who came to the United States without money, without professional resources, often without the language, and commonly without support—even from the church—to deal head on with the social justice questions of their time and so saved the church in the process.

"Women & Spirit," the traveling museum exhibit mounted by the Leadership Conference of Women Religious that reviews the story of women's religious communities in the United States, bears witness to the role of religious life in church and society.

It is the visual history of women who made astounding choices at all the crossroads in national history and made them when women were allowed to make few, if any, choices at all.

It is a story too often forgotten and too easily domesticated. "That's just what sisters were supposed to be doing," people say. Oh, please.

These were women who opened schools for girls in a world that considered the education of women a useless and uppity waste.

These were women who nursed soldiers on both battlefields of the Civil War, North and South, in an age when sisters didn't work with men at all, let alone nurse them.

These were women who worked with what was left of a Native American society that had been stripped of its dignity, robbed of its lands and denied its civil rights in a culture that defined both the American Indian and the women who served them as less than fully human.

These were women who taught blacks for centuries and then walked with them in Selma, Alabama, to claim their full humanity—attack dogs at their heels, fire hoses in front of them—and met disdain everywhere from Christians who used religion to justify first slavery and, after it, segregation.

These were women who gave their lives to insert Catholic children into a Protestant society as equal participants in the democratic dream all the way to a Catholic presidency. Indeed, for hundreds of years, over and over again, women religious have found themselves at the junction between past and future. For hundreds of years they have consistently, persistently, confidently, and courageously chosen for a necessary future—whatever difficulties the doing of it meant for them in the present. Over and over again, they chose for tomorrow rather than settle for a more convenient past.

The entire history of religious life in this nation has been a history of crisis and response, of need and resistance, of response and reaction.

It was not an easy time.

At a time when the sick died uncared for, and the uneducated died illiterate, and the poor or addicted died destitute, and minorities died invisible to the rest of society, women religious chose to challenge any and every system for the sake of the coming of the reign of God.

And in the end, they succeeded. But don't be fooled: They did not succeed because their numbers were large or their influence was great or their social support was either broad-based or obvious. They succeeded because they refused to allow the ideas of the past to become the cement of the future. They succeeded because of the courage of women who went where they were told not to go.

Now we are at another crossroads moment in time. This is a time, too, of deep crisis and great needs, of the rejection of those who raise new questions and a reaction against those who raise new ideas in a system trying to preserve the old ones in order to preserve itself.

It is a time, as it has always been, for leadership.

But leadership and authority are not the same thing. It can take a long time to learn the difference between the two, but there is nothing in life that demonstrates the difference between the two better than a crossroad.

At the crossroads in life, authority goes in one direction: back. Authority goes in the direction that's already in the book; the path that has been clearly trod before now, the way that is safe and sure, clear and certain, obedient and approved, applauded and rewarded.

Leadership, on the other hand, rewrites the book. It takes the direction that leads only to the promise of a better tomorrow for everyone however difficult it may be to achieve it now. "The seed," the Zen master teaches, "never sees the flower."

The times are clear. The needs are now. The time for new decisions is upon us. Authority is not enough for times such as these. We need leaders now.

As women religious meet in Dallas these days as a "Leadership Conference" rather than as a conference of "Major Superiors," may God raise up women among them who will lead. It is a new period of crisis. We must determine to meet this challenge to spiritual maturity, to human adulthood now, as our foremothers before us met theirs. We, too, must move beyond fear to the real, real faith that can, we have seen, move mountains.

It is another period in which public and even ecclesiastical approval must be second again to the needs of those who look to us for both vision and voice.

It is a period in which we must not forego reaching for what is necessary because others tell us it is not acceptable.

For the sake of religious life, for the sake of women everywhere, and, in the end, for the sake of the very integrity of the church itself, we are looking to you now to be "Women of Spirit." May we be to our age what our ancestors were to theirs. Whatever the cost to ourselves.

For that, we are depending now on you.

—*National Catholic Reporter,* August 11, 2010

Coming Soon to a Church Near You

This is a critical commentary on the liturgical changes imposed by the Vatican in 2012 through the revision of the Roman Missal and the restoration of the Tridentine Latin Rite. Sister Joan contrasts the latter with the liturgical changes created by Vatican II. Two different ecclesiologies result with momentous consequences for the future of the church.

It used to be that if you asked a question about the Catholic Church, you got very straightforward answers. No, we did not eat meat on Friday. Yes, we had to go to church every Sunday. Not anymore.

In fact, the answers are getting more confusing all the time. Consider the question of how the newly revised Roman Missal is better than the last, for instance.

They tell us now that Mass texts—including even hymns— may not include feminine references to God. And this in a church that has routinely addressed God as Key of David, Door of Life, wind, fire, light and dove. God who is also, they tell us, "pure spirit" can never, ever, be seen as "mother." Are we to think, then, that even hinting at the notion that the image of God includes the image of women, as well as the image of men, as God in Genesis says it does, is dangerous to the faith? Antithetical to the faith? Heresy?

Or, too, we learned that the words of the consecration itself would soon be edited to correct the notion that Jesus came to save "all"—as we had been taught in the past—to the idea that Jesus came to save "many." The theological implications of changing from "all" to "many" boggles the mind. Who is it that Jesus did not come to save?

Does such a statement imply again that "only Catholics go to heaven?" And, if read like that by others, is this some kind of subtle retraction of the whole ecumenical movement?

Now, this week, we got the word that the pope himself, contrary to the advice and concerns of the world's bishops, has restored the Tridentine Latin Rite. It is being done, the pope explains, to make reconciliation easier with conservative groups.

But it does not, at the same time, make reconciliation easier with women, who are now pointedly left out of the Eucharistic celebration entirely, certainly in its God-language, even in its pronouns. Nor does it seem to care about reconciliation with Jews who find themselves in the Tridentine Good Friday rite again as "blind" and objects of conversion. It's difficult not to wonder if reconciliation is really what it's all about.

What's more, where, in the intervening years, bishops had to give permission for the celebration of Tridentine Masses in the local diocese, the new document requires only that the rite be provided at the request of the laity.

But why the concerns? If some people prefer a Latin Mass to an English Mass, why not have it?

The answer depends on what you think the Mass has to do with articulating the essence of the Christian faith.

The Latin Mass, for instance, in which the priest cele-brates the Eucharist with his back to the people, in a foreign language—much of it said silently or at best whispered—makes the congregation, the laity, observers of the rite rather than participants in it.

The celebrant becomes the focal point of the process, the special human being, the one for whom God is a kind of private preserve.

The symbology of a lone celebrant, removed from and independent of the congregation, is clear: ordinary people have no access to God. They are entirely dependent on a special caste of males to contact God for them. They are "not worthy," to receive the host, or as the liturgy says now, even to have Jesus "come under my roof."

The Eucharist in such a setting is certainly not a celebration of the entire community. It is instead a priestly act, a private devotion of both priest and people, which requires for its integrity three "principal parts" alone—the offertory, the consecration, and the Communion. The Liturgy of the Word—the instruction in what it means to live the Gospel Life—is, in the Tridentine Rite, at best, a minor element.

In the Latin Mass, the sense of mystery—of mystique—the incantation of "heavenly" rather than "vulgar" language in both prayer and music, underscores a theology of transcendence. It lifts a person out of the humdrum, the dusty, the noisy, the crowded chaos of normal life to some other world. It reminds us of the world to come—beautiful, mystifying, hierarchical, perfumed—and makes this one distant. It takes us beyond the present, enables us, if only for a while, to "slip the surly bonds of earth" for a world more mystical than mundane.

It privatizes the spiritual life. The Tridentine Mass is a God-and-I liturgy.

The Vatican II liturgy, on the other hand, steeps a person in community, in social concern, in the hard, cold, clear reality of the present. The people and priest pray the Mass together, in common language, with a common theme. They interact with one another. They sing "a new church into being," non-sexist, inclusive, centered together in the Jesus who walked the dusty roads of Galilee curing the sick, raising the dead, talking to women, and inviting the Christian community to do the same.

The Vatican II liturgy grapples with life from the point of view of the distance between life as we know it and life as the Gospel defines it for us. It plunges itself into the sanctifying challenges of dailiness.

The Vatican II liturgy carries within it a theology of transformation. It does not seek to create on earth a bit of heaven; it does set out to remind us all of the heaven we seek. It does not attempt to transcend the present. It does seek to transform it. It creates community out of isolates in an isolating society.

There is a power and a beauty in both liturgical traditions, of course. No doubt they both need a bit of the other. Eucharist after all is meant to be both transcendent and transformative. But make no mistake: In their fundamental messages, they present us with more than two different styles of music or two different languages or two different sets of liturgical norms. They present us with two different churches.

The choice between these two different liturgies brings the church to a new crossroads, one more open, more ecumenical, more communal, more earthbound than the other. The question is, which one of them is more likely to create the world Jesus models and of which we dream?

There are many more questions ahead of us as a result of this new turn in the liturgical road than simply the effect of such a decree on parish architecture, seminary education, music styles, language acquisition, and multiple Mass schedules.

The theological questions that lurk under the incense and are obscured by the language are far more serious than that. They're about what's really good for the church—ecumenism or ecclesiastical ghettoism, altars and altar rails, mystique or mystery, incarnation as well as divinity, community or private spirituality?

From where I stand, it seems obvious that the Fathers of Vatican Council II knew the implications of the two different

Eucharistic styles then and bishops around the world know it still. But their concerns have been ignored. They don't have much to do with it anymore. Now it's up to the laity to decide which church they really want—and why. Which we choose may well determine the very nature of the church for years to come.

—*National Catholic Reporter*, July 10, 2007

Greed

I heard a story a long time ago that helped me to understand three things: the daily newspaper, the tenth commandment, and the difference between most lives and some lives.

The story tells of an exhausted American businessman who traveled to a faraway island for a vacation. Every day he went to the beach to swim, and every day he found a native there slowly cleaning fish in his boat.

"Do you catch fish every day?" the visitor asked. "Oh, yes," the native said. "Plenty fish here." "Well," the visitor asked, "how often do you fish?" "I fish every morning," the native said.

"But what do you do then?" the businessman asked. "Well," the native said, "first I clean the fish for supper, then I take a little siesta, then I build a bit of my house, then I eat with my family, and then, for the rest of the night, I play my guitar, visit with my friends, and drink my homemade wine."

"But don't you see?" the visitor asked. "If you fished all day, you could sell your fish, buy a U boat, hire helpers, can, pack, and sell your fish all over the world, and make a lot of money."

"But what would I do with it?" the native replied.

"Why, you could buy a house, quit working, enjoy your family, take big vacations, and party with your friends for the rest of your life!"

"Mister," the native said to the businessman, "that's what I'm doing now and I only have to catch one fish a day to do it."

"You shall not covet your neighbor's goods," the tenth commandment teaches, and like the old native, the tenth commandment knows what it's talking about. It's warning us about the gnawing, groaning, smothering effects of greed on the human soul. It's talking about dooming ourselves to the spiritual disease of "perpetual dissatisfaction."

Every day our newspapers demonstrate the effects of it: Billionaires cheat to get more money. Businesses cheat customers and workers and one another to make greater profits. Governments collude with other governments to cheat their own people out of wages and workers' benefits for the sake of the personal payoffs that come to those who choose graft over just gains.

And for what? For the very same things that average hard-working people get all the time: a house, a car, a family, a few good friends, decent food, an education, a social life. Nothing else. The same things, all priced to provide what the traffic can afford. Cotton sheets or silk sheets, a resort or a cabin in the woods, perch or lobster, wood or vinyl interiors. Depending.

When you come right down to it, at the end of the day there's not all that much different in the things to be gotten by money at either end of the financial spectrum, except to get more of them. A TV in every room that nobody watches, a car collection, the same kind of condo in the same kind of places, most of them empty all of the time. And people everywhere to pay for taking care of them.

"Those who have cattle have care," the Kenyans say. But remember, God said it first.

Most of us have everything we need. Greed is the compulsion to get more because we refuse to enjoy what we have.

My advice? Remember the native fisherman.

Perhaps one of the greatest philanthropists of modern times, John D. Rockefeller, understood the difference between greed and gain best. He said, "I know of nothing more despicable and pathetic than a person who devotes all the hours of the waking day to the making of money for money's sake." It is not wealth, in other words, that is in question. It is why we make it and what we do with it when we have it that makes the difference.

The compulsive need to amass things may be nothing more than a signal of the emptiness of our souls. To work hard, to play well, to enjoy life, to give to others, and to be satisfied with what we have may be the only criteria we need to know whether or not we have really succeeded in life.

In this culture a sense of "enoughness" is a sign of mental aberration. A need for "moreness" is considered normal. What a pathetic way to go through life, always grasping, always greedy—always discontented with the self.

Greed can lead to jealousy, which means that I not only never get enough of the things I want, but the more things I see, the more friends I lose. "Whenever a friend succeeds," Gore Vidal wrote, "a little something in me dies." Pitiable. Truly pitiable.

To cure greed we must learn to love something enough to be willing to do without everything else but it. If you want to break the tendency to greed, when you get something new, unless you go on using the first one as well as the second one, try giving the old one away. If you find yourself simply storing it, beware.

If the Northern Hemisphere is unduly rich, it can only be because the Southern Hemisphere is unduly poor. "International business may conduct its operations with scraps of paper," Eric Ambler wrote, "but the ink it uses is human blood." What we do as a people to other peoples of the world will surely come back on our own heads. If for no other reason than that one, that is why international law is everyone's concern.

Beware what you value in life. You may get exactly what you're looking for without any of the cure for it. Or as Imelda Marcos said once with great indignation: "I did not have 3,000 pairs of shoes; I had 1,060." I know that Imelda Marcos had at least a thousand pairs of shoes because I saw them with my own eyes. But all I could think of when I looked at them was that if she wore one pair a day, every day of the year, each pair would be worn, on average, no more than once every three years. Or from twenty-five to thirty times in a person's entire life. Outside the palace, though, children walked through the streets wearing no shoes at all. That's not a hobby; that's greed. The question, I knew, was what is it in my life that is the equivalent of Imelda Marcos's shoes?

Greed eats away at the soul, distracts us from friendship, consumes us with want. "There is," the Buddha says, "no fire like passion, there is no shark like hatred, there is no snare like folly, there is no torrent like greed."

It isn't that greed is a sin against others that is its only evil. It is that greed is self-destructive that makes it so pathetic. Greed eats out the center of our own lives. We exhaust ourselves with envy instead of learning to enjoy what we already have.

Give one thing away every day for a month. It's called oiling the soul so it works better.   —*The Ten Commandments*

PEACE AND NONVIOLENCE

An Open Letter to the Bishops

In 1983, the U.S. National Conference of Bishops issued its historic peace pastoral, "The Challenge of Peace: God's Challenge and Our Response." Though the pastoral morally condemned the use of nuclear weapons, it did not condemn nuclear deterrence. In 1989, Pax Christi USA, the Catholic Peace Movement, issued a publication, "Dear Bishops: Open Letters to the U.S. Catholic Bishops Concerning the Immorality of Deterrence." Joan Chittister was one of the contributors to that publication

Dear Bishops,

One of my most hopeful moments of church came when the bishops of the United States were willing to wrestle with the questions of nuclear morality in a nuclear world. One of my most disappointing moments, on the other hand, came when you failed to say that deterrence that is aimed at the destruction of the globe is morally unacceptable, that a defense system that has already begun to erode the social fiber of our country with its lustful, gluttonous profligate use of resources, which could and should be better used to assure human development rather than to plot human destruction, could possibly be a sinless activity.

How can we possibly say that what is immoral to use is moral to design and develop and deploy?

How can we possibly say that to abort a fetus is morally wrong but that the weapons intended only to abort the entire human race are not?

How can we possibly make ourselves and our generation more worthy of the ultimate act of retaliation than at any other possible moment in history?

Isn't the arrogance of those postures alone a sin against the Holy Spirit?

How is it that we can ask people to be prepared to die in nuclear warfare in the name of a "defense" that is destructive, but refuse to ask them to be prepared to die in passive resistance in the name of the Gospel? All that would happen to us if we faced a nuclear attack without weapons is that we would die, but isn't that the very posture that we clearly espouse even now in the name of "defense"? And isn't that precisely the kind of deterrence that we expect from the nonnuclear world even now?

The point is that we say that nuclear weapons alone can be a deterrence to nuclear war. But surely there is a rational and Christian deterrence as well that would be equally effective. All that would happen to us if we faced a nuclear attack, with nuclear weapons, is that we would die. And in each case the enemy would simply destroy what they wanted and threaten their own existence as well. The posture that we now espouse in the name of "defense," then, makes us no less vulnerable, but it takes from the poor while we practice it and it holds the world hostage to fear which we stockpile more and always more demonic danger. The difference is that in refusing to threaten a nuclear retaliation, or worse, "pre-emptive strike," we would not have set out to destroy Creation in the doing.

An even graver question, perhaps, for us as church may be, Why is it it is that the unilateral initiatives for weapons destruction must come from an atheist general secretary of a communist state rather than from the Roman Catholic bishops of a professedly Christian nation?

The fact is that governments and political systems, economic theories and institutionalized philosophies, kings and presidents, emperors and premiers—all come and go. Is this system, culture, era, epoch, or political arena of ours really worth the price: the loss of all our futures, as well as the cost of all glories of our past, the possible loss of the planet itself? Would any other era think so? Is any form of self-defense, then, acceptable, regardless of its consequences and its cost? Is becoming what we hate the Christian answer to the fears of this world? Is this the message of the Gospel for which we stand?

It was a Christian state that designed the Holocaust, and Christian countries that waged the Inquisition, and Christian states that burned witches and napalmed Vietnamese villages and used the atomic bomb, not once but twice, for experimental purposes. Now, with all the planet and universal human morality and civilization itself at stake, in an age when errors cannot be forgiven, we are begging you, lead this Christian state to more than that.

We are asking you to reject the balance-of-terror game in favor of turning this country to Truth and Light as you have in so many other issues: the labor movement and religious freedom and human rights.

The *Rule of Benedict* requires humility as the cornerstone of a spirituality built in the patriarchal culture of imperial Rome. We need that same humility now from the church. Call this country to negotiations, to human respect, to faith, and to humility in our dealing with both the little and the great ones of this world. As long as the bishops of the country give credence to a militarism based on arrogance and fear and paranoia and power and pride, it will be called moral even though it isn't. There is an ancient proverb that teaches, "Wherever there is excess in anything, something is lacking."

One of my most hopeful moments of church came when the bishops of the United States were willing to wrestle with the questions of nuclear morality in a nuclear world. One of my most disappointing moments, on the other hand, came when you failed to say that deterrence that is aimed at the destruction of the globe is morally unacceptable, that a defense system that has already begun to erode the social fiber of our country with its lustful, gluttonous profligate use of resources, which could and should be better used to assure human development rather than to plot human destruction, could possibly be a sinless activity. Finish the fine work you have begun and give this nation what it lacks, to its peril , in its excessive militarism—the challenge of peace.

— Dear Bishops: Open Letters to the U.S. Catholic Bishops
Concerning the Immorality of Deterrence

Aggression and Nonviolence: A New Road to Peace

Nonviolent resistance, derived from Mahatma Gandhi and modeled in this country by Martin Luther King Jr.'s civil rights movement of the sixties, rests on six clear concepts, none of them cowardly, insipid or weak. They are, rather, a demonstration of the kind of strength no amount of violence can extinguish.

First, nonviolent resistance is pacifism, not passivism. People who are passive in the face of evil create the climate that enables it to exist. The major difference between armed resistance and nonviolent resistance is not that one opposes evil and the other allows it. The difference between armed resistance and nonviolent resistance lies simply in the means by which the resistance is waged. Both types of resistance rest on the conviction that evil must be challenged, but nonviolent resistance insists that evil must not be repeated in the effort to defeat it. Injustice done in the name of justice is still injustice. The strength of nonviolent resistance lies in its determination to do no harm to the other in the course of resisting harm. Gandhi wrote, "If there is blood in the streets, it must be no one's but our own."

Second, nonviolent resistance is committed to making friends out of enemies. To win a war but keep an enemy makes no progress toward peace. To win the point at the expense of the other does nothing to resolve the tension. The goal of nonviolent resistance is to concentrate on issues rather than on belittling, demeaning, destroying the people who hold positions different from our own. Nonviolent resistance calls us to distinguish between enmity and opposition.

Third, nonviolent resistance condemns systems, ideas or policies that oppress but never launches personal attacks against individuals who are the agents of the system itself. If we cannot assume the good will of those who oppose us we must at least not judge their motives. Ideas and systems are bigger than any single person. To attack individuals in order to curb a sinful system only plays into the hands of the system itself by failing to focus attention where attention is necessary. We can wage war against the local mayor and miss the meaning of the fascism that makes oppression possible. We can focus on males and miss the assumptions of sexism that underlie every law, policy, and program in the world. We can turn against men and soldiers and husbands and sons and sexist women and fail to change the language, the educational programs, the economic structures, the theology that taught them to demean women in the name of God's will and moral righteousness. Hating leads to the destruction of people we learn to destroy.

Fourth, nonviolent resistance absorbs physical attack without striking back physically. Suffragettes went to jail to win the vote and never struck a blow. Women, jeered at and pummeled, supported the demands of underpaid miners by banging kitchen pans to stampede coal-carrying donkeys coming out of the offending mines. Women and men faced attack dogs in Selma, Alabama, to win the right to be human beings without themselves becoming barbaric in the process. Nothing is learned from force but force. Striking a child teaches the child to strike others. Bringing brute force to bear where brute force is possible simply teaches that might does indeed make right. Giving our bodies to the blows of those for whom physical assault is their only power to persuade does no harm to the other except what they do to themselves. Allied military forces may have defeated the Axis, but it was the thought of Jews standing defenseless on the edge of mass graves that quashed any possible image of a valiant Nazism forever. It was row upon row of Indians falling to their knees under the gratuitous blows of their English masters that sent a chill up the spine of a colonial world. Nonviolent resistance unmasks the inhumanity of oppression, a consciousness that is of the essence of feminism, and gives all of us another chance to repent and begin again to be thinking, feeling human beings.

Fifth, nonviolent resistance refuses to sow hate for the enemy. Hate gives foundation to hate until hate becomes a cycle that never ends. Nonviolence vows not only to end the oppression but to end the hate as well. "Love your enemy" is not poetry; it is strategy. Those we want to have love us, we will have to love first.

Sixth, nonviolent resistance is based on the faith that in the end justice will come because justice is right and God is good. Two commandments undergird nonviolence and ring in every heart: The first is "Love your neighbor as yourself," and the second is "Vengeance is mine, says the Lord. I will repay." Love is our responsibility. Justice is God's.

Each of these principles taxes courage, demands great spirituality and promises opposition equal to the length of the struggle and the depth of the issue.

Nonviolent resistance is the weapon of those who need no weapons to be effective. It breeds questions that do not go away until governments lose the right to rule because they have lost the hearts and minds of the people.

What the world fails to understand rises to haunt it as struggle after struggle solves nothing and simply breeds the next one. In our own time, World War I, "the war to end all wars," bred World War II. The ruthless suppression of national states by Russia led in the long run to genocide in Bosnia, revolt in Chechnya, rejection in the Ukraine. The obvious has escaped us: Violence never solves anything; it simply opens wounds that fester in wait for centuries until the tables turn and the guns are bigger and the damage is beyond repair.

The idea that weapons defend a people is bogus at every level—physical, social, and psychological. To resist an enemy unarmed is no guarantee of success, true. But to go into conflict armed is no guarantee of success either. Witness the body bags in every armory of the world.

More than that, armed nations fall in brutal and pitiless ways. Weapons are no surety that a nation will not fall to external pressure. They are also no guarantee that the nation will not deteriorate from within while it stockpiles weapons but neglects roads and Medicare and education and housing and employment and internal investment. The United States concentrated on defense after World War II while countries we disarmed, thanks to our insistence, concentrated on making computer chips and cars, electronic peripherals, and consumer goods. Now we have new problems, not because other countries are better armed than we are but because they are internally more nonviolent or educationally superior, financially more balanced or morally more defined, while we ourselves are still attempting to recover from the militarism spawned by World War II and its effects on the soul of this nation. The question of the most militarized generation in the history of humankind after two world wars is not who won the wars but who won the peace.

Armed individuals, too, are killed despite their weapons or, armed to the teeth, suspicious of everyone and everything, they destroy their own inner peace and openness. They make themselves targets for other people's fear. Witness the gurneys at every gang fight in the United States. Witness the eternal damage done in every family, in every relationship that relies for resolution of conflict on force. Just as the damage to human development is a high price to pay for military victory so, too, the surrender of human serenity and personal growth is an exorbitant price to pay for enmity.

The fundamental question of spirituality today is whether or not the spirit that rises in our hearts and overflows into our daily routine rids the world of one more beaten child, leads to a lower military budget, insists on an equality that is based more on genuine respect than on tokenism, demands a hearing for the voiceless, refuses to do harm whatever the glory of the cause, reaches out instead of striking out, and pledges to resist evil whatever the cost without doing evil ourselves.   —*Heart of Flesh*

Unleashing a Power Such as the World Has Never Seen

Everybody wants to know, in a world ravaged by war, what can possibly be missing in the multiple attempts being made to stop it. Israel and Palestine, for instance, have been embroiled in negotiations for at least fifty years. So why does the violence go on?

Kofi Annan, Secretary General of the United Nations, points to the voices invariably absent in every set of deliberations: the voice of spiritual leaders and the voice of women.

This first meeting of the "Women's Partnership for Peace" will not make the headlines it should. While Ariel Sharon, Mahmoud Abbas, and George Bush were deciding whom to bomb, blast and terrify next, Israeli, Palestinian and other religious, politicians, and businesswomen from the international community held their own meeting in Norway. The choice of site was itself significant: Women were setting out to revive the spirit of the Oslo Peace Accords that are in danger of being scrapped by the men in the conflict.

The very notion of the meeting raises eyebrows. How could such a thing be happening? Why would it be happening? What do women have to do with war? Answer: Women have everything to do with war.

It isn't true that women do not go into combat, that women are spared the barbarisms of war. Women go into combat in the worst way: They go unprepared, unarmed, and unasked whether they really want to be defended defenselessly or not.

Women, who have nothing whatsoever to do with the planning of wars and the making of wars and the declaring of wars, have everything to do with the losing of wars! Women are the booty of war. Their bodies have become an instrument of war. Their children have become the fodder of war. Their homes have become the rubble of war. Their daily struggles to live have become one of the horrors of war and their futures have been left shattered in the shambles of war though they have nothing whatsoever to say about the raging of wars.

Instead, they die from its bombs and bullets. They die in large cities and small villages for lack of food. They die from lack of water or they die from drinking water filthy with human feces.

They die in tent cities without medicines, without clothing, without sons and husbands, and hope. Or they live raped, ravaged, and beaten. And they die seeing their daughters in the same circumstances—helpless to avoid it, powerless to stop it.

Oh, yes, when all the warriors have finally left their battlefields, women are left in the ashes of war and the cemeteries of anguish. If truth were ever told, war falls hardest, longest, cruelest on the backs of women.

Indeed, women must have a role, not only in the reconstruction of societies already ravaged by war. More than that, women intend to take a voice until they are given a voice in the development of peaceful alternatives to war.

But it is not simply the experience and agendas and values of women that are not being heard. It is also the spiritual wisdom of the world's spiritual traditions that are suppressed in favor of the dictates of power and profit.

Surely the history of the world confirms that insight. Religion has been at the bottom of almost every major conflict the world has ever known and, according to a U.N. report, to over half of them even now. Truth claims on all sides, absolutism made divine, political issues masked as theological differences, theological differences justifying exclusion or domination have wracked the globe. Indeed, do wrack the globe. And continue to wrack the globe. It's an old story.

The Crusades divided the Christian and the Arab world; the Wars of Religion divided Europe; tension between Hinduism and Islam lies at the heart of the division between India and Pakistan; sectarian convictions divide Iraq itself; religious differences still mark the lines of division in Northern Ireland; and religious figures in the United States go on spreading religious rancor at a time of intense political tension. Islam, they argue, is an "evil" religion, intent on the destruction of the West, the United States, Christianity. It's an awesome charge against an entire body of religious believers, most of whom have never made a hostile move against anyone, let alone in the name of religion.

However benign and enlightened the world may now claim to be, the fact remains that politicians use religion as a fan to inflame the ire of people who have too many daily worries to even think about arguing politics but who will gladly die to preserve their religion.

At the same time, the forgotten reality is that every religion teaches peace and respect for the other. And that truth has a way of seeping up and spilling over into the human psyche even when religions do everything they can to avoid it. For instance, "mixed marriages"—the union of Catholics and Protestants, who, it was said, were divided by an irreconcilable theological gulf—is now a given in every Christian culture. Christians and Muslims have lived in peace in every country in the Middle East and in the West, as well. In fact, one-third of the world's 1.5 billion Muslims live outside a Muslim country in peace and in tune with the laws of the country and the people of other religions around them. Mosques and temples, churches and synagogues face each other on every corner in every part of the world now. In peace. With respect.

Nevertheless, in the name of religion, radical fundamentalists of every stripe have gone on arguing the union of God's will, the purpose of civil society and their own theological views. Christian states have persecuted other Christians as well as non-Christians. Theocratic states have excluded nonbelievers from the body politic. We have all sinned.

Obviously, religion itself is not really the problem. But, from where I stand, until religion is part of the answer, until religions everywhere refuse to be used to advance the very secular ends of power and greed and control and domination that the secular world seeks, then religion will continue to be the hot ashes under every conflict.

In Oslo, women brought both dimensions of life—the feminine and the spiritual—to a new level of meeting point. The British poet Matthew Arnold wrote, "If ever the world sees a time when women shall come together purely and simply for the benefit of (hu)mankind, it will be a power such as the world has never seen." I think it may be beginning to happen.

—*National Catholic Reporter*, June 24, 2003

What Kind of People Are These?

On October 2, 2006, a shooting occurred at the West Nickel Mines School, an Amish one-room schoolhouse in Lancaster County, Pennsylvania. The gunman shot ten girls (aged six to thirteen), killing five, before committing suicide. What made this massacre different from so many that occur in the United States was the Amish response of forgiveness and reconciliation. Sister Joan's commentary on the Amish response made this one of her most requested columns.

The country that went through the rabid slaughter of children at Columbine high school several years ago once again stood stunned at the rampage in a tiny Amish school this month.

The kind of ferocity experienced by the Amish as they buried the five girl-children murdered by a crazed gunman has not really been foreign to Amish life and the history of this peaceful people.

This is a people born out of opposition to violence and, at the same time, persecuted by both Catholics and Protestants in the era before religious tolerance. Having failed to adhere to the orthodoxy of one or the other of the controlling theocracies of their home territories, they were banished, executed, imprisoned, drowned, or burned at the stake by both groups.

But for over three hundred years, they have persisted in their intention to be who and what they said they were.

Founded by a once-Catholic priest in the late seventeenth century, as part of the reformist movements of the time, the Mennonites—from which the Amish later sprung—were, from the beginning, a simple movement. They believe in adult baptism, pacifism, religious tolerance, separation of church and state, opposition to capital punishment, and opposition to oaths and civil office.

They organize themselves into local house churches. They separate from the "evil" of the world around them. They live simple lives opposed to the technological devices—and even the changing clothing styles—which, in their view, encourage the individualism, the pride, that erodes community, family, a righteous society. They work hard. They're self-sufficient; they refuse both Medicare and Social Security monies from the state. And though the community has suffered its own internal violence from time to time, they have inflicted none on anyone around them.

Without doubt, to see such a peaceful people brutally attacked would surely leave any decent human being appalled.

But it was not the violence suffered by the Amish community last week that surprised people. Our newspapers are full of brutal and barbarian violence day after day after day—national and personal.

No, what really stunned the country about the attack on the small Amish schoolhouse in Pennsylvania was that the Amish community itself simply refused to hate what had hurt them.

"Do not think evil of this man," the Amish grandfather told his children at the mouth of one little girl's grave.

"Do not leave this area. Stay in your home here," the Amish delegation told the family of the murderer. "We forgive this man."

No, it was not the murders, not the violence, that shocked us; it was the forgiveness that followed it for which we were not prepared. It was the lack of recrimination, the dearth of vindictiveness that left us amazed. Baffled. Confounded.

It was the Christianity we all profess but which they practiced that left us stunned. Never had we seen such a thing.

Here they were, those whom our Christian ancestors called "heretics," who were modeling Christianity for all the world to see. The whole lot of them. The entire community of them. Thousands of them at one time.

The real problem with the whole situation is that down deep we know that we had the chance to do the same. After the fall of the Twin Towers, we had the sympathy, the concern, the support of the entire world.

You can't help but wonder, when you see something like this, what the world would be like today if, instead of using the fall of the Twin Towers as an excuse to invade a nation, we had simply gone to every Muslim country on earth and said, "Don't be afraid. We won't hurt you. We know that this is coming from only a fringe of society, and we ask your help in saving others from this same kind of violence."

"Too idealistic," you say. Maybe. But since we didn't try, we'll never know, will we?

Instead, we have sparked fear of violence in the rest of the world ourselves. So much so, that they are now making nuclear bombs to save themselves. From whom? From us, of course.

The record is clear. Instead of exercising more vigilance at our borders, listening to our allies and becoming more of what we say we are, we are becoming who they said we are.

For the 3,000 dead in the fall of the Twin Towers at the hands of 19 religious fanatics, we have more than 2,700 U.S. soldiers now killed in military action, more than 20,600 wounded, more than 10,000 permanently disabled. We have thousands of widows and orphans, a constitution at risk, a president that asked for and a Congress that just voted to allow torture, and a national infrastructure in jeopardy for want of future funding.

And nobody's even sure how many thousand innocent Iraqis are dead now, too.

Indeed, we have done exactly what the terrorists wanted us to do. We have proven that we are the oppressors, the exploiters, the demons they now fear we are. And—read the international press—few people are saying otherwise around the world.

From where I stand, it seems to me that we ourselves are no longer so sure just exactly what kind of people we have now apparently become.

Interestingly enough, we do know what kind of people the Amish are—and, like the early Romans, we, too, are astounded at it. "Christian" they call it.

—*National Catholic Reporter*, October 9, 2006

My Enemy Has Become My Friend

It was a hot and honest session in that meeting of Palestinian and Israeli women in Oslo, Norway. The Palestinian women said that they supported the Israelis' right to an independent state; the Israeli women said that they supported the Palestinians' right to resources, political integrity, and freedom to live in the land. It was a significant political moment.

Nevertheless, what happened after the conference adjourned may, in the end, prove to be even more significant.

On the last night of the assembly, one of these women went to the other and asked to continue the discussion about what had been lost and what must be gained if the two peoples are ever to live together well. They went out for coffee together. I don't know what was said. I only know that the conversation went on until after midnight.

When it came time to leave, the Israeli woman—old enough to be the Palestinian's mother—decided she would walk the young woman to her hotel. But then the young Palestinian realized how far the older woman would have to walk alone back to her own place of residence and insisted that she walk her halfway back again.

"I've had a wonderful night," the Israeli woman said as they parted. "This time with you was itself worth the conference."

The young Palestinian woman went silent for a moment. "I'm glad for you," she said, "but I'm confused."

The Israeli woman winced inside, "Why? What's wrong?" she asked.

"Oh, nothing is wrong," the younger woman said. "I'm just confused. I don't know what to do now that my enemy has become my friend."

The next day, in the Tel Aviv airport, the Israeli women whisked through customs and baggage claim. The Palestinian women did not. When the Israeli women realized that all the Palestinians had been detained, they turned around, went back and refused to leave the customs hall themselves until all the Palestinians were released.

That, I learned, is what it means to proceed in the "ways of peace." It means having the courage to make human connections with those we fear, with those we hate, with those who think differently than we do. It means refusing to leave the other behind as we go.   —*National Catholic Reporter,* July 8, 2003

Road to Damascus: Still a Place for Conversions

Our small delegation from the Woman's Global Peace Initiative went to Syria with one thing in mind: We went to do some citizen-to-citizen diplomacy.

We decided that this time we would go straight to the religious leaders of the country to ask them what kind of a place they thought Syria to be.

Our first appointment, they told us, would be a trip to "meet with the Iraqis."

The Iraqis? What did that mean? We were, after all, in Syria.

As we wound our way through the narrow back lanes of the city, I realized that Paul of Tarsus had walked in this very area, too. "Not in this area," our translator said. "Paul walked here. Here. On this street. I will show you." And, all of a sudden, we emerged on the street called "Straight" talked about in scripture.

The impact of the statement was far more than biblical. Damascus is the longest continuously populated city in human history. More than seven thousand years old, they tell us. We were on the very street that ties the early moments of Christianity with today's struggles.

When the car stopped, we found ourselves in the front courtyard of a huge marble building. Fronted by narrow marble steps and great columned portico, it had all the marks of a standard Roman Catholic installation. Except that we were not in Rome. We were in a convent in Damascus run by a feisty old nun, Regina, a sister of St. Basil. It was a classic institution confronted by a very current situation.

The four sisters there work with Iraqi refugees. "Four thousand Iraqi refugees a day come to Syria," Sister Regina told us.

The sisters feed the refugees three times a week on fresh soups and casseroles, vegetables, bread and meat donated by the members of the parish and their Muslim friends around them. The people come with old pots and pans, the sisters fill them to the brim. The people take the food back for the rest of the family to make meals and home and family life as normal as possible in a totally abnormal situation.

Four sisters, older but undaunted, collect clothes for them, manage a medical clinic to care for them and try to get them housing. "Come and see them," she said.

I was a bit reluctant to go with her, afraid to embarrass them, concerned that the very presence of Americans could break the thin thread of strength that gave them a last semblance of dignity. But since she and I had made a personal contact—she a Basilian, I a Benedictine—she pushed me out into the midst of them in the inner courtyard where they were all watching us through the windows. I could hardly get out the door. They pressed around me, all talking at once. We were Americans and they knew it.

The rest of the time is almost a blur, meaning I don't know what happened in what order. But I do know what happened. I looked into their faces while the translator pointed each of them out: this one's son had been killed, these lost their homes, this one saw her family shot to death by American soldiers, these here have nowhere to go . . . the list was endless. "I am so sorry," I said to them. "I am so sorry this happened to you. Many, many Americans tried to stop this. All I can do is apologize to you from the center of my heart for the millions of Americans who are concerned for you."

"And what good does that do?" a young teenager said, a sharp edge to her voice.

"They are still working very hard to stop this destruction," I went on. "Yesterday in a national election, American people said 'No' to the present direction. There is no way to justify what has happened to you—and to your country—and we know that."

Suddenly, a woman pushed forward from the back of the jostling crowd, big black eyes fixed on me intently. She turned to the translator for help. "I accept your apology," she said quietly. "I accept your love." Then she put her arms around me, kissed me firmly on the cheek, put her head on my shoulder and began to cry. And so did I. The rest of the group pressed tightly against us, all of them with tears on their faces.

I had never seen the faces of my victims before and they had not seen the face of the enemy who was not an enemy. It was a profound moment for all of us.

Then, the Reverend Joan Brown-Campbell—chair of the Global Peace Initiative of Women—came forward quietly and began to do what ministers do: She made the sign of the cross on first one forehead, then another. And, instantly, the whole crowd fell into line waiting for the blessing, Muslims and Christians.

It was a scene of frustration, care, trust, anger, hurt, and commitment I will never forget.

From where I stand, it seems that road to Damascus is still the place of conversion. Maybe before we name any more enemies, politicians should go there.

—*National Catholic Reporter,* November 16, 2006

WOMEN IN
CHURCH AND SOCIETY

Nature of Oppression

People come to know who they are by virtue of what other people tell them they are. The fact is that self-image is largely a social construct. People defined as unworthy by a society come to define themselves as unworthy. People learn that they are slow or shy or pretty or smart because other people, significant people—their parents, their teachers, their heroes—tell them that they are. The way we view the other, in other words, has a great deal to do with the way they come to view themselves. The implications of these findings have serious consequences for women, as well as for any other minority in any society.

Prejudice studies indicate that oppressed people deal with the effects of prejudice in four ways: First, they become what the dominant class defines them to be. Second, they live down to the stunted expectations their society has of them. Third, they seek the approval of the oppressor. Fourth, they turn their anger at the situation inward on themselves rather than outward on the oppressor. The results of such a situation shrink and shrivel the souls of everybody concerned.

The situation is clear: Women become what men want them to be. They wear what men want them to wear, do what men want them to do, think what men say they should think. Women know from every theology book they ever read, every survey-of-philosophy course they ever took, every psychological study conducted before 1970 that they are weak, inferior, and intellectually deficient. By nature. They learn to doubt their own judgments, their own insight, their own instincts, their own abilities not less, but more and more as they get older. They become, with a few outstanding exceptions, exactly what the patriarchal world has defined them to be: its helpers, its servants, its handmaidens in every field.

Whatever women, in the innocence and excitement of childhood, aspire to has been carefully culled across time. Women learn young to live down to the stunted expectations imposed on them by the society around them. They were taught that they could be cook but not chef, nurse but not doctor, teller but not manager of the bank. The patriarchal system told women they could not run marathons, and so women didn't run them. Patriarchal men told women they were too weak to play basketball on the whole court, and women never tried the game. Patriarchal society told women that they could not do math and science, and few women did. Patriarchal society told women that politics was a male preserve and so women never ran for office. Patriarchal society told women that they were responsible for the sexual responses of men, so mothers dutifully taught their daughters whose fault rape really was. No wonder it is women who say that women can't be president, can't be priests, can't be airline pilots, can't be the primary wage earner in the family. Or worse, no wonder it is women who reject women who are.

Oppressed peoples, ironically, look to the oppressor for their standard of achievement and measure of approval. Blacks straightened their hair and lightened their skin before they discovered a black beauty independent of white culture. Women find themselves locked into male academic models, male corporate uniforms, male structures, and male models of the world's major institutions, all designed to facilitate a world designed from the perspective of men for the convenience and comfort of men. To succeed in this world, women conform to norms they never had a chance to help create. The archetype of female achievement lies in becoming like men at the male game. Being approved by men as one of the team, a good nun, the perfect wife, a good Christian, a real scholar, a good mother, marks the highest level of female accomplishment. It's these women who don't want to be thought of as strident feminists for asking for the same compensation for women as for men in the same situation. They want to be nice feminists—if they will use the word at all. It's these women who don't make the changes in family life that would enable their own lives to flower because change would upset their husbands and cost the kind of uneasy peace that is built on their confinement in exchange for his satisfaction. It is these women who want other women to be quiet, to be pleasant, to be grateful for whatever they get, however little it is on the human scale.

In the end, women, like other minorities who have been taught their natural limitations by the dominant culture in which they live, turn their anger against themselves. They come to realize their weakness, their defects, their natural disabilities and, mistrusting themselves, they mistrust women in general. After that, the conquest is complete. They believe anything that a patriarchal system tells them about themselves, about what God wants for them, about the value of their souls, about the nature of their relationship with God, about the plans that God has for them, about the potential that is theirs to parlay into fullness of life, about the ceiling that God has put on a woman's potential, about the fact that God gave women brains, apparently, so that they could suffer the ache of not being allowed to use them. They know that women cannot do what men can do, and they resent and scold and criticize any woman who tries to do it. They become instruments of the system, its perfect product, its most important achievement. Max Weber says that power is most complete when the powerless themselves accept it without question. No doubt about it: Patriarchal power is, for far too many, most complete.

For these women, the price of patriarchy requires the price of personhood. Patriarchal women turn into oppressors of other women, true, but only because they have been victimized themselves. Spiritually, they live without ever knowing the full scope of life, the real extent of their potential, the real depth of their own souls. At the same time, the rest of the world loses the value of their unpursued ministries, the quality of their unrecorded insights, the power of the unsought wisdom in them that is waiting to be tapped like sap from a tree in winter. Most painful of all, perhaps, the daughters of the world never see modeled in these patriarchal women—for their own future use—the resurrection of soul that, once buried by a patriarchal system, has come to fullness of life. —*Heart of Flesh*

A Feminist Spirituality

The ostracism of women as a class from public policy and the long-time elimination of women from the theological development of the Western world has limited the vision of the world. It makes discrimination generic. It entombs half the people of the world. Clearly, it is a feminist spirituality—a heart of flesh—that we need if the church is to survive. More than that, if the planet is to survive.

There are points of tension, however. First, it is necessary for all of us, at all times, to understand that female and feminist are not the same things. Feminists are people who believe that the notion of gendering, of defining the sexes by traits and limiting them in life on physical grounds to separate roles, should be replaced by the notion of universal personhood. Surely God did not make one sex simply for the sake of waiting on the other. Surely God did not give women minds in order to taunt them by not allowing them to use them—an argument which is now losing ground somewhat in the secular community but which is alive and well in the synods and seminaries and sacristies and chanceries of the church. To feminists, then, a spirituality that does not release the feminine dimension in both women and men leaves all of humanity half-souled, the church half-graced, and the world half-developed.

Second, it is necessary to realize that feminists come in two genders—female sometimes, but not always, and male, often, though too rarely recognized either by women or the men themselves. In fact, it is only my feminist brothers who are any proof to me whatsoever that humanity and creation as God made it is really possible. To those brothers, I owe my love. Each of them, male and female, reflects a different experience, yes, but each is searching for the same thing—a heart of flesh and a soul that's soft. And each of them feels the weight of sexism in body and spirit, men as well as women. Men know the price of ignoring the feminine dimensions in themselves as well as women know the price of its being obstructed and suppressed in them. Reason, forbidden to women, has diminished by cauterizing their hearts and calling the suffering "virtue." Patriarchy denies men feeling and substitutes heart attacks and alcoholism—Hiroshima and Holocaust—instead. Power consumes men, literally. They are prodded from little boys to "get ahead," "to become something," "to succeed," until the seed of dissatisfaction saps all the energy in their souls and makes of every man around them a potential threat to their own achievement. Trained to be aggressive, men know the sexist pain of being hunted and hazed, beaten and sneered at, of having courage and character confused.

The man who seeks a family life rather than status knows what it is to be disdained by both men and women for whom manliness means wealth, image and public "recognition." Universalism—the epitome of humanity in maleness—requires that men never fail, are always right, have all the answers, are responsible for everything and everyone, and show no doubts, until sick of having to bluster their way through life, weighed down by the pressure of it, they crumble both inside and out, raging as they do.

Authoritarianism—the male sexist model—demands control, sees disloyalty everywhere, and insists on submission from those who will not, ultimately, submit. That is the war between the sexes. It's the weight of sexism on men versus the search for life among women. It is not a war; it is a loss of life in both of them. Life for men in a patriarchal society becomes one long struggle to stay in charge, whatever the cost.

Feminist men know how it feels to refuse to compete. Feminist men know how it feels to be a wimp in the eyes of those around them—friends and family—who see failure to get to the top as failure to be a "man." Feminist men know the ridicule that comes to the man who admits his fear, his compassion, his love. Men know they must be self-sufficient, that little boys are taught not to cry, ever, for anything; that being able to kill, maim, and destroy without flinching marks their passage to manhood. Indeed, they know the ridicule and the loneliness of it. No doubt about it: patriarchy erases, excises, patronizes and diminishes women, but it is killing men! Men are trained, taught, expected to work, to succeed, to get ahead, to get money. And they literally drop dead from sexism. And men are the ones who benefit from the system?

Feminism is a new worldview. Feminism is a spirituality that the world and the church ignore to the peril of us all. Feminism is about another way of looking at life, about another set of values designed to nurture a dying globe and rescue any people too long ground under foot, too long ignored, unseen, invisible. Feminism is about a new way of thinking for both women and men who are tired of the carnage, sickened by the exploitation of the globe, disillusioned by the power struggles and searching—as Ezekiel promises—for a heart of flesh in a world of stone. Feminism is, in other words, not a women's question: It is the human question of the century. It is the spiritual question of all time. It's not about getting what men already have. Not on your life. What men have is not nearly enough. Feminism is about getting a better world, for everybody.

Feminism, a different cluster of values, a distinct worldview, comes to correct patriarchy's skewed concepts of who should be rulers and who are ruled, of who are weak and who are strong, of what is right and what is wrong, of what is a man and what is a woman. Feminism does not come to destroy men. If anything, it comes to save men from imprisonment by a system that cramps the human development of men all the while it purports to give them power. Feminists are not asking men to be less than manly. Feminists are asking women and men not to buy into patriarchal systems that destroy them both. Feminism comes to bring both men and women to the fullness of life, and wholeness of soul for which we are all made "in the image and likeness of God."

Feminists—both women and men—call us to the Christianity of a Jesus who preceded the patriarchal church, the corporate world, and the nuclearized government. They call us to listen to the Canaanites in our midst, to include women in our groups, to do away with rigid roles, to open synods and seminaries and chanceries everywhere, to see ourselves as part of the whole rather than its potentates, to go through life as partners rather than as power mongers, to devote ourselves to more than ourselves.

Those concepts would change domestic legislation and foreign policy, theology and corporate life, families and churches. The world would begin to operate on a spirituality of compassion, of empowerment, of dialogue, of community, of openness, of nonviolence, of feeling as well as reason, of circles rather than pyramids, of hearts of flesh—instead of hearts of stone. Those concepts would turn the world around us upside down. They are holy-making ideas for our time. In a world exhausted by, dying from, and destroying itself by power plays, these concepts are the spirituality of the twenty-first century.

If this church is to be true to itself, if this nation is to prosper, if this world is to survive, feminism is a moral imperative. Feminism is not a heresy; it is the spirit of Jesus written anew. No wonder it threatens the system so much.

The question arises repeatedly: Is it possible for a person to be a feminist and a Christian at the same time? The answer must surely be: How is it possible to be a Christian without being a feminist? This is not an option; it is the fundamental mandate of Christianity. Or to put it another way: Is God inclusive or not?

"Rabbi," the disciples asked, "How is it that the Messiah has not come, neither yesterday nor today? Has the heart of the Messiah changed toward us?"

And the rabbi answered, "The reason the Messiah did not come, neither yesterday nor today, has nothing whatsoever to do with a change of heart in the Messiah. It is because our own hearts are no different today than they were yesterday. For the Messiah to come, it is our hearts that much change."

For the sake of the world, for the sake of the church, you and I must demand otherness. We must refuse to be imprisoned by a one-sided world in a one-minded church. We must change our hearts of stone to hearts of flesh, so that the Messiah who has surely come, may finally, rise again in us.

—*Call to Action*, keynote address,
November 1997

Dangerous Disciple

This is an edited version of a talk given by Sister Joan for the Women's Ordination Worldwide First International Conference held in Dublin, Ireland in 2001. The Vatican sought to prohibit Joan from speaking because they argued her participation in this conference would be a public contradiction of church teaching as laid out in Pope John Paul II's decree, Ordinatio Sacerdotalis. *In this decree, the pope clearly stated that Roman Catholic women would never be ordained to the priesthood, and, moreover, no further public discussion of this issue was allowed. The prioress at the time, Sister Christine Vladimiroff, after extensive dialogue with Joan, Vatican officials, and several other bishops, canonists, Benedictine prioresses, and religious leaders, declined to support the Vatican's request. Sister Christine upheld the tradition of monastic obedience, which is defined as the concept of listening—listening to the community, to the prioress, and to the Word of God. Hence, authority and obedience are discerned in the context of interpersonal and communal dialogue—a fifteen-hundred-year tradition at odds with the Vatican's understanding of obedience. As a result, Joan's Benedictine community voted overwhelmingly to support her response, as a Benedictine, to speak at the conference.*

> *Whenever people discover that they have rights, they have the responsibility to claim them.*
>
> —Pope John XXIII, *Pacem in Terris*

Up at the top of a Mexican mountain, up beyond miles of rutted road and wet, flowing clay, I toured an Indian village that was visited by a priest only once a year. That was years ago. Now the mountain is just as high but the priest is fifteen years older.

Five years ago, I spoke in an American parish of six thousand families—a "mega-church" that is served by three priests. There is no priest shortage there, however, the priests want you to know, because the bishop has redefined the optimum priest-to-people ratio from 1 priest for every 250 families to 1 priest for every 2,000 families.

In diocese after diocese, Catholic parishes are being merged, closed, or served by retired priests or married male deacons designed to keep the church male, whether it is ministering or not. The number of priests is declining, the number of Catholics is increasing, and the number of lay ministers being certified is rising in every academic system, despite the fact that their services are being rejected.

Clearly, the Catholic Church is changing even while it reasserts its changelessness. But static resistance is a far cry from the dynamism of the early church. Prisca, Lydia, Thecla, Phoebe, and hundreds of women like them opened house churches, walked as disciples of Paul, "constrained him," the scripture says, to serve a given region, instructed people in the faith, and ministered to the fledgling Christian communities with no apology, no argument, and no tricky theological shell games about whether they were ministering in persona Christi or in nomini Christi.

So what is to be done at a time like this, when what is being sought and what is possible are two different things? To what are we to give our energy when we are told no energy is wanted?

The answer is discipleship. The fact is that we cannot possibly have a renewed priesthood unless we have a renewed discipleship around us and in us as well. The temptation is to become weary in the apparently fruitless search for office. But the call is to become recommitted to the essential, the ancient, and the authentic demands of discipleship.

Christian discipleship is a very dangerous thing. It is about living in this world the way that Jesus the Christ lived in his— touching lepers, raising donkeys from ditches on Sabbath days, questioning the unquestionable and—consorting with women! Discipleship implies a commitment to leave nets and homes, positions and securities, lordship and legalities to be now—in our own world—what the Christ was for his. Discipleship is prepared to fly in the face of a world bent only on maintaining its own ends whatever the cost.

But to understand the nature of discipleship is not enough. The church must not only preach the Gospel; it must be what it says. It must demonstrate what it teaches. It must be judged by its own standards. The church that preaches the equality of women but does nothing to demonstrate it within its own structures is dangerously close to repeating the theological errors that upheld centuries of church-sanctioned slavery.

The pauperization of women in the name of the sanctity of motherhood flies in the face of the Jesus who overturned tables in the temple, contended with Pilate in the palace, and chastised Peter to put away his sword. Jesus, despite the teaching of that day, cured the woman with the issue of blood and refused to silence the Samaritan woman on whose account, scripture tells us, "thousands believed that day." Indeed, as the life of Jesus shows us, the invisibility of women in the church threatens the very nature of the church itself.

What does the theology of discipleship demand here? What does the theology of a priestly people imply here? Are women simply half a disciple of Christ? To be half-commissioned, half-noticed, and half-valued? If discipleship is reduced to maleness, what does that do to the rest of the Christian dispensation? If only men can really live discipleship to the fullest, what is the use of a woman aspiring to the discipleship that baptism implies, demands, and demonstrates in the life of Jesus at all? What does it mean for the women themselves who are faced with rejection, devaluation, and a debatable theology based on the remnants of a bad biology theologized? What do we do when a church proclaims the equality of women but builds itself on structures that assure their inequality?

The answers are discouragingly clear on all counts. Christian discipleship is not simply in danger of being stunted. Discipleship has, in fact, become the enemy. Who we do not want to admit to full, official, legitimated discipleship—something the church itself teaches is required of us all—has become at least as problematic for the integrity of the church as the exclusion of women from those deliberations of the church that shape its theology and form its people. And therein lies the present challenge of discipleship. Some consider faithfulness to the Gospel to mean doing what we have always done. Others find faithfulness only in being what we have always been. The distinction is crucial to our understanding of tradition. The distinction is also essential to the understanding of discipleship in the modern church. When "the tradition" becomes synonymous with "the system," and maintaining the system becomes more important than maintaining the spirit of the tradition, discipleship shrivels. It becomes at best "obedience" or "fidelity" to the past but not deep-down commitment to the presence of the living Christ confronting the leprosies of the age.

How can a church such as this call convincingly to the world in the name of justice to practice a justice it does not practice itself? How is it that the church can call other institutions to deal with women as full human beings made in the image of God when their humanity is precisely what the church itself holds against them in the name of God?

It is the question that, like slavery, brings the church to the test. For the church to be present to the women's question, to minister to it, to be disciple to it, the church must itself become converted by the issue. Men who do not take the women's issue seriously may be priests but they cannot possibly be disciples. They cannot possibly be "Other Christs." Not the Christ born of a woman. Not the Christ who commissioned women to preach him. Not the Christ who took faculties from a woman at Cana. Not the Christ who sent women to preach resurrection and redemption of the flesh to apostles who would not believe it then and do not believe it now. Not the Christ who sent the Holy Spirit on Mary the woman as well as on Peter the man. Not the Christ who announced his messiahship as clearly to the Samaritan woman as to the rock that shattered.

Thomas Carlyle wrote, "Our main business is not to see what lies dimly in the distance, but to do what lies clearly at hand." A priestly people in a priestless period must keep the ultimate vision clearly in mind. But we must also keep the tasks of the present clearly in mind. The task of the present is not simply preparation for priestly ordination in a church that denies the right even to discuss this festering question of whether or not women can participate in the sacrament of orders. Clearly, preparation for ordination to the priesthood would be premature, at best, if not downright damaging to the Spirit itself in a climate such as this.

No, the task of the present in a time such as this is to use every organization to which we belong to develop the theology of the church to a point of critical mass. The task now is to practice a dangerous discipleship. We need a group free of mandatums that will organize seminars, hold public debates in the style of the great medieval disputations that argued for and against the full humanity of indigenous peoples, hold teach-ins, sponsor publications, write books, post educational websites, and hold more and more gatherings where women speak freely. It is time to bring into the light of day the discussions that lurk behind every church door, in every seeking heart. If, as Vatican II says, priesthood requires preaching, sacrifice, and community building, then proclaiming the coming of a new church, sacrificing ourselves to bring it, and shaping a community new with the notion of a new kind of priest and permanent women deacons may be the greatest priestly service of them all right now.

As John XXIII says in *Pacem in Terris*, "Whenever people discover that they have rights, they have the responsibility to claim them." And a proverb teaches clearly, "If the people will lead, the leaders will eventually follow." Therefore, what must we do now as priestly people? We must take responsibility. We must take back the church. We must lead leaders to the fullness of Christian life!   —*Sojourners Magazine*, January–February 2002

The Bishop Who Said "Sorry"

In 1977, Joseph Bernardin, then archbishop of Cincinnati, was president of the National Conference of Catholic Bishops in the

United States. We went to a lot of meetings together, Bishop Bernardin and I.

One occasion was the twelfth Inter-American Conference of Bishops, a regular gathering. A few "observers" would attend: in this case, one male religious and three women—a Canadian, a Central American, and myself, then president of the Leadership Conference of Women Religious in the United States. The bishops—twenty-six of them—were not a large group, and so the "official observers" were unusually close to the center of the meeting. We all met together at the same table, ate together in the same dining room, prayed together at the beginning and end of every session, and sat in a tight circle in front of the altar for daily Mass together—until the day before the conference ended.

When I came into the large circular arena-like chapel that particular afternoon, no one was sitting in the Mass circle at all. "Joan," the other women stage-whispered to me from the pews that surrounded the altar area, "we're not allowed to sit in the circle anymore. We have to sit back here," they motioned.

I felt the heat rise in my brain. Here I was in a church that never used a feminine pronoun in liturgical prayer, forbade altar girls, and refused women the right to preach even when they had doctorates in theology.

What's more, women were supposed to bear their treatment as secondary members of the church with a docile smile, an unquestioning mind. But this was too much. Now they wanted us to be "observers" at the Mass, as well. So this is what I became.

I moved to the back pews and sat through the entrance procession with my arms folded and my hymn books closed. "Are you going to sit through the Gospel?" the other women whispered.

"There is no Gospel being proclaimed in a situation like this," I said with my jaw set, and sat through the collect and the Gospel and the Communion, as well.

Joe Bernardin gave the homily on this Feast of Corpus Christi. His theme was the priesthood. He talked straight to the bishops but, judging by his furtive glances in our direction, was clearly aware of the women in the back pews. Immediately after the Mass, he headed straight for me.

"Joan," he said, "I told my secretary you wouldn't like the homily."

"Homily?" I spluttered. "What in the holy name of God does the homily have to do with it?"

He stopped. "You aren't upset because of the homily?" he said, incredulous.

"Joe," I said. "I happen to think that women are called to be priests, too, but that doesn't mean that I don't respect and love the priesthood for its own sake."

"Then what are you mad about?" he demanded. "What is it? Come and have a drink with us before dinner."

"Never," I said. "If I can't be at the community table for the Mass, I have no intention whatsoever of going to any other table so that everybody can go on pretending that everything is all right for women in the church."

The conversation was a hard one. "We had been put out of the circle by the bishops," I said.

"You were not," he said. "But I intend to find out just who it was who did it."

I was chagrined. "I'm sorry, Joe," I said. "I jumped to conclusions. We were told that the bishops didn't want us with them and I believed it. I apologize. It's not necessary to do anything. We'll just forget it."

"Oh, no, we won't," he said as he guided me down the hall to cocktails and dinner.

The next morning, before the opening of the final session, the bishops of North America and South America made a public apology for the exclusion of women from the closing Mass of the week. A zealous sacristan, for whom Vatican II and women in the church were still at best a rumor, had made a judgment and been corrected for it.

I WAS impressed. But it wasn't over yet. That afternoon, we departed via the small airport in Medellín, Colombia. As we waited in a long line for the security checks, I realized that the women further up the queue had suddenly veered to the right. I stopped for a second.

Up ahead, two signs marked separate stations. The one to the left said, "Hombres." The one to the right said, "Damas."

Suddenly, I heard a call from the top of the line. "Joan! Jooooooannn!"

There was Joseph Bernardin at the head of the row, head back, pointing up at the male-female placards and laughing. "Joan!" he shouted for all the bishops of the Americas to hear. "I just want you to know that I didn't have a thing to do with this!"

I laughed all the way to the plane—a little more wryly than he, perhaps.

Last year at Cambridge, when I heard about his death, memories of the laughter came through tears. Who is left who will apologize now?   —*The Tablet* (London), January 18, 1997

Loss

The Book of Ruth begins in tragedy. Three women are left with three dead husbands and no means of support. It is a crossover moment in time. It is the moment that leads these women—and we ourselves, perhaps—to God's new time.

Like everyone ever born who goes through sudden, defining loss of any kind, these women find themselves faced with the question: Who am I when I am no longer who and what I was? Like the rest of us for whom the very foundations of our lives are given to shifting from day to day, there are no miracles in sight to save them, no angels on the road to point the way. Nothing. Everything they had, everything they ever thought they wanted, is gone. There are no anchors to steady them, no safety nets to catch them. Now they have only themselves on which to depend. Only the Spirit of God to lead them on through a world that has little place for them at all.

Women everywhere know the feeling, have felt the helplessness that attends abandonment and marginalization. Women know what it's like to be the eternal outsider looking in. Women know the sense of powerlessness that comes from being only a woman in a world shaped primarily for men. What can possibly be the will of God for a woman at a time like this? What does God have in mind for women when it seems that the world has little or nothing in mind for women at all—once motherhood ends, or there is no man to support them, or there is no institution to define them, or there is no one and nothing whose need legitimates their existence? In the Book of Ruth, God takes a stand on the side of the woman alone in the world. In the Book of Ruth, God pronounces her whole and capable of her own direction.

There is a difference between great misfortune and great loss. Misfortune is a temporary detour through a jungle of opportunities. It is a case of "If not this, then that." "If I can't get to medical school, then I'll be a lawyer." "If I can't own a farm, I'll work on one." When my young father died, my twenty-one-year-old mother had nowhere to go, no professional education to fall back on, no place in the circle of men who did the hiring, opened the businesses, controlled the credit in town. Institutions did not invest in women. Thirty years later when her second husband, my stepfather, died as well, little had really changed. She still had few options. She was still a woman in a society of male organizations. She still had only what his job enabled him to leave her to live on. Today, over half the national workforce are women, but over 80 percent of them are employed only in the service industries, where wages are low and benefits are nil. If women earned what men earn, current studies show, the national poverty rate would be cut in half. For these women, too, losing the men in their lives is still to be left on the brink of destitution.

Clearly, women left to fend for themselves in this world even today do not have great "misfortunes"; they have life-changing losses. God, it seems, leads them down dark roads from which there is no dignified egress, little hope of earthly salvation. But God, the Book of Ruth is clear, has more in mind for them than that.

Loss, any kind of loss—rejection, abandonment, divorce, death—is a shocking, numbing, gray thing that at the outset, at least, freezes the heart and slows the mind. Loss changes life at the root. Irrevocably. What was once the center of life—the person, the position, the plan, the lifestyle—is no more. What shaped our identities, what fashioned our days and filled our sleep, what gave us meaning and direction, comfort and support, has disappeared like sunset on a cloudless night. And with the loss, time stands still; thought stops in mid-configuration. Life is never the same again. What we have known, almost unconsciously, often for years, to be good—to be at least familiar, sure, certain—is gone, snatched away without warning. Vanished, and without our permission. Withdrawn, and with nothing in its place.

For no acceptable reason, loss destabilizes even the most sophisticated of us, spilling us off the carousel of commonplaces we thought would never end. With little warning, with less compensation, we find ourselves left to cope with an abandoned pattern of happy yesterdays left spinning in a blur of bleak tomorrows.

It is the habitual that dies with every death, the comfortable that dissolves with every ebb and loss of the familiar. What we took for granted, what has been the unquestioned gravity of our existence, shifts and tilts and weakens. Emptiness becomes our new companion, God more a rumor than a fact. Even our spiritual certainties can fade a little: Where is God now when our world is tilting and tipping and we are left in a sea of disorientation?

To be left without the mainstay of a life is to be plunged into questioning the rest of it. To what end is life without this position, this support, this thing, this person? To what purpose is a future that has no living past? The tomorrow that, once a given, now has no design? The hope that has gone to dust, the prospect turned to mist? What can possibly be left to live for, even though, for whatever reason, live we must? Where is the will of God for us in loss?

And yet loss, once reckoned, once absorbed, is a precious gift. No, I cannot be what I was before but I can be—I must be—something new. There is more of God in me, I discover in emptiness, than I have ever known in what I once took to be fullness.

There are spiritual lessons to be learned from loss that can be barely divined by any other means and often despite ourselves. We learn, just when we think we have nothing, just when it feels that we have not one good thing left in the world, that what we do still have is ourselves. We have, deep down inside us, what no one can take away, what can never be lost either to time or to chance: We have the self that brought us to this point—and more. We have gifts of God in abundance, never noticed, never touched, perhaps, but a breath in us nevertheless and waiting to be tapped. And more, whatever we have developed over the years in the center of ourselves—the grit, the hope, the calm, the bottomless, pulsating, irrepressible trust in the providence of God despite the turns of fortune—is here now to be mined like gold, scratched out and melted down, shaped and shined into a whole new life. We have within us the raw material of life. And we have it for the taking.

For most women anywhere, even now in fact, loss takes on a special character. Women the world over have limited control of the world around them. They are commonly at the mercy of the social mores in which they live. They ordinarily have access to fewer resources, either economic or political. They bear more rigid role definitions. They have fewer options because less money always means fewer options. In Naomi we see clearly that, if Creation goes on creating in us all our lives, then the function of loss is to bring us all back to the completion of ourselves just when it seems that there is nothing left in us to develop. No one is one thing only. We are all a medley of possible beginnings, all of them straining toward fulfillment. The pain of loss lies in the fact that we so seldom realize the fullness of ourselves until the rest of life lies open in the ashes of the past. When loss finally happens, as loss inevitably will, then we get the opportunity to say either yes or no to the other parts of creation in ourselves.

—*The Story of Ruth*

Litany of Women for the Church

Dear God, creator of women in your own image
born of a woman in the midst of a world half women,
carried by women to mission fields around the globe,
made known by women to all the children of the earth,
give to the women of our time,
the strength to persevere,
the courage to speak out,
the faith to believe in you beyond
all systems and institutions,
so that your face on earth may be seen in all its beauty,
so that men and women become whole,
so that the church may be converted to your will
in everything and in all ways.

We call on the holy women
who went before us,
channels of Your Word
in testaments old and new,
to intercede for us
so that we might be given the grace
to become what they have been
for the honor and glory of God.

Saint Esther, who pleaded against power
for the liberation of the people; —*Pray for us.*
Saint Judith, who routed the plans of men
and saved the community;
Saint Deborah, laywoman and judge,
who led the people of God;
Saint Elizabeth of Judea, who recognized
the value of another woman;
Saint Mary Magdalene, minister of Jesus,
first evangelist of the Christ;
Saint Scholastica, who taught her brother Benedict
to honor the spirit above the system;

Saint Hildegard, who suffered interdict
for the doing of right;
Saint Joan of Arc, who put no law above the law of God;
Saint Clare of Assisi, who confronted the pope
with the image of woman as equal;
Saint Julian of Norwich, who proclaimed for all of us
the motherhood of God;
Saint Thérèse of Lisieux, who knew the call
to priesthood in herself;
Saint Catherine of Siena, to whom the pope listened;
Saint Teresa of Avila, who brought women's gifts
to the reform of the church;
Saint Edith Stein, who brought fearlessness to faith;
Saint Elizabeth Seton, who broke down boundaries
between lay women and religious;
by wedding motherhood and religious life;
Saint Dorothy Day, who led the church
to a new sense of justice;
Mary, mother of Jesus,
who heard the call of God and answered;
Mary, mother of Jesus,
who drew strength from the woman Elizabeth;
Mary, mother of Jesus,
who underwent hardship bearing Christ;
Mary, mother of Jesus, who ministered at Cana;
Mary, mother of Jesus, inspirited at Pentecost;
Mary, mother of Jesus, who turned the Spirit of God
into the body and blood of Christ, pray for us. Amen.
                                                    —Benetvision

4

A FINAL WORD

This is the culminating piece that Sister Joan wrote as an after-word in a collection of essays published in 2001 to celebrate Joan as she turned sixty-five. In academic circles the presenta-tion of such a volume is a singular tribute to someone whose exceptional intellectual, artistic and spiritual contributions have uniquely impacted the academy and the wider world. The key question all contributors to the volume addressed was "What do you think is the most important spiritual ques-tion of our time?" Here Joan, first, affirms the very process of questioning and, second, reveals how doing so shaped her own spiritual and intellectual journey as a woman, a Catholic, and a Benedictine.

Almost twenty-five hundred years ago, the philosopher Plato wrote one of the most commonly cited dictums in the English language. "The unexamined life," he said, "is not worth living." Here, clearly, is an insight that the world knows to be impor-tant. It carries a truth—a challenge—that clings like a tick to the human soul. And yet it takes years to understand it completely, perhaps. The longer I live, the more convinced I become of the fundamental truth of it, the more I wonder at the same time how many people really—consciously—rummage the ground, search out the underpinnings of the lives they lead. After all, it's a dan-gerous process.

There is something very frightening about looking at the tru-isms of our lives and wondering how true they really are. To examine what is and find it wanting could threaten the boggy shoals on which we stand. The tidal wave called Truth could sweep in, then, and wash it all away. What if I look and find that there are tiny little fissures, obscure little lacunae in the systems on which I have staked my life? I heard of a woman who, finding herself drifting toward the middle of a dangerously feminist conversation, stopped the group around her in the midst of the process. "I don't want to hear any more about any of this," she said, "because if I did, I would have to change my life." A wise woman. It is always so much easier to assuage pain than it is to cure it, so much easier to accept a thing than it is to question it.

This reflection is dedicated to the questions that brought me to this one. It is an exercise in the power of questions. It recognizes the necessity of questions to test the truth of our own lives. Without experience in a culture of questions we become the pawns of every period, however noble, however muffling of the human spirit it may be. Just because a thing does not seem to need to be questioned does not make the question ignoble.

The ability—the commitment—to question, to examine, every aspect of the human journey is the only form of fidelity worth the price of admission to this sojourn called life. Otherwise, no sector of the social anatomy to which we swear emotional allegiance can trust us to serve it well. It is the questions we ask that move us from stage to stage of our growing, that take us from level to level of our thoughts, however simple the questions may seem. I have just realized, in fact, how boring my own questions have been over the years: Do non-Catholics go to heaven? Is sin the center of life? Or to put it another way, what is a "good" life? Does what we give up in life make for more holiness than what we do? Is religious life incarnational or transcendent? Don't we really need to be violent sometimes? What is a woman? Can a woman be Catholic? (No mention, you notice, of birth control, which also had a lot to do with radicalizing me, or divorce, which I have always believed in, even when it was a sin, and "the role of women in the home," which I knew was wrong by the time I was five.) And yet, without those questions there was no coming beyond the naïve simplicity of all the early answers to them: Only Catholics go to heaven. Sins are the things against the law, and the purpose of life is to avoid them. Good things are bad for you. Or—the second version—really good people give up good things. Religious life requires separation from "the world." The Crusades and Vietnam were noble ventures fought to make the world safe for Christianity. Woman is man's help-mate. The reason women can't minister to the people of God sacramentally is because God wants it that way.

It was an age of absolute certainty in the face of growing complexities. It was an age that absolutely dismissed questions. It was an age that needed questions badly, but had been forbidden to ask them.

We each have our own personal set of questions. For those of us who lived the greater part of the twentieth century—during the wars, before and after Vatican II, in the midst of the second wave of the women's movement—maybe the questions I find so mundane today were common ones. Maybe they were quite different from the ones asked by the people around me. But whatever the ilk of them, the process of writing them out—like this—is a humbling experience. It exposes the level of inquiry with which a life has been consumed. It also unmasks the questions behind the questions that agitate the very pilings of the world around me.

At the same time, it is a worthwhile excursion into the soul to look at the questions that have shaped our lives and ask what it was about them that intrigued us in the first place, that changed us as we dealt with them, that brought me, as a result of them, to be the person that I am today. After all, it is only in the light of our past that we understand the present with which we grapple as well the future toward which we strive.

But questions never exist in a vacuum. Or at least they never get answered in one. They happen when Galileo finds himself fascinated by these particular swinging lampstands in this particular church and then begins to time them by his own pulse rate. They happen when Columbus comes ashore on the wrong island in the wrong sea. They happen when something vital founders in our own lives. My own questions of the last half of the twentieth century did not come out of textbooks. They came out of the protean pieces of what was otherwise a quite ordinary paradigm: I was Irish Roman Catholic, woman, religious. Those were the filters through which I saw my world. The questions that emerged out of each of them were, by any means of measure, few. But they changed me completely.

What Kind of God Is This?

My Irish Catholic mother was a very young widow when she remarried. I was five years old. Dutch Chittister, my new father, had been raised Presbyterian, but churchgoing had had little meaning to him. He liked to show me the small Bible he'd been awarded for perfect Sunday school attendance, of course, but I never saw him read it and I never, ever heard him talk about anything in it. He went to the local parish priest for marriage preparation discussions as a concession to my mother, but the thought of his continuing with instructions in the faith was not out of the question. He was, after all, not intensely committed to any tradition and "mixed" marriages were not anyone's definition of the ideal relationship.

Father O'Connell, the parish priest, was the stern, dogmatic type. No foolishness allowed. Instructions were basic and direct. You either believed or you didn't. "To be saved," he taught, "it is necessary to be Catholic." My new father seemed suddenly alert. "Wait a minute," he paused the process. "Are you saying that my mother didn't go to heaven when she died?" Father O'Connell pushed the pamphlet across the table. "You can read," he said. "Read it yourself." My mother, years later, was still saying that it might not have been nearly so bad if the priest had just not shoved the pamphlet so hard. Dutch got up out of his chair, suddenly, harshly. His face burned red. "You're completely mad," he said tautly. "I'm leaving this place." Then he looked at my mother. "Make up your mind: Are you leaving with me or staying with him?" She reached out and picked up her coat. They never talked about his taking instructions again and our family life changed drastically from what it might have been.

Somehow or other, the two of them figured out how to negotiate the problem, but the question stayed with me forever. What was at stake here? His salvation? My grandmother's salvation? Yes, but far more than that. What was really at stake was the kind of God who would create a world full of people who had come thousands of years before Christ and thousands of years after Christ and decree that belief in Christ was essential to their souls. What was at stake was the fact that these people, too, were religious, were good, were holy. What was at stake was faith in a God who would create a world in order to damn the greater part of its inhabitants through no fault of their own.

I had two problems. The first was that I simply could not believe in a sadistic God. The second was that so much evil had been done in the name of conversion to the true faith—starting in the great religious conversion campaigns and ending, for me as a small child, in that rectory. In the final analysis, I found it harder to believe in a hierarchical heaven, where some people are "higher" than other people than I did to believe that everyone is meant to enjoy whatever heaven itself might be. But how is it possible to deal with such problems when the law of your life says otherwise? It took a while.

I spent years awash in values that made the parochial the ultimate. But after years of *lectio*, years of immersion in scripture, years of a monasticism that predated the divisions in the church and so was naturally ecumenical, what finally saved me from a faith too small was the memory of the Jesus who talked to Canaanite women and sent Samaritans to speak his name to a different people in a different way. There was, I came to see, no mention in scripture that the Samaritans who came to believe in him became Jews. Like my father, they stayed Samaritan, it seemed.

The question of heaven, of God, of truth led me to realize that if God is truly a creating God, a loving God, we all have a special role in God's design. I began to seek out what there was to learn, to appreciate God in each religion around me and, eventually, in every religion everywhere. Vatican II, with its insight that we were to respect "all that was good and true" in non-Christian religions, brought me beyond Father O'Connell to the center of my own soul, where the God of creation waited to give me into the embrace of the entire world, to teach me a more total truth. I came to realize that the more I learned about differences in all things, the more I would understand myself in all my weaknesses, all my strengths. As the years went by and I began to work with Buddhists and meet Bahai and talk with Muslims, I also began to recognize the fact that coming from a "mixed" marriage—a marriage where truth came in different designs—was one of the graces of my life.

Is Sin the Center of Life?

Everyone in the novitiate was near the same age, most of us just out of high school, some of us not yet graduated. The early days in the convent were a panoply of interesting things: veils to adjust and office books to mark, stiff ways to walk and new ways to eat, silence to keep and books to read. There was only one major problem: When the confessor came every Wednesday, no one in the novitiate wanted to go. When I couldn't avoid the situation anymore, I simply remember saying to the priest, "Bless me, Father, for I have sinned—but to tell you the truth I haven't been here long enough to do anything." I heard him shift in the box. I shifted, too. The whole context of sin had changed for me. Was it really "sin" to break silence, or eat between meals, or speak to people on the street, or keep a gift box of candy rather than hand it in to the novice mistress? Each week we "spoke fault" for being human: for spilling things, walking heavily, eating between meals. I admit that I never really repented any of them, but I became more and more aware of the weakness of the self and less and less aware of its glory. Life was one long slippery slope away from God.

Sin had become the center of a life that the presence of God was supposed to occupy. What we did—the silly, schoolgirl peccadilloes—became the focus of the spiritual life. I heard Fulton Sheen say once, "My fear for the religious of the church is that they will be fit only for the sandboxes of heaven." It was a chilling thought. It was also a very real one.

The Korean War, McCarthyism, trade union problems came and went, but we knew very little about them because reading newspapers was forbidden. Someone was making sure that "worldliness" would not creep into us. As a result, nothing crept in that was touching the lives of the world around us—not the deep political tensions, not the great atomic questions, not the first soundings of the racial divide, not the tentacles of militarism that were strengthening their choke hold on U.S. society. We were oblivious to it all. We said not a word as a community about any of it.

All the time we worried about sin we had lost a sense of what it really was. We had managed to confuse the moral, the immoral, and the amoral. We were learning, literally, to be good for nothing. Religious life, however well-intentioned, had become little more than a relic of the proclamations of Palestine, the memory of martyrdoms no longer tolerated, a mental construct of great gospel valor without a skeleton to hang it on.

When Pope John XXIII talked about "the signs of the times"— poverty, nuclearism, sexism—I began to read these new signs with a new conscience and with a new sense of religious life in mind. Most of all, I began to read scripture through another lens. Who was this Jesus who "consorted with sinners" and cured on the Sabbath? Most of all, who was I who purported to be following him while police dogs snarled at black children and I made sure not to be late for prayer or leave my monastery after dark? What was "the prophetic dimension" of the church supposed to be about if not the concerns of the prophets—the widows, the orphans, the foreigners and the broken, vulnerable, of every society?

We prayed the Psalms five times a day for years, but I had failed to hear them. What I heard in those early years of religious life was the need to pray. I forgot to hear what I was praying. Then, one day I realized just how secular the psalmist was in comparison to the religious standards in which I had been raised: "You, O God, do see trouble and grief. . . . You are the helper of the weak," the psalmist argues. No talk of fuzzy, warm religion here. This was life raw and hard. This was what God called to account (Psalm 10:14). This was sin.

When the Latin American bishops talked about a "fundamental option for the poor," I began to see the poor in our inner-city neighborhood for the first time. When Rosa Parks and Martin Luther King Jr. finally stood up in Birmingham, Alabama, I stood up, too. I was ready now. Like the blind man of Mark's Gospel, I could finally see. The old question had been answered. The sin to be repented, amended, eradicated was the great systemic sin against God's little ones. For that kind of sin, in my silence, I had become deeply guilty.

I had new questions then but they were far more energizing than the ones before them. I began to look more closely at what "living a good life" could possibly mean in a world that was so full of suffering, so full of greed.

I began to realize that "a good life" had something to do with making life good for other people. Slowly, slowly I began to arrive at the oldest Catholic truth of them all: All of life is good and that sanctity does not consist in denying that. Sanctity consists in making life good for everyone whose life we touch.

The question, "What is sin?" had changed my life completely. I came to understand that selfishness, self-centeredness, and the kind of self-indulgence that is bought at the expense of the other was the real essence of sin. The private little wrestling matches, the pitfalls that come and go with the process of personal development, were all part of all our secret struggles to resist the predisposition to sin that is part of being human. Those were all part of my growing up process, yes, but it was not of the real essence of either sin or sanctity. Sanctity had far more to do with building up the reign of God here and now for everyone. All the saints were "sinners" in the narcissistic sense of the word. But all the saints were also those who overturned tables in every temple of every system in which exploiting the little ones of the world was one of the givens of the social game. Since God lives in us all, the destruction of the other has got to be a sin against God.

I had discovered that life was for the living and that to live a good life meant that we had to live it in such a way that we made it even better for everyone else.

What Is Holy Violence?

I was a graduate student at Penn State when the word came. A young cousin, Norman Chittister, had been killed in Vietnam just before his twenty-first birthday and two weeks away from being discharged. He would have been best man at his best friend's marriage one week later. Instead, he would be buried in the family plot at the end of the week. He was an only child. I was on my way to the funeral.

The Vietnam War was raging all around me on the campus at the time. Young men who were in class one week had left the country for Canada by the next in order to escape the draft. I never took part in any demonstrations, but I watched mystified as the silent candle light parades passed nightly down College Avenue under my dormitory window. Students disrupted classes, streaked naked across lecture halls carrying anti-war slogans, smoked marijuana, and dyed their long hair green, as if all the moral standards they'd been given had simply come to boil, gone to pus, and erupted all over the generation before them that had concentrated on private piety but failed to recognize public sin. What was happening to patriotism? To obedience? To the defense of democracy? I passed through the main gates of the university every day—on my way to class, of course—as they read the names of the war dead in one unending monotone day and night, day and night, day and night for weeks. I was getting my doctorate. I had no time for the political rebellion of naturally rebellious youth.

I was also a child of World War II, the "good war," the war between the forces of freedom and a ruthless, genocidal dictator. We had won a "holy war." We were the Messianic people, the City on the Hill, the New Jerusalem. We had saved the world for democracy and were now girding to repel atheistic communism, as well, something every Catholic child dreaded far more than we did Hitler. Hitler would make us Germans, yes, but communism would make us godless.

At the funeral parlor with the family, I searched for words of comfort for a grieving aunt and uncle. I stood at the coffin and gave myself all the old answers, but none of them worked.

Soon after Norman's funeral, elsewhere in the United States, soldiers shot into a crowd of American students on an American campus, while babies ran through the streets of Vietnam aflame in napalm, and one of my best friends, a young nun, was arrested for being part of a sit-in at one of the companies that supplied the chemicals. The questions stirred in my heart and no amount of patriotism, of "obedience," could quiet them. The questions grated against a part of the human soul that I had never before realized I had.

We had become what we hated. And we were prepared to do it again. "Mutually assured destruction," the commitment to a nuclear first strike if we ourselves feared being struck—to destroy first what might destroy us—was the order of the day. It was called a "deterrent," but it had already started to kill people everywhere, even here, by virtue of the funds it took away from education and medicine and housing and food.

I questioned the value of the war; I questioned the effectiveness of violence; I questioned the integrity of the country; I questioned the theology of the church. Most of all, I remembered the Jesus who told Peter to put away his sword and went to his death killing no one on the way.

Life became a nightmare of contradictions. Prayer became a searing truth. How was it possible to "love your enemies" and then set out consciously, designedly, to annihilate them? "We had to destroy this village in order to save it," the papers quoted a commander as saying by way of explanation for the rout of civilian rice growers in the Asian farmland. I struggled between the church of the martyrs and the church of the crusaders. Violence was clearly not the road to love. Violence was clearly not the way of Jesus. Where were we as a church in the middle of this? How could we teach one thing and say not a public word about the other on the pretext of the separation of church and state? Is that what silenced us during the Holocaust, too? How could any of this be "holy"?

Exhausted by the spiritual wrenching that came with having lived through a "good war" and now watching as we ourselves conducted an evil one, I became part of a Christian peace movement that challenged the continuing viability of any theory of a just war in a world where disproportionality was now official government policy and discrimination in targeting a theological joke. The questions simply would not, could not, quit in me. The personal effects of the spiritual scuffle were cataclysmic for me.

Once a very standard-brand U.S. Roman Catholic, I now found myself inside some new circles and outside some old ones. I was suddenly considered "radical" to most, "communist" to some, at best "misguided" to many, including priests who previously had called me "a good sister." But there was no turning back. The gentle Jesus of my daily prayer was far too clear to be ignored at a time of social convenience. I found myself certain that, though conflict resolution might not be able to guarantee peace, violence certainly could not. And after Selma and South Africa, Kosovo and Bosnia, I knew that my questions had brought me to a whole new place in both church and state. Violence launched for the sake of political ends was a sin. It lurked under false pretenses of honor and righteousness but it was evil. And the seed of it lived in my own soul or no government would ever be able to tap it there so easily for the sake of its crusades and inquisitions and carpet bombings and ethnic cleansings and genocides.

Systemic violence was not holy, and I could not support any country that was doing it, not even my own; and further, scripture showed me quite clearly, never, ever, could I give such support in the name of Jesus.

What Is a Woman?

I grew up on stories. Every night my mother and father took turns telling me a bedtime story. I was in fourth grade before the process finally tapered off to a halt and I began reading my own. But over the years, I had developed a list of favorites out of the repertoire which I requested over and over again. In one of them my mother told the story of the only black family in the small, all-white Pennsylvania hill town in which she grew up. My entire family, including my grandfather, was quarantined because one of the many children had some kind of childhood disease. No one could go out and no one could come in. It was a desperate time. With no money to count on and grandfather's job in jeopardy if he didn't return to it quickly, grandma was scrimping on everything. His was the only income, the only support.

Then one day, Mamie Galloway, the black woman from the other side of the dam and the mother of a large family herself, who seldom, if ever, ventured into town, showed up on Donegal Hill in front of our house. She was carrying a basket. "Come out, madam," she shouted to my grandmother, who was watching from the front window. "I'll roll these eggs down the porch one at a time. You catch them carefully." Mamie Galloway kept a garden and raised chickens. "Where did she get those chickens?" I asked myself again and again as I listened to the story. The white man's business and labor problems meant nothing to her. Mamie Galloway supported herself.

Every day for the duration of the quarantine, Mamie Galloway came with a dozen eggs and rolled them down the porch to grandma and never charged a penny. "And that, Joan," my mother always said at the end of the story, "means that prejudice is wrong. Everyone is good and everyone is capable. You must always accept everyone. And you must always do your best whether people accept you or not." It was a story about prejudice, true. But only on one level. How to account for Mamie Galloway herself was my problem.

I learned early that some people, whatever their talents, whatever their goodness, ranked lower than other people in life. I discovered that "Irish need not apply," that there were "black water fountains" and "white lunch counters." And I learned it was wrong. But it took me awhile to realize that I was one of them.

My mother, undereducated and dependent all her life, trained me fiercely for independence. What she could not have, she wanted for me. I got no speeches about "women's role" and "women's place" from her. Instead, I got a vision and a direction. I was to study hard so that I could "take care of myself." I was to realize that I could do "anything I set my mind to." I was to understand that I was a person first, and possibly, but not necessarily, a mother as well.

But it was a schizophrenic situation. At home, I was geared for equality. I went fishing with my father, laid a roof or two, helped plan the family budget and, in the idiom of the time, studied hard to "get ahead." But in the world around me, I was only a girl. And girls did not get ahead, my mother my own best proof of that. Boys led the band. Boys played sports. Boys became doctors. Boys made the money. Boys traveled. Boys became politicians. Boys had clubs and businesses and fishing trips and adventures. Boys did it all. And whatever the talents of a girl, eventually she put them all down to be "a woman."

Suppressing part of the human community for the sake of its other parts was not a new trick. But everywhere men controlled the system and everywhere men taught other men that such was the way it should be. When other races, peoples, nations were freed, women were never completely freed. What they got to do in society, if they got to do much at all, they did by virtue of concession or necessity, not by reason of human right. Women were allowed to get jobs because there weren't enough men there to take them. Women were allowed to school because men needed educated women to support their industries. Women, for the most part, were relegated to the home because raising children "was the most important thing a person could do in life." But if it was really so important, why weren't men doing their share of it?

The question I grew up with in the center of my soul was, Why all this? Why this diminishment of women? Unfortunately, the question has not really changed. Today, women are still being beaten, enslaved, raped, murdered, and married into intolerable degradation simply because they are women. The woman who does not deal with the women's question, if not for herself, for women everywhere, has yet, I came to understand, to really become a woman. But she does not know it.

These questions were my questions. Either I had to deal with them or know that my life had failed—not only my own life, my mother's, and my grandmother's, but all the daughters of all our days. It was my life or theirs, and since the questions were mine, the answer was obvious. I simply did not anymore believe in the natural inferiority of women, whatever the male theology of depreciation taught me to revere about men and reject about me. What we had was the social diminishment of one half the human race for the sake of the other and yet, ironically, to the peril of them both. The God who would create half of humanity to be half as good as the other half, half as whole as the other half, is a teasing, taunting bully. Not my God. Not the God who created all humanity as "bone of my bone, flesh of my flesh, somebody just like me." Not the God who looked at humanity and said, "That's good." Not "some" are good. Or some are "half good." I must believe, then, that women are really fully human, human beings. And, to be true to the theology of creation, I must contest any system that teaches otherwise.

Can a Woman Be Catholic?

The question of the place of women in the church did not emerge for me with the advent of Gloria Steinem and Simone de Beauvoir. The truth is that, at that time, I had yet to read either of them. No, I had confronted the issue years before they came along to tell me that I'd been right all along about my concerns. One of my cousins was the bishop's pageboy. I wasn't even allowed on the altar, unless, of course, I was cleaning the church floor on Saturday. Sister ran the school, but Father had the last word about everything we did. Women put on all the church parties, but men were the ushers and wore the great plumed hats and marched in the processions and carried the candles and crosses and canopy that covered the Blessed Sacrament as the priest carried it down the aisle. Men were in the church; women were in the church hall. I knew early on in life that there was a problem. A serious one. But no one said so out loud.

In regard to men and women, the church was no different from the rest of the world, and that was the problem. In the church, I expected to see a model of the reign of God, a template of the way things would be in heaven, a sign of the way God wanted things to be on earth. Instead they told me that God was the problem. God had made women but clearly did not want to traffic with women directly—to wit, the Bible stories they read to us about Abraham and Moses and David and the apostles. No mention of the angel who came to announce that Sarah was to be blessed outside the natural order of things. Not a word about the exploits and contributions to the economy of salvation in Judith or Deborah or Esther or Naomi or Ruth. No talk of Martha's messianic proclamation, only Peter's. No notice that the rabbi taught theology to a woman at the Samaritan well. No awareness that Mary was treated as a free agent in the birth of Christ. No memory of the women at the foot of the cross, at the announcement of the empty tomb to the men who should have been there. No understanding that the church took root in house churches started and presided over by women. They gave us half a scripture, half a history, half a worldview, and told us that it was all there was.

Indeed, it was a bare and sterile church for you if you were a girl. Even most of the sisters, the only image I had of a woman doing church, took the names of male saints. And why not, when 75 percent of the canonized saints of the church were men? The message was clear: the church was a male preserve. Eucharist was the acme of the faith and the sacraments were required of both women and men, of course, but women could not expect to have either Eucharist or sacraments unless there was a man around who was willing provide it for them. Clearly, there was a pale, even in the church, and women were outside of it.

Slowly, slowly I began to ask myself a different question: Could a woman really be a Catholic at all? The fullness of the faith was surely not meant for us. And that, according to Roman catechesis, was because God wanted it that way, and much as they might like, they could not do otherwise. So surely God, too, does not really want us. Not really. Not completely. So why would a woman be there?

The answer came out of the stuff of the question itself: God. I no more believed that God made women half human, half capable of grace, half available to the divine than I believed that no one else except Catholics went to heaven or that those who were not white were not fully human or that we could perpetrate whatever violence we chose on anyone else we named lesser than ourselves and call it holy. I did not believe in a God who created half the human race in order to reject it.

Until the church answers the women's question in a way that makes the Gospel real and all of humanity human, the integrity of its sacraments, its theology and its structures are all at stake. It is the question that will not go away, for it makes every other dimension of the faith either true or false. Either baptism makes new people of us all or it does not. Either we are all receptacles of grace or we are not. Either incarnation redeems all of us or it does not. Either what the church teaches about the redemption of the flesh—all flesh—female as well as male—in Jesus is true or it is false. Either Jesus became flesh or he became only male. Either we are all responsible for the deposit of faith or we are not.

When the women's movement emerged from the hibernation caused by the gain of the vote, women with questions were standing there waiting for it. When Pope John XXIII named feminism as one of the signs of the times, and a church that had forever denied women found itself with the biggest women's question of them all, women were standing there waiting for the church, which had taught them the answer to their own question, to make real a theology that until now had been only theoretical. We were all waiting all our lives, whether we realized it consciously or not. And we are waiting still. I among them.

Some New Questions

A series of things has happened that raised another question in me. The first happened long ago, gestated for years and is only now becoming plain in its implications. One of my most long-standing memories of the wrestling match between reason and feeling came as a young nun, when reason (the objective adherence to the rules of the game) reigned and feeling (the error of the particular) was a failure to be avoided if a person was to be truly strong, truly holy. When the telephone rang in the local priory that day, none of us was prepared for the response to it.

The mother of Eileen Condon, a seventeen-year-old junior in the local parochial school, had just been found dead on her kitchen floor. There was one other girl in the family, a younger Down's Syndrome child, and no father. A sad and shocking situation, surely, but no immediate concern of ours. After all, we were nuns. In our commitment to separation from the world, we didn't go into people's homes. Good nuns stayed in their convents, kept the rule, and prayed.

I saw her get up from the community room table and go to the shawl cupboard. "I don't know when I'll be back," she said. The superior sat at the head of the table. "Where are you going, Sister Lois Marie?" she asked. "To the Condon's," Lois said, adjusting her shawl. "You can't do that without permission," the superior said. "I'll call Erie and ask Mother Alice if it's all right for you to go." By this time, Lois was on her way down the hall. "Fine," she called back. "You call if you want to, but I'm going over there regardless. I do not intend to leave that child alone." I heard the back door close and felt my stomach lurch. How could she possibly do that? I asked myself. As the years went by I knew that the real question was, How could the rest of us not? The answer to that question has become more and more clear as the years have gone by. We, as a culture, have repressed feeling to the point where law supersedes love and people without feelings make the laws. We act as if a world that operates without feeling can possibly live a higher law.

The second impetus in my quest for a resolution of the tension between reason and feeling came with the statement of Pope John Paul II that women had "a special vocation" for which they were uniquely fitted. I resented the comment at the time as simply another way of saying that the purpose of women was primarily and solely to bear children, despite the fact that even those who do, do so for only a very small portion of their lives. But I have begun to think other of the insight now. I have begun to see how dearly we need in society what we have suppressed in our idolization of a male culture and the value system it spawns. We train young people to sit at the bottom of nuclear missile silos and, when the light goes to green, to press the buttons that will annihilate the world without ever seeing the faces of their enemies. We abstract feeling from the rationality of war and do grossly irrational things as a result. We plot economy in terms of profit figures and have no feeling for the pain, the starvation, caused by our "cyclical corrections." We "downsize" our businesses with no care for the feelings of the long-time workers whose lives are ruined by them. We put no faces on our graphs. We allow no feelings to affect the figures we use to chart our growth curves. We abstract feeling from decision-making and call ourselves "objective." We equate feelings with women and so diminish both.

It defrauds the human spirit, this lack of regard for the feelings of those who suffer and the feelings of those who feel for them. It is a signal of the depth and gravity of the spiritual question that is even now looming on the horizon of the human soul. The fact is that we have gone as far as rationality will take us.

Rationality and the power to enforce it gave us the encomienda system, slavery, segregation, sexism, religious intolerance, nuclearism and ecological ruin. It has drained the soul of feeling for the truly human, human concerns.

The papal statement is surely correct, however inadequate the present response to such an obvious truth. Women do have something to bring to the world that the world has too long eschewed. Women are expected to provide feeling in the private arena but denied the right to bring it to the public arena, where it is so obviously missing. Blamed for being "irrational" and "too emotional," they may be the only hope we have to redeem rationality and bring the grace of feeling to the ruthlessness of pure thought. They may be all we have left that can once again show us, men and women alike, what it is to be fully human. If feeling is not affirmed in women and released in men, if reason is not tempered by feeling in men and brought to wholeness in women, we all are surely doomed spiritually.

More than that, if reason and feeling are not soon balanced in the public arenas of our world, in congresses and consistories alike, we may also be doomed physically. We must now begin to integrate reason and feeling, or we confine ourselves to the paucity of the human mind and the sterility of the soul that comes with the denial of sensitivities. We have taken the objective, the emotionless, the pragmatic, the powerful to the ultimate. We have wrung the human soul dry of the kind of thinking that feeling brings.

Consequently, we face the question now of the tension between the catechetical and the mystical, the dogmatic and the spiritual that is infecting every dimension of modern life. We want rules and dogmas and systems and hierarchies so that we can tell who has the power, who's right and who's wrong, who's on top and who doesn't count at all. That way we can dispose of the earth, the animals, and the women without contest and call all of it God's will.

Until feeling becomes as important as thinking, as important to the spiritual life as rituals and rules, we will continue to have religion but we will never find spirituality, we will have countries but we will never have culture, we will have liturgy but we will never have holiness, we will have religious life but we will never have religious.

Until we concern ourselves with how people will feel as a result of what we do, we have not really thought a thing through—at all. Feeling is not nonthinking. Feeling is another way of thinking. Feeling may be the only thing that, in the end, can finally take us beyond the structures and politics and shifting dogmas of the church into the heart of God.

None of the questions that have consumed my life is completely answered, of course. We are still struggling to bridge religious differences. We have yet to define social sin adequately. We are still in search of peace in an increasingly brutal world. We are still dealing with a male power structure everywhere. We have yet to deal with the role of women in the church in a theologically persuasive and coherent way. And we are only beginning to recognize that we are spiritually crippled by the fact that we fail to bring the godliness of feeling to our most serious thoughts and policies and plans and programs. But each of them has, at least, come to a head in my lifetime. Some of them are even showing signs of resolution: The Catholics and the Lutherans have signed an accord that says that it was all a great misunderstanding and, yes, Lutherans can go to heaven. I have prayed in international meetings and even on Catholic altars with Buddhist and Hindu friends in whose eyes I see the light of God. The Catholic bishops wrote a peace pastoral affirming the religious commitment to conscientious objection.

Even though I realize that all of my questions are admittedly a long way from resolution, missing something else that convinces me that I would rather be asking them than not. "Everything that deceives," Plato said, "can be said to enchant." I have been enchanted by far too many falsehoods in life. I would rather go on living the struggle than go comatose in the face of answers that are not true, were never true, cannot possibly be true. Most of all, I have indeed found that the very process of examining them has made my life worthwhile.

—from the Afterword to *Spiritual Questions for the Twenty-First Century*

MODERN SPIRITUAL MASTERS
Robert Ellsberg, Series Editor

This series introduces the essential writing and vision of some of the great spiritual teachers of our time. While many of these figures are rooted in long-established traditions of spirituality, others have charted new, untested paths. In each case, however, they have engaged in a spiritual journey shaped by the challenges and concerns of our age. Together with the saints and witnesses of previous centuries, these modern spiritual masters may serve as guides and companions to a new generation of seekers.

Already published:

Simone Weil (edited by Eric O. Springsted)
Dietrich Bonhoeffer (edited by Robert Coles)
Henri Nouwen (edited by Robert A. Jonas)
Charles de Foucauld (edited by Robert Ellsberg)
Pierre Teilhard de Chardin (edited by Ursula King)
Anthony de Mello (edited by William Dych, S.J.)
Oscar Romero (by Marie Dennis, Rennie Golden, and Scott Wright)
Eberhard Arnold (edited by Johann Christoph Arnold)
Thomas Merton (edited by Christine M. Bochen)
Thich Nhat Hanh (edited by Robert Ellsberg)
Mother Teresa (edited by Jean Maalouf)
Rufus Jones (edited by Kerry Walters)
Edith Stein (edited by John Sullivan, O.C.D.)
Modern Spiritual Masters (edited by Robert Ellsberg)
John Main (edited by Laurence Freeman)
Mohandas Gandhi (edited by John Dear)
Mother Maria Skobtsova (introduction by Jim Forest)
Evelyn Underhill (edited by Emilie Griffin)
St. Thérèse of Lisieux (edited by Mary Frohlich)
Flannery O'Connor (edited by Robert Ellsberg)
Clarence Jordan (edited by Joyce Hollyday)
G. K. Chesterton (edited by William Griffin)

Alfred Delp, S.J. (introduction by Thomas Merton)
Bede Griffiths (edited by Thomas Matus)
Karl Rahner (edited by Philip Endean)
Pedro Arrupe (edited by Kevin F. Burke, S.J.)
Sadhu Sundar Singh (edited by Charles E. Moore)
Romano Guardini (edited by Robert A. Krieg)
Albert Schweitzer (edited by James Brabazon)
Caryll Houselander (edited by Wendy M. Wright)
Brother Roger of Taizé (edited by Marcello Fidanzio)
Dorothee Soelle (edited by Dianne L. Oliver)
Leo Tolstoy (edited by Charles E. Moore)
Howard Thurman (edited by Luther E. Smith, Jr.)
Swami Abhishiktananda (edited by Shirley du Boulay)
Carlo Carretto (edited by Robert Ellsberg)
Pope John XXIII (edited by Jean Maalouf)
Jean Vanier (edited by Carolyn Whitney-Brown)
The Dalai Lama (edited by Thomas A. Forsthoefel)
Catherine de Hueck Doherty (edited by David Meconi, S.J.)
Dom Helder Camara (edited by Francis McDonagh)
Daniel Berrigan (edited by John Dear)
Etty Hillesum (edited by Annemarie S. Kidder)
Virgilio Elizondo (edited by Timothy Matovina)
Yves Congar (edited by Paul Lakeland)
Metropolitan Anthony of Sourozh (edited by Gillian Crow)
David Steindl-Rast (edited by Clare Hallward)
Frank Sheed and Maisie Ward (edited by David Meconi)
Abraham Joshua Heschel (edited by Susannah Heschel)
Gustavo Gutiérrez (edited by Daniel G. Groody)
John Howard Yoder (edited by Paul Martens and Jenny Howells)
John Henry Newman (edited by John T. Ford, C.S.C.)
Robert McAfee Brown (edited by Paul Crowley)
Joan Chittister (edited by Mary Lou Kownacki and
    Mary Hembrow Snyder)